Past and Future Presence

Past and Future Presence

APPROACHES FOR IMPLEMENTING XR
TECHNOLOGY IN HUMANITIES AND ART
EDUCATION

Edited by

Lissa Crofton-Sleigh and Brian Beams

Amherst
College
Pr ss

The complete manuscript of this work was subjected to a partly closed ("single-
blind") review process. For more information, visit https://acpress.amherst.edu/
peerreview/.

Published in the United States of America by Amherst College Press
Manufactured in the United States of America

Library of Congress Control Number: 2023948683

DOI: https://doi.org/10.3998/mpub.14371789
ISBN (Print) 978-1-943208-69-2
ISBN (OA) 978-1-943208-70-8

Contents

INTRODUCTION

Brian Beams and Lissa Crofton-Sleigh

Extended reality (XR) technology (that is, virtual reality, augmented reality, mixed reality, and other 3D technologies) offers many opportunities and benefits for education in the humanities and arts. However, after attending many education-technology workshops and having read countless books and journal articles on the uses of XR in education over the past decade, it has been overwhelmingly apparent that most of the research and conference presentations tend to focus on the use of this technology in science, technology, engineering, and mathematics (STEM) education. While in many ways this is understandable, given the obvious applications of the technology to the fields and study of science, engineering, technology, and mathematics, the focus is still too limited and even to some extent exclusionary, failing to see and/ or acknowledge the potential benefits and creative opportunities in education outside of these areas of research and teaching. Additionally, though a multitude of digital humanities projects exist at many, if not all, institutes of higher education, the push for STEM education and careers in colleges and universities can be viewed as contributing to the lack of concentration on innovation in humanities education, as well as to declining enrollments in many non-STEM courses. Finally, for many scholars and teachers in fields outside of STEM, who are already incorporating this and similar types of technology into their teaching and research agendas, their work may not always be recognized or appreciated as scholarly effort in the same sense or worth as traditional research methods by those judging tenure cases, grant proposals, funding opportunities, and the like.

In this volume we aim to counteract some of the narrower views mentioned earlier through highlighting how XR technology can be used in (sometimes) less obvious but equally sophisticated and fruitful ways to create innovative, immersive, and interactive learning experiences for students in the arts and humanities.[1] By presenting case studies from several arts and humanities fields at the undergraduate and graduate levels, our goals are to help: 1) inspire outside-the-box thinking; 2) move conversations from isolated silos into national and international discussions (and eventual collaborative projects) among researchers, scholars, teachers, and developers about how to best utilize this technology to complement and enhance current humanities teaching and learning practices in higher education and beyond; and 3) argue that performing research and creating teaching materials with this technology qualify as important scholarly endeavors and ought to be judged and valued as such by university administrators, faculty and other colleagues, grant committees, and more. This collection incorporates academic sources, project write-ups, and case studies that are intended to be used by instructors and administrators in secondary and post-secondary education to introduce or procure a better understanding of the benefits and drawbacks of XR technology in the humanities classroom. While academic in nature, this volume is also intended to be read as a practical document, and we encourage the reader to learn from the authors' successes and mistakes which they encountered in the process of exploring this emerging medium.

DEFINITIONS AND DESCRIPTIONS OF CONTEMPORARY XR TECHNOLOGY

Most people understand XR through the context of consumer technology, entertainment, or the past few decades of literature, which often portray immersive virtual technology with a degree of fantasy, whimsy, or societal dread. But XR technology has a long lineage of academic study and research fueled by interest in innovative technologies that aim to immerse people into virtual worlds, augment their perception of the world around them, or use any number of novel technologies to create some hybrid of the two.

The term XR has been adopted as a catch-all term for a myriad of related technologies, including virtual reality (VR), augmented reality (AR), or mixed reality (MR). And while the approaches differ considerably in execution, these technological concepts are taxonomically placed on what can be called the "mixed-reality continuum" or "virtuality continuum," a heuristic model for understanding where a technology exists between virtual and real world environments.[2]

This continuum is useful when trying to contextualize how people understand immersive technology. VR is likely the easiest

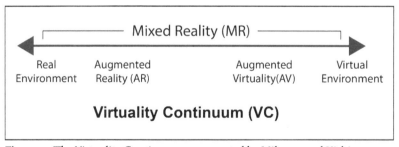

Figure 1: The Virtuality Continuum as presented by Milgram and Kishino, 1994.

to understand, as it involves placing an individual into an immersive virtual environment using a head-mounted display (HMD). It is also the most mature of the technologies that exist along the virtuality continuum. At the time of writing, the world's largest social network has recently made a pivot fully into virtual reality with the sustained support and development of the Quest-branded headsets, the best-selling VR headset in history. By putting on these VR "goggles," users can be instantly transported into artificial yet realistic worlds. What users can view in these virtual worlds typically falls into two categories: 360° capture, and 3D-rendered immersive virtual environments (IVR). 360° cinema is the simplest form of VR, in that it uses specialized cameras to capture footage instead of creating 3D geometrical models. The strength of this is that one can make content quickly and affordably, but it is limited to head rotations with only three degrees of freedom (3DoF). It is less interactive than IVRs, which utilize computer graphics to render environments in 3D and can offer six degrees of freedom (6DoF). IVRs are typically built using game engines and involve the use of more computer software engineering, user experience design, and more "gamified" experiences.

Augmented reality is more difficult to define,[3] as the technology exists more broadly along the virtuality continuum. AR can be fully integrated into an HMD, such as Microsoft's HoloLens or the Magic Leap, or it can be an application that uses the various sensors embedded into a smart phone. Common uses for AR utilize the camera of a smartphone to manipulate pictures or videos of faces posted on social media platforms, or add a new image or animation to a piece of art or a billboard. Companies like Apple and Google have invested in making their iOS and Android operating systems "AR-capable" as the cameras and sensors on their devices follow a trajectory of nearly exponential improvement. All of the AR-related projects in this volume use smartphone-based technology to create their experiences. Because of the ubiquity of smartphones in modern society, AR is often seen as the more democratized XR platform when compared with other immersive technology platforms, such as VR.

Similarly, mixed reality (MR) can also be hard to define. While historically this term has been used for projects like immersive art installations, which use projection mapping in the vein of work produced by art collectives such as teamLab or Meow Wolf, hardware companies have also begun designating the term 'mixed reality' for wearable hardware that is capable of both augmented and virtual reality.[4] While MR is not an umbrella term like XR, it covers a lot of ground. In the context of this volume, we will consider MR anything that significantly alters the real environment to create an immersive experience that is interpreted as a different space or world without putting participants in a fully virtual environment (cave systems also fall into this category). This volume will focus on VR and AR projects, but understanding the whole virtuality continuum is important when developing any XR project.

WHY XR IS USEFUL IN HUMANITIES AND ART EDUCATION

Over the past twenty years, a multitude of researchers and scholarship have recognized the benefits of XR technology for education; this brief literature review section can hardly claim to be a comprehensive review of all (or even some) of the research, but it will attempt to cover those benefits particularly pertinent to education in the humanities and arts. However, it is important to recognize that potential benefits applicable to STEM fields are typically also useful for the humanities and arts, and will be discussed below as such. As a group of scholars argued recently:

> If entering 3D virtual worlds assists students with understanding scientific language, then what could a 3D VR to teach reading or writing add to this preliminary knowledge related to language acquisition? Additionally, using a 3D VR for students to

not only enter an environment, but a community of people in a place and time, could offer powerful social and historical learning experiences.[5]

Recent teaching and learning practices in both STEM and humanities classrooms have trended toward collaborative or social constructivist learning (knowledge actively constructed in one's mind through interaction with others in a specific social context),[6] problem- or inquiry-based learning, and blended online/in-person learning environments (particularly after the beginning of the COVID-19 pandemic).[7] XR technology lends itself well to these practices with its many learning affordances in cognitive, affective, and social domains. To start, VR has been shown to increase student motivation and engagement in learning through its collaborative[8] and immersive nature, leading to high level interaction[9] and more concrete realizations of abstract concepts.[10] Immersion is attained in part through the simulation of reality, particularly with first-person avatars, causing users to feel as if the scenarios are not removed from life, but in fact true to life or even part of it.[11] These virtual scenarios, because of their lifelike character, and a user's presence within them, then enable the user to more directly transfer the knowledge or skills gained through the virtual experience into real life scenarios.[12] Additionally, the presence of classmates and teachers in the virtual experience creates community and offers opportunities for immediate feedback.[13] The communal aspect, involving role play and mentoring, allows for new opportunities for creativity,[14] while individual users themselves are given virtual and cognitive space to experiment, explore, research, investigate, and create content, engaging in what is known as self-guided or even autonomous learning.[15] Exposure to virtual scenarios can help to enhance spatial knowledge and improve problem solving skills.[16]

Finally, virtual reality offers unprecedented access to users, in the sense that it enables them to experience sites and scenarios which may be otherwise inaccessible in the real world, due to financial, time, distance, safety/security, or personal constraints.[17] For example, cultural heritage projects, such as the PARTHENOS project, SmartMarca, or *Rome Reborn*, reconstruct lost or fragmentary monuments, archaeological sites, and works of art, and allow the user to immerse themselves in the structure or artwork, not only providing an engaging experience of an otherwise unknowable place or object, but also effecting a desire in users to recognize the value in preserving what is still extant.[18] In addition to reducing limitations of time and history, virtual environments can offer access and benefits to special education students and students with physical disabilities or other learning difficulties, providing a multisensory experience in a safe environment which can aid mental health and reduce anxiety.[19]

Augmented reality also offers similar benefits to its users. As Prodromou observes, when AR technology is used in educational settings, it:

1. Helps students to engage in authentic explorations in the real world.
2. Facilitates the observation of events that cannot easily be observed with the naked eye by displaying virtual elements alongside real objects.
3. Increases students' motivation and helps them to acquire better investigation skills.
4. Creates immersive hybrid learning environments that combine digital and physical objects, thereby facilitating the development of processing skills (e.g., critical thinking, problem solving, and communicating through interdependent collaborative exercises).[20]

Like VR, AR increases the opportunities for student collaboration, student-faculty interaction, motivation, and autonomy,[21] creating experiential tasks unable to be replicated in traditional classroom settings[22] and leading to deeper thinking and engagement in the subject matter.[23] Projects such as the EU-sponsored "Living Book: Augmenting reading for life" offer professional development opportunities for educators regarding the teaching of reading and literacy. Mobile augmented reality applications have been shown to have positive impacts on emotional, cognitive, and social development in foreign language learning,[24] and have also helped students to develop English writing and composition skills.[25] Many of these mobile AR apps (in addition to many VR applications) utilize the benefits of gamification in order to increase motivation and achieve more positive thinking regarding learning goals.[26] Additionally, the mobile AR apps enable opportunities for learning in more informal environments, such as home, library, or even outside (utilizing the same functions as games such as Pokemon GO), allowing users to educate themselves and further solidify their knowledge and skills nearly anytime and anywhere.[27]

DRAWBACKS OF XR

Although XR can offer various benefits and affordances, potential drawbacks must also be acknowledged. While some mobile AR apps may be free or low cost, much of the equipment involved in running these technologies (VR headsets and so on) can be very expensive for schools or individuals to acquire, which means that many potential users, including those in underrepresented groups, may not have access to them. Even when access can be provided, training of students and teachers can be time-consuming and costly. The current state of VR technology, where users can occasionally experience motion sickness or headaches from wearing (ill-fitting) headsets for too long, means that immersions into virtual environments have to be short in duration (typically 20–30 minutes or less). People with health concerns that could be triggered or exacerbated by use of the headset may be less inclined or even unable to use the technology.

There are also risks, and ethical and legal concerns, associated with using and abusing the immersive and sensational nature of the technology. First, issues regarding privacy, security, and the like must be taken into consideration. When using technology in the classroom it is important to know the best ways to protect students' personal information in accordance with the Family Educational Rights and Privacy Act (FERPA), and the amount of data collected by XR hardware and software should be scrutinized and carefully considered before instructors commit to incorporating the technology into their curricula.[28] Additionally, while one of the most touted benefits of VR, as promoted by content creators and media publications,[29] has been to enhance empathy in a user, which could lead to prosocial behavior, recent research has called this benefit into question, suggesting that the correlation between XR users and an increased sense of empathy is not as strong as previously thought.[30] Furthermore, personal and cultural biases can greatly affect a user's perception of the VR experience and potentially lead to negative outcomes.[31] At this time a greater, continued focus on longitudinal studies on the effects of XR exposure is needed, in order to understand its long-term effects, both positive and negative, on users.

Misinformation in VR is yet another concern for would-be XR educators. In 2022, 90 percent of all VR headsets were sold by either Meta or ByteDance, two of the largest social media companies in the world. With so much misinformation originating in social media, pairing these social issues with the immersive potential of XR can create a scenario where people experience things that are perceptually "real" but are factually incorrect.[32] This scenario, coined "mis-experience" by Brown et al., is not well-researched or documented. However, when comparing existing misinformation in online spaces, it is not unreasonable to believe a scenario where bad actors influence beliefs and behaviors in realistic virtual environments. To combat these scenarios, social media companies continually require more validation for online accounts, which further complicates the structural implementation of wearable XR hardware in the classroom. As technology becomes more internet-connected, the greater safety risks it poses to students, which necessitates organizational solutions for widespread adoption.

From a pedagogical, ethical, or inclusive standpoint, educators, researchers, and developers should not consider these technologies as a one-size-fits-all tool capable of benefiting or transforming any lesson plan or pedagogical goal. They are best used in collaboration with or as a complement to other established or traditional teaching methods—not as replacements for these methods. Context, pedagogical approaches, and learning theories are all necessary for best usage and practice with XR technologies, allowing for customization within a range of educational settings and to best suit each user.[33] Additionally, if a lesson plan or unit utilizing this technology seeks to elicit empathy, XR and VR content developers should "design experiences that challenge people to engage in empathic effort."[34] While the pitfalls of XR are a valid concern for many educators, we believe that for this volume it is more helpful to focus on how VR *can* be successfully implemented in the classroom. We encourage all educators to observe the risks and benefits of this powerful medium and proceed accordingly.

THE CONTRIBUTIONS

In this volume, we present contributions comprised of a broad range of disciplines under the larger scope of the humanities and arts in higher education, with chapters focused on English and world language arts and instruction, art and art history, women's and gender studies, history, archaeology and architecture, classics (ancient Greek and Roman studies), and American studies. In order to provide a wider array of perspectives and possibilities for the use of XR technology, we also looked to be inclusive in representation within the authorship; the authors come from diverse backgrounds, locations (both within the United States and internationally), and stages of their careers (graduate student to full professor; early career to mid–late career). Some of the authors work at universities in other educational settings (libraries, for instance), and others are artists who have worked at or in collaboration with universities. Some of the chapters are more theoretical in nature, while others offer case studies and preliminary results. Yet even with the variety of backgrounds, fields, and approaches, similarities and common themes occur throughout the chapters. First of all, an eye toward creativity, ingenuity, and teamwork has helped to make these projects possible. The flexibility offered by XR technologies allows for instruction to occur in a variety of locations, from traditional classroom spaces to the library to one's home to a museum to other public buildings to outside in nature. As educators we celebrate the opportunities afforded by the ability for students, users, and participants to learn anywhere at any time, but we also note the efforts involved in the collaboration between those various formal and informal learning environments to create a cohesive educational experience. Perhaps most significantly, the projects discussed in this volume demonstrate how XR technology and experiential learning can help put *humanity* back into the humanities, creating deeper connections between participants and the people (or topics) they are learning about, with several of the projects actively engaging in social justice aims and facilitating more accurate understandings of cultures, places, and peoples across time and space.

CHAPTER SUMMARIES

Laura Surtees' and Molly Kuchler's chapter, "Coloring Outside the Classroom: Digital Technology Restores Color to Ancient Sculpture in the Library," discusses the implementation of the "Coloring the Past" project at Bryn Mawr College. This project uses augmented reality and 3D modeling to noninvasively project hypothetical, but historically accurate, reconstructions of color and pigmentation onto ancient Greek and Roman sculptural reliefs, which have lost their original polychromatic natures. Surtees and Kuchler highlight the interdisciplinary nature of the project, as well as the collaborative process among students, faculty, and library staff to research and set up the installation in the Rhys Carpenter Library on campus. The authors also trace the problematic history of the reception and idealization of ancient "white" sculpture, from early Renaissance to modern-day white supremacist groups, and explain how XR and 3D technologies can be utilized to reshape the conversation surrounding color in antiquity and to help us come to a more realistic understanding of the past (and its effects on the present).

In the second chapter, "Beyond Reconstruction: Alternative Realities and Breaking Barriers in Classical Archaeological Pedagogy," by Elizabeth Wolfram Thill, Matthew Brennan, and Ryan Knapp, the authors explore the technical and ideological challenges inherent in the traditional teaching methods and goals of classical archaeology courses, and argue that VR enables the students to better understand and engage with ancient archaeological material in more meaningful and sophisticated ways. They stress the collaborative process involved in creating 3D VR builds of ancient Greek and Roman architectural structures for use in the classroom, and explain how various types of VR experiences are utilized to fulfill pedagogical goals in the traditional classroom setting. The authors conclude by discussing future possibilities and goals.

Similar to the previous chapter on classical archaeology, Brian Beams and Lissa Crofton-Sleigh's chapter, "*Lingua Vitae*: Teaching the Latin Language in Virtual Reality," explains the challenges involved in teaching what is considered a "dead language", and advocates for VR as a useful and plausible methodology by which to engage students in meaningful dialogues with humans of the past. In support of VR as a tool for learning ancient languages, the authors present their development of a VR learning experience in conjunction with *Wheelock's Latin*, a traditional introductory Latin textbook. The experience allows students to develop conversational skills and learn more about ancient Roman culture through the completion of task-based exercises in a virtualized Roman Forum with ancient Roman characters. Beams and Crofton-Sleigh offer a synopsis of relevant literature, then discuss the development of the project, preliminary user results, and future goals, arguing that VR cannot replace traditional teaching methods for language instruction, but can supplement and enhance them.

In "Designing and Teaching a Virtual Field Trip Course in American Studies," Tim Gruenewald explains how the COVID-19 pandemic-related cancellation of a US study abroad program for his students at the University of Hong Kong led to his creation of a two-week intensive virtual study abroad program, or field trip course. After a brief summary of relevant scholarship, the author discusses the guiding pedagogical philosophies and principles behind his design of the VR experience, then highlights two of the units of the virtual field trip as example case studies, followed by a review of student experience and feedback as well as key lessons learned from teaching the virtual field trip course. Gruenewald recognizes that VR travel certainly cannot replace real-life travel, but advocates for using these immersive experiences as a supplement for either traditional abroad programs or regular courses in classrooms.

David Lindsay and Ian R. Weaver's chapter, "Developing a Site-Specific Art and Humanities Platform," explores the evolution of the Popwalk mobile app, which offers an augmented reality platform for the exhibition of more than 450 pieces of art at specific locales and the exposition of such art through artist-created cultural videos. Site-specific art, as well as its meaning and interpretation, is inherently linked to the environment in which it is exhibited, and benefits in its viewing from the dialogue created between the visual art and the artist's audiovisual component in the app. Lindsay and Weaver discuss three case studies in various national and international university and public settings, which aided in the understanding of site-specific cultural video, and thus, in the development of Popwalk.

Another AR project is presented in Elham Hajesmaeili's chapter, "An Embodied Arts-Based Research Methodology: Augmented Reality (AR) Portrait Painting in Dialogue," in which she describes the theoretical and philosophical frameworks used in the creation of AR companions for physical paintings of Iranian women living in the United States. She uses a combination of audio and visual augmentations to the original artworks to create new contexts and immersive engagement with the artwork. This, she argues, creates a cyclical, dialogic relationship between the viewer, the art, and the researcher, leading to increased engagement with the artwork.

Finally, the chapter "The Imperative of Preparing Language Teaching Professionals for XR/VR Environments", by Fabiola Ehlers-Zavala and Jay Schnoor, considers how technology, particularly XR technology, can enable more meaningful and valuable conversational skills in foreign language learning. However, the training curriculum for foreign language instructors, particularly in the United States, has not typically included study and preparation in these types of technologies, unless the faculty and the instructors in training take a personal interest in learning the technologies on their own time and through their own expertise. The authors argue that these technologies must become a formal part of the curriculum in order to better prepare students for foreign language interaction in the digital age. They provide a literature review highlighting the benefits (as well as challenges) of XR technology in foreign language teaching and learning, then advocate for partnerships between universities and the public and private sector in order to bridge the digital divide and the often exorbitant costs of acquiring these technologies at a large scale, and conclude by offering future avenues for research.

These chapters have been grouped into two sections, *Reinvigorating and Reinvestigating the Past,* and *Considering and*

Questioning the Present, followed by a concluding chapter on *Preparing for the Future,* where we mull on some of the possibilities of XR in times to come.

NOTES

1. This volume is, of course, not the first to include studies in humanities-based fields. For example, an early systematic review (Hew and Cheung, "Use of three-dimensional (3-D) immersive virtual worlds") explores the use of 3D environments in the arts as well as health and environmental fields. Special issues in educational and pedagogical journals (for example, *The Journal of Interactive Technology & Pedagogy* 17, edited by Licastro et al.) and volumes concerning VR and 3D applications in library settings (Grayburn et al., eds., *3D/VR in the Academic Library*) have looked into extended reality in humanistic projects, while a recent volume, *Virtual and Augmented Reality in Education, Art, and Museums,* edited by Guazzaroni and Pillai (2020), offers another type of model for our project. Individual case studies (e.g., Wilson, "Immersive Education"; Biedermann, "Virtual museums"; Kim, "Another Type of Human Narrative"; Rose and Hedrick, "Multisensory and Active Learning Approaches"; Bozia, "Reviving Classical Drama"; see also the review by Hutson and Olsen, "Digital Humanities and Virtual Reality," 491–500) can also be found if one knows where to look. But by and large, recent systematic reviews of XR technology in education, including Kavanagh et al., "A systematic review of virtual reality in education", and Siposova and Hlava, "Uses of Augmented Reality," indicate that the majority of studies are completed in STEM subjects.
2. Milgram and Kishino, "A Taxonomy of Mixed Reality Visual Displays."
3. And should not be confused with augmented virtuality, which incorporates elements, including objects and people, from the physical world into the virtual world and allows for user interaction and manipulation of those real-world elements within the virtual world. It differs from augmented reality, because in AR interaction occurs in the real world. For recent studies of augmented virtuality, see, e.g., Gonzalez, Richards, and Bilgin, "Making it Real."
4. Devices such as the Lynx R1 are capable of both augmented and virtual reality: https://www.lynx-r.com/
5. Tilhou, Taylor, and Crompton. "3D Virtual Reality," 181–182.
6. For more on the constructivist learning theory, see, e.g., Liu et al., "Potentials and Trends."
7. For more on these trends, with particular relevance to language learning, see Chong, "Ten trends and innovations."

8. To name just a few references: Freina and Ott, "Literature Review"; Dalgarno and Lee, "What are the learning affordances of 3-D virtual environments?"; Huang, Rauch, and Liaw, "Investigating learner's attitudes"; and Ott and Tavella, "What makes young students genuinely engaged in computer-based learning tasks."

9. Lau and Lee, "Use of virtual reality."

10. Also known as reification: Dalgarno and Lee, "What are the learning affordances?"

11. Fedeli, "Virtual Body."

12. See also Dede, Jacobson, and Richards, "Introduction"; Slater, "Implicit Learning through Embodiment"; Pederson and Irby, "VELscience Project"; and Mikropoulos and Natsis, "Educational virtual environments."

13. Monahan, McArdle, and Bertolotto, "Virtual reality for collaborative e-learning."

14. DeFreitas and Veletsianos, "Editorial: Crossing boundaries."

15. DeFreitas and Veletsianos, "Editorial: Crossing boundaries." For more on autonomous learning, see Liu et al., "Potentials and Trends."

16. Leite, Svinicki, and Shi, "Attempted validation of the scores."

17. For more on accessibility, see, e.g., Geris and Özdener, "Design Models," 4; Tilhou et al., "3D Virtual Reality"; Todd, Pater, and Baker, "(In)Accessible Learning"; Freina and Ott, "Literature Review"; Pederson and Irby, "VELscience Project."

18. Pierdicca et al., "Evaluating Augmented and Virtual Reality," 234 (this article also discusses SmartMarca in greater detail). For more on the Parthenos project, see Cook and Lischer-Katz, "Integrating 3D and VR." For further benefits and discussion of cultural heritage in relation to VR and AR technology, and gaming, see Mori, "Gamification," 87; Tilhou et al., "3D Virtual Reality," 176–81; Bekele et al., "Survey"; Bertacchini and Tavernise, "NetConnect Virtual Worlds"; Mortara et al., "Learning cultural heritage"; Frischer et al., "New digital model," 167–9.

19. Anderson, *Virtual Reality*.

20. Prodromou, "Introduction," xxix.

21. Siposova and Hlava, "Uses of Augmented Reality," *passim*. They also recognize that, given the greatest benefits of AR (visualization and interaction with virtual content), it is typically implemented into courses of fields that are, "logically, based on working with concrete objects built from real matter" and acknowledge the challenge to aid learning processes in disciplines grounded in "abstract concepts and multidimensional systems of relations" (196). In many ways, the challenges they recognize occur in disciplines common to the

humanities; however, as we see above, AR has been successfully implemented into many humanities-based courses and pedagogy.

22. Schachter, "How AR and VR will revolutionize the classroom"; Bower et al., "Augmented Reality in education."

23. Kamarainen et al., "Using mobile location-based augmented reality."

24. Diță, "A foreign language learning application"; Liu, Holden, and Zheng, "Analyzing students' language learning experience"; Perry, "Gamifying French language learning"; McGonigal, *Reality is Broken*.

25. Liu and Tsai, "Using augmented-reality-based mobile learning."

26. For more on gamification and its benefits, see, e.g., Mori, "Gamification"; and Klopfer, "Massively Multiplayer Online Roleplaying Games." Mori also considers cultural heritage in relation to gamification and VR/AR, with her discussion of the *Assassin's Creed Odyssey Discovery Mode Tour* exhibit at the British Museum in 2018, which combined meticulous digital reconstructions of Ancient Greece with opportunities for engaging, self-guided, subjective learning, where one can repeat their experiences, for instance walking through the same building twice, and move at will.

27. For more on the uses of XR technology in informal environments, such as libraries, see Varnum, ed., *Beyond Reality*.

28. For more on these ethical and legal concerns, see Royakkers et al., "Societal and ethical issues"; Tabatabaie, "Introduction to Laws"; Madary and Metzinger, "Real virtuality."

29. Three such examples (of many) are Bailenson, "How to create empathy in VR"; Zhang, "Can VR really make you more empathetic?"; and Milk, "How virtual reality can create the ultimate empathy machine."

30. On this topic, see, e.g., Sora-Domenjó, "Disrupting the 'empathy machine'"; Martingano, Hererra, and Konrath, "Virtual Reality Improves"; Rose, "The immersive turn"; Bollmer, "Empathy machines"; Nash, "Virtual reality witness"; and Sutherland, "The Limits of Virtual Reality."

31. Sora-Domenjó, "Disrupting the 'empathy machine.'"

32. On this topic, see Brown, Bailenson, and Hancock, "Misinformation in Virtual Reality."

33. On the necessary collaboration between XR technology and learning/teaching goals, see, e.g., Meccawy, "Creating an Immersive XR Learning Experience"; Rizk, "Considerations for Implementing Emerging Technologies"; Southgate, *Virtual Reality in Curriculum and Pedagogy*; Farley, "The Reality of Authentic Learning"; Eutsler and Long, "Preservice Teachers"; and Fowler, "Virtual reality and learning."

34. Martingano et al., "Virtual Reality Improves."

WORKS CITED

Anderson, Ange. *Virtual Reality, Augmented Reality, and Artificial Intelligence in Special Education: A Practical Guide to Supporting Students with Learning Differences*. London and New York: Routledge, 2019.

Bailenson, Jeremy. "How to create empathy in VR." Wired UK, February 26, 2018. https://www.wired.co.uk/article/empathy-virtual-reality-jeremy-bailenson-stanford

Bekele, Mafkereseb Kassahun, Roberto Pierdicca, Emanuele Frontoni, Eva Savina Malinverni, and James Gain. "A Survey of Augmented, Virtual, and Mixed Reality for Cultural Heritage." *Journal on Computing and Cultural Heritage (JOCCH)* 11, no. 2 (2018), https://doi.org/10.1145/3145534

Bertacchini, Francesca, and Assunta Tavernise. "NetConnect Virtual Worlds: Results of a Learning Experience." In *Learning in Virtual Worlds: Research and Applications*, edited by Sue Gregory, Mark J.W. Lee, Barney Dalgarno, and Belinda Tynan, 227–40. Athabasca: Athabasca University Press, 2016.

Biedermann, Bernadette. "Virtual museums as an extended museum experience: Challenges and impacts for museology, digital humanities, museums and visitors – in times of (Coronavirus) crisis." *Digital Humanities Quarterly* 15, no. 3 (2021). http://www.digitalhumanities.org/dhq/vol/15/3/000568/000568.html

Bollmer, Grant. "Empathy machines." *Media International Australia* 165, no. 1 (2017): 63–76. https://doi.org/10.1177/1329878X17726794

Bower, Matt, Cathie Howe, Nerida McCredie, Austin Robinson, and David Grover. "Augmented Reality in education – cases, places, and potentials." *Educational Media International* 51, no. 1 (2014): 1–15. https://doi.org/10.1080/09523987.2014.889400

Bozia, Eleni. "Reviving Classical Drama: virtual reality and experiential learning in a traditional classroom." *Digital Humanities Quarterly* 12, no. 3 (2018). http://digitalhumanities.org:8081/dhq/vol/12/3/000385/000385.html

Brown, James G., Jeremy N. Bailenson, and Jeffrey Hancock. "Misinformation in Virtual Reality." *Journal of Online Trust and Safety*, (March 2023). https://www.stanfordvr.com/mm/2023/03/Misinformation-in-Virtual-Reality.pdf

Chong, Chia Suan. "Ten trends and innovations in English language teaching for 2018." British Council, June 11, 2018. https://www.britishcouncil.org/voices-magazine/ten-trends-innovations-english-language-teaching-2018

Cook, Matt, and Zack Lischer-Katz. "Integrating 3D and Virtual Reality into Research and Pedagogy in Higher Education." In *Beyond Reality: Augmented, Virtual, and Mixed Reality in the Library*, edited by Kenneth J. Varnum, 69–85. Chicago: ALA (American Library Association) Editions, 2019.

Dalgarno, Barney, and Mark J.W. Lee. "What are the learning affordances of 3-D virtual environments?" *British Journal of Educational Technology* 41, no. 1 (2010): 10–32. https://doi.org/10.1111/j.1467-8535.2009.01038.x

Dede, Christopher J., Jeffrey Jacobson, and John Richards. "Introduction: Virtual, Augmented, and Mixed Realities in Education." In *Virtual, Augmented, and Mixed Realities in Education*, edited by Dejian Liu, Christopher Dede, Ronghuai Huang, and John Richards, 1–16. Singapore: Springer, 2017.

DeFreitas, Sara, and George Veletsianos. "Editorial: Crossing boundaries: Learning and teaching in virtual worlds." *British Journal of Educational Technology* 41, no. 1 (2010): 3–9. https://doi.org/10.1111/j.1467-8535.2009.01045.x

Diță, Florentin-Alexandru. "A foreign language learning application using mobile augmented reality." *Informatica Economică* 20, no. 4 (2016): 76–87. http://revistaie.ase.ro/content/80/07%20-%20Dita.pdf

Eutsler, Lauren, and Christopher S. Long. "Preservice Teachers' Acceptance of Virtual Reality to Plan Science Instruction." *Educational Technology & Society* 24, no. 2 (2021): 28–43. https://www.jstor.org/stable/27004929

Farley, Helen S. "The Reality of Authentic Learning in Virtual Worlds." In *Learning in Virtual Worlds: Research and Applications*, edited by Sue Gregory, Mark J.W. Lee, Barney Dalgarno, and Belinda Tynan, 129–49. Athabasca: Athabasca University Press, 2016.

Fedeli, Laura. "Virtual Body: Implications for Identity, Interaction, and Didactics." In *Learning in Virtual Worlds: Research and Applications*, edited by Sue Gregory, Mark J.W. Lee, Barney Dalgarno, and Belinda Tynan, 67–85. Athabasca: Athabasca University Press, 2016.

Fowler, Chris. "Virtual reality and learning: Where is the pedagogy?" *British Journal of Educational Technology* 46, no. 2 (2015): 412–22. https://doi.org/10.1111/bjet.12135

Freina, Laura, and Michela Ott. "A literature review on immersive virtual reality in education: State of the art and perspectives." In *Proceedings of the International Scientific Conference "eLearning and Software for Education" (eLSE 2015): Rethinking education by leveraging the eLearning pillar of the Digital Agenda for Europe, Volume 1*, edited by Ion Roceanu, Florica Moldoveanu, Stefan Trausan-Matu, Dragos Barbieru, Daniel Beligan, and Angela Ionita, 133–41. Bucharest: "CAROL I" National Defence University Publishing House, 2015. https://doi.org/10.12753/2066-026X-15-020

Frischer, Bernard, Dean Abernathy, Fulvio Cairoli Giuliani, Russell T. Scott, and Hauke Ziemssen. "A new digital model of the Roman Forum." In *Imaging Ancient Rome: Documentation – Visualization – Imagination. Proceedings of the Third Williams Symposium on Classical Architecture, Journal of Roman*

Archaeology: Supplement 61, edited by Lothar Haselberger and John Humphrey, 163–82. Portsmouth, RI: Journal of Roman Archaeology, 2006.

Geris, Ali, and Nesrin Özdener. "Design Models for Developing Educational Virtual Reality Environments: A Systematic Review." In *Virtual and Augmented Reality in Education, Art, and Museums*, edited by Giuliana Guazzaroni and Anitha S. Pillai, 1–22. Hershey, PA: IGI Global, 2020. https://doi.org/10.4018/978-1-7998-1796-3.ch001

Gonzalez, Dilian Alejandra Zuniga, Deborah Richards, and Ayse Aysin Bilgin. "Making it Real: A Study of Augmented Virtuality on Presence and Enhanced Benefits of Study Stress Reduction Sessions." *International Journal of Human-Computer Studies* 147 (2021), 102579. https://doi.org/10.1016/j.ijhcs.2020.102579

Grayburn, Jennifer, Zack Lischer-Katz, Kristina Golubiewski-Davis, and Veronica Ikeshoji-Orlati, eds. "3D/VR in the Academic Library: Emerging Practices and Trends." Arlington, VA: Council on Library and Information Resources, 2019. https://www.clir.org/wp-content/uploads/sites/6/2019/02/Pub-176.pdf

Gregory, Sue, Mark J.W. Lee, Barney Dalgarno, and Belinda Tynan, eds. *Learning in Virtual Worlds: Research and Applications*. Athabasca: Athabasca University Press, 2016. https://doi.org/10.15215/aupress/9781771991339.01

Guazzaroni, Giuliana, and Anitha S. Pillai, eds. *Virtual and Augmented Reality in Education, Art, and Museums*. Hershey, PA: IGI Global, 2020.

Hew, Khe Foon, and Wing Sum Cheung. "Use of three-dimensional (3-D) immersive virtual worlds in K-12 and higher education settings: A review of the research." *British Journal of Educational Technology* 41, no. 1 (2010): 33–55. https://doi.org/10.1111/j.1467-8535.2008.00900.x

Huang, Hsiu-Mei, Ulrich Rauch, and Shu-Sheng Liaw. "Investigating learners' attitudes toward virtual reality learning environments: Based on a constructivist approach." *Computers & Education* 55, no. 3 (2010): 1171–82. https://doi.org/10.1016/j.compedu.2010.05.014

Hutson, James, and Trent Olsen. "Digital Humanities and Virtual Reality: A Review of Theories and Best Practices for Art History." *International Journal of Technology in Education* 4, no. 3 (2021): 491–500. https://doi.org/10.46328/ijte.150

Kamarainen, Amy, Joseph Reilly, Shari Metcalf, Tina Grotzer, and Chris Dede. "Using Mobile Location-Based Augmented Reality to Support Outdoor Learning in Undergraduate Ecology and Environmental Science Courses." *Bulletin of the Ecological Society of America* 99, no. 2 (2018): 259–76. https://doi.org/10.1002/bes2.1396

Kavanagh, Sam, Andrew Luxton-Reilly, Burkhard Wuensche, and Beryl Plimmer. "A systematic review of virtual reality in education." *Themes in Science and*

Technology Education 10, no. 2 (2017): 85–119. https://files.eric.ed.gov/fulltext/EJ1165633.pdf

Kim, Eugenia S. "Another Type of Human Narrative: Visualizing Movement Histories Through Motion Capture Data and Virtual Reality." *Digital Humanities Quarterly* 15, no. 1 (2021). http://digitalhumanities.org:8081/dhq/vol/15/1/000514/000514.html

Klopfer, Eric. "Massively Multiplayer Online Roleplaying Games and Virtual Reality Combine for Learning." In *Virtual, Augmented, and Mixed Realities in Education*, edited by Dejian Liu, Christopher Dede, Ronghuai Huang, and John Richards, 179–92. Singapore: Springer, 2017.

Lau, Kung Wong, and Pui Yuen Lee. "The use of virtual reality for creating unusual environmental stimulation to motivate students to explore creative ideas." *Interactive Learning Environments* 23, no. 1 (2015): 3–18. https://doi.org/10.1080/10494820.2012.745426

Leite, Walter L., Marilla Svinicki, and Yuying Shi. "Attempted validation of the scores of the VARK: Learning styles inventory with multitrait-multimethod confirmatory factor analysis models." *Educational and Psychological Measurement* 70, no. 2 (2010): 323–39. https://doi.org/10.1177/0013164409344507

Licastro, Amanda, Angel David Nieves, and Victoria Szabo, eds. "Virtual Reality, Augmented Reality, and Extended Reality." Special issue, *Journal of Interactive Technology & Pedagogy* 17 (2020).

Liu, Dejian, Chris Dede, Ronghuai Huang, and John Richards, eds. *Virtual, Augmented, and Mixed Realities in Education*. Singapore: Springer, 2017. https://doi.org/10.1007/978-981-10-5490-7

Liu, Dejian, Kaushal Kumar Bhagat, Yuan Gao, Ting-Wen Chang, and Ronghuai Huang. "The Potentials and Trends of Virtual Reality in Education." In *Virtual, Augmented, and Mixed Realities in Education*, edited by Dejian Liu, Christopher Dede, Ronghuai Huang, and John Richards, 105–30. Singapore: Springer, 2017.

Liu, Pei-Hsun Emma and Ming-Kuan Tsai. "Using augmented-reality-based mobile learning material in EFL English composition: An exploratory case study." *British Journal of Educational Technology* 44, no. 1 (2013): E1–E4. https://doi.org/10.1111/j.1467-8535.2012.01302.x

Liu, Yang, Daniel Holden, and Dongping Zheng. "Analyzing students' language learning experience in an augmented reality mobile game: An exploration of an emergent learning environment." *Procedia – Social and Behavioral Sciences* 228 (2016): 369–74. https://doi.org/10.1016/j.sbspro.2016.07.055

Madary, Michael, and Thomas K. Metzinger. "Real virtuality: A code of ethical conduct. Recommendations for good scientific practice and the consumers of

VR-technology." *Frontiers in Robotics and AI* 3 (2016), 3. https://doi.org/10.3389/frobt.2016.00003

Martingano, Alison Jane, Fernanda Hererra, and Sara Konrath. "Virtual Reality Improves Emotional but Not Cognitive Empathy: A Meta-Analysis." *Technology, Mind, and Behavior* 2, no. 1 (2021). https://doi.org/10.1037/tmb0000034

McGonigal, Jane. *Reality Is Broken: Why Games Make Us Better and How They Can Change the World.* New York: Penguin Press, 2011.

Meccawy, Maram. "Creating an Immersive XR Learning Experience: A Roadmap for Educators." *Electronics* 11, no. 21 (2022), 3547. https://doi.org/10.3390/electronics11213547

Mikropoulos, Tassos A., and Antonis Natsis. "Educational virtual environments: A ten-year review of empirical research (1999–2009)." *Computers & Education* 56, no. 3 (2011): 769–80. https://doi.org/10.1016/j.compedu.2010.10.020

Milgram, Paul, and Fumio Kishino. "A Taxonomy of Mixed Reality Visual Displays." *IEICE Transactions on Information Systems* E77-D, no. 12 (1994): 1321–29.

Milk, Chris. "How virtual reality can create the ultimate empathy machine." Talk given March 18, 2015 at TED2015, Vancouver, Canada. Video, 10 min, 16 sec. https://www.ted.com/talks/chris_milk_how_virtual_reality_can_create_the_ultimate_empathy_machine.

Monahan, Teresa, Gavin McArdle, and Michela Bertolotto. "Virtual reality for collaborative e-learning." *Computers & Education* 50, no. 4 (2008): 1339–53. https://doi.org/10.1016/j.compedu.2006.12.008

Mori, Biancamaria. "Gamification: To Engage Is to Learn." In *Virtual and Augmented Reality in Education, Art, and Museums,* edited by Giuliana Guazzaroni and Anitha S. Pillai, 81–92. Hershey, PA: IGI Global, 2020. https://doi.org/10.4018/978-1-7998-1796-3.ch005

Mortara, Michela, Chiara Eva Catalano, Francesco Bellotti, Giusy Fiucci, Minica Houry-Panchetti, and Panagiotis Petridis. "Learning cultural heritage by serious games." *Journal of Cultural Heritage* 15, no. 3 (2014): 318–25. https://doi.org/10.1016/j.culher.2013.04.004

Nash, Kate. "Virtual reality witness: Exploring the ethics of mediated presence." *Studies in Documentary Film* 12, no. 2 (2017), 119–31. https://doi.org/10.1080/17503280.2017.1340796

Ott, Michela, and Mauro Tavella. "A contribution to the understanding of what makes young students genuinely engaged in computer-based learning tasks." *Procedia: Social and Behavioral Sciences* 1, no. 1 (2009): 184–8. https://doi.org/10.1016/j.sbspro.2009.01.034

Pederson, Susan, and Travis Irby. "The VELscience project: Middle schoolers' engagement in student-directed inquiry within a virtual environment for learning." *Computers & Education* 71 (2014): 33–42. https://doi.org/10.1016/j.compedu.2013.09.006

Perry, Bernadette. "Gamifying French language learning: A case study examining a quest-based, augmented reality mobile learning-tool." *Procedia: Social and Behavioral Sciences* 174 (2015): 2308–15. https://doi.org/10.1016/j.sbspro.2015.01.892

Pierdicca, Roberto, Emanuele Frontoni, Maria Paola Puggioni, Eva Savina Malinverni, and Marina Paolanti. "Evaluating Augmented and Virtual Reality in Education Through a User-Centered Comparative Study: SmartMarca Project." In *Virtual and Augmented Reality in Education, Art, and Museums*, edited by Giuliana Guazzaroni and Anitha S. Pillai, 229–62. Hershey, PA: IGI Global, 2020. https://doi.org/10.4018/978-1-7998-1796-3.ch012

Prodromou, Theodosia, ed. *Augmented Reality in Educational Settings*. Leiden: Brill, 2019.

Prodromou, Theodosia. "Introduction." In *Augmented Reality in Educational Settings*, edited by Theodosia Prodromou, xxix–xxxv. Leiden: Brill, 2019.

Rizk, Jessica. "Considerations for Implementing Emerging Technologies and Innovative Pedagogies in Twenty-First-Century Classrooms." In *Emerging Technologies and Pedagogies in the Curriculum*, edited by Shengquan Yu, Mohamed Ally, and Avgoustos Tsinakos, 447–60. Singapore: Springer, 2020.

Rose, Mandy. "The immersive turn: Hype and hope in the emergence of virtual reality as a nonfiction platform." *Studies in Documentary Film* 12, no. 2 (2018), 132–49. https://doi.org/10.1080/17503280.2018.1496055

Rose, Marice, and Tera Lee Hedrick. "Multisensory and Active Learning Approaches to Teaching Medieval Art." *Art History Pedagogy & Practice* 3, no. 1 (2018). https://academicworks.cuny.edu/ahpp/vol3/iss1/4.

Royakkers, Lambèr, Jelte Timmer, Linda Kool, and Rinie van Est. "Societal and ethical issues of digitization." *Ethics and Information Technology* 20 (2018): 127–42. https://doi.org/10.1007/s10676-018-9452-x

Schachter, Bart. "How AR and VR will revolutionize the classroom." ReadWrite, May 10, 2018. https://readwrite.com/2018/05/10/how-ar-and-vr-will-revolutionize-the-classroom/.

Siposova, Martina, and Tomas Hlava. "Uses of Augmented Reality in Tertiary Education." In *Augmented Reality in Educational Settings*, edited by Theodosia Prodromou, 195–216. Leiden: Brill, 2019. https://doi.org/10.1163/9789004408845_009

Slater, Mel. "Implicit Learning through Embodiment in Immersive Virtual Reality." In *Virtual, Augmented, and Mixed Realities in Education*, edited by

Dejian Liu, Christopher Dede, Ronghuai Huang, and John Richards, 19–33. Singapore: Springer, 2017.

Sora-Domenjó, Carles. "Disrupting the 'empathy machine': The power and perils of virtual reality in addressing social issues." *Frontiers in Psychology* 13 (2022). https://doi.org/10.3389/fpsyg.2022.814565

Southgate, Erica. *Virtual Reality in Curriculum and Pedagogy: Evidence from Secondary Classrooms.* London and NY: Routledge, 2020.

Sutherland, Ainsley. "The Limits of Virtual Reality: Debugging the Empathy Machine." MIT – docubase, September, 29 2016. https://docubase.mit.edu/lab/case-studies/the-limits-of-virtual-reality-debugging-the-empathy-machine/.

Tabatabaie, Layla F. "Introduction to Laws Relevant to Virtual Worlds in Higher Education." In *Learning in Virtual Worlds: Research and Applications*, edited by Sue Gregory, Mark J.W. Lee, Barney Dalgarno, and Belinda Tynan, 275–93. Athabasca: Athabasca University Press, 2016.

Tilhou, Rebecca, Valerie Taylor, and Helen Crompton. "3D Virtual Reality in K-12 Education: A Thematic Systematic Review." In *Emerging Technologies and Pedagogies in the Curriculum*, edited by Shengquan Yu, Mohamed Ally, and Avgoustos Tsinakos, 169–84. Singapore: Springer, 2020. https://doi.org/10.1007/978-981-15-0618-5_10

Todd, Robert L., Jessica Pater, and Paul M.A. Baker. "(In)Accessible Learning in Virtual Worlds." In *Learning in Virtual Worlds: Research and Applications*, edited by Sue Gregory, Mark J.W. Lee, Barney Dalgarno, and Belinda Tynan, 87–115. Athabasca: Athabasca University Press, 2016.

Varnum, Kenneth J., ed. *Beyond Reality: Augmented, Virtual, and Mixed Reality in the Library.* Chicago: ALA (American Library Association) Editions, 2019.

Wilson, Andrew. "Immersive Education: Virtual Reality and Project-Based Learning in the History Classroom." *Journal of Interactive Technology & Pedagogy* March 11, 2021. https://jitp.commons.gc.cuny.edu/immersive-education-virtual-reality-and-project-based-learning-in-the-history-classroom/.

Yu, Shengquan, Mohamed Ally, and Avgoustos Tsinakos, eds. *Emerging Technologies and Pedagogies in the Curriculum.* Singapore: Springer, 2020.

Zhang, Sarah. "Can VR Really Make You More Empathetic?" Wired, September 1, 2016. https://www.wired.com/2016/09/can-vr-really-make-people-empathetic/.

PART 1

REINVIGORATING AND
REINVESTIGATING THE PAST

CHAPTER 1

COLORING OUTSIDE THE CLASSROOM: DIGITAL TECHNOLOGY RESTORES COLOR TO ANCIENT SCULPTURE IN THE LIBRARY

Laura Surtees and Molly Kuchler

On Friday April 23, 2021, 60 people gathered on Zoom for a Bryn Mawr College Friday Finds talk to celebrate the *Coloring the Past* project, a digital scholarship project restoring color to two plaster casts of ancient Mediterranean sculpture housed in Rhys Carpenter Library, a research library dedicated to the study of archaeology, classics, history of art, and architecture. To restore color to the reliefs, we used projection mapping, a form of projected augmented reality that uses a 3D object as a canvas for displaying images or videos. We had hoped to give this talk in person and debut the exhibit in the library in front of the objects themselves, but the COVID-19 pandemic forced us to adjust to our circumstances and be flexible and creative in the approach, execution, goals, and scale of *Coloring the Past*. Even over Zoom the audience's reactions to the projected colorful images on the full-size plaster casts were palpable. Eyes widened, heads crooked, and gasps were heard as the audience watched the plaster casts transition from the appearance of bare stone to brightly colored sculpture. We juxtaposed the two views to challenge the audience's preconceptions of ancient sculpture as white and encourage them to confront their reactions to its colorful reality. For many, the contrast is jarring. Colored sculpture is often described as garish, tacky, or gaudy because of cultural conditioning established by the prevalence of bare stone statues as a definition of beauty.[1] White unpainted sculpture is the expected and familiar aesthetic due not only to poor preservation of the original paint, but also the value attached to bare sculpture since the Renaissance. This misunderstanding has been corrected to some extent in academic circles but has not been consistently addressed in public education. As a cross-departmental, interdisciplinary project, *Coloring the Past* experimented with non-invasive and non-destructive digital technologies of 3D modeling and projection mapping to explore new methods of conveying traditional archaeological and art historical research on polychromy (a term referring to the use of many colors as decoration on architecture and sculpture). Projecting color provides vivid and immersive visual representations of the colorful nature of the original sculpture, creating an alternative sensory experience for the general public and underscoring the incomplete nature of these artifacts.

Coloring the Past is a project led by Laura Surtees, Research and Instruction Librarian, Coordinator of Rhys Carpenter Library, and archaeologist, and Molly Kuchler, digital scholarship graduate assistant and MA student in Greek, Latin and classical studies in collaboration with Digital Scholarship Specialist Alice McGrath. Together we designed a six-week program for two undergraduate students that combined traditional archaeological and art historical library research with the acquisition of digital skills. We capitalized on the interdisciplinary nature of the project by distributing responsibilities according to expertise while collaborating closely throughout the process. Surtees led the research component and logistics while Kuchler designed the curriculum for the digital technologies in consultation with McGrath. Our focus was on developing students' skill sets and the acquisition of knowledge, so no previous experience with digital tools or the ancient world was required. We chose two undergraduate students from different backgrounds and fields of study: Vimbai Mawoneke (Math and Chemistry '21) and Mira Yuan (Classical and Near Eastern Archaeology and Museum Studies '21).[2] The project ran from June to mid-July 2020 with additional time dedicated to the exhibit opening and talk in spring of 2021.

DEVELOPING THE PROJECT

The seed for the *Coloring the Past* project was planted after attending a digital scholarship conference, *Apps, Maps & Models: Digital Pedagogy and Research in Art History, Archaeology & Visual Studies* by the Wired! Group at Duke University in 2015.[3] There, Mark Olson and Mariano Tepper presented their interactive projection mapping exhibit *Medieval Color Comes to Light* at the Nasher Museum as part of 2014–2015 *The Lives of Things* project at Duke University. This interdisciplinary project was part of an academic course where they projected color onto stone reliefs of medieval saints. An interactive iPad component allowed museumgoers to choose the colors for each section of the relief and receive information about the different pigments used for paint.[4] This exhibit showed how projection mapping could be a fun, interactive, and sustainable method of visually introducing ancient polychromy to people and recognizing the value of seeing the ancient world in color. The Nasher Museum is one of many museums that have incorporated extended reality (XR) technologies into their exhibits as tools for audience engagement by amplifying their sensory experience through the transformation of stone into colorful and life-like objects from the past.[5] Since the initial adoption of this technology in museums, advancements in 3D modeling programs, the availability of free online tools and resources, a manageable learning curve of digital skills, and the relatively low cost of high-quality projectors make projection mapping a feasible and engaging method of integrating XR technologies into humanities curricula and public discourse.

At its conception, the intended aim of *Coloring the Past* was to habituate viewers to seeing colorful images of ancient art in their everyday spaces on campus. But the value and importance of *Coloring the Past* became evident in the years between its inspiration and inception as modern reception of ancient Mediterranean art continued to evolve in harmful ways, particularly in the overt misuse and misappropriation of its "whiteness" by white supremacist groups and the violent pushback against scholars who advocate for the inclusion of ancient polychromy in conversations about the past.[6] The urgency of rectifying the reception of ancient Mediterranean sculpture hit closer to home during an informal discussion about making the library a more welcoming environment. One student mentioned how "white" the art is in Carpenter Library: that is, both visually "white" and culturally "white."[7] It was a stark reminder that the images around us are laden with symbolism and meaning that can be manipulated to be exclusionary and racist. We must be aware of and be proactive in countering the false portrayal of ancient society as homogenous and white by rethinking how objects are displayed and their impact on our communities. As stewards of these spaces, it is incumbent on us to engage with the historiography of the discipline and to rethink how the integration of alternative methods of displaying objects could combat these false narratives of the past and lead to the creation of a more inclusive space in the library.

While the idea for the project began in 2015, *Coloring the Past* was not set into motion until we received the financial support of a Digital Bryn Mawr Grant in late 2019.[8] We selected two relief sculptures on display in Rhys Carpenter Library as our canvases. These plaster casts were teaching aids in the early years of Bryn Mawr College but were resigned to storage until recently. Currently mounted side-by-side on the back wall of the Digital Media and Collaboration Lab are plaster casts of the Sandalbinder (late 5th century BCE) from the parapet wall of the Temple of Athena Nike in Athens, hanging on the left (Figure 1.1), and the Borgia Stele, an Archaic grave stele from an unknown context depicting a man and his dog (late 6th/early 5th century BCE) now in the Naples Museum, on the right (Figure 1.2).[9] We chose these reliefs because of their high visibility in a public setting and practical consider- ations, such as lighting and spatial configuration.[10] The students each picked a sculpture to research and reconstruct digitally; Mawoneke investigated the Sandalbinder, while Yuan worked on the Borgia Stele.[11]

Plans quickly changed in early 2020 as the COVID-19 pandemic brought a unique set of challenges. Most significantly, because campus access was restricted, the program pivoted to remote learning using Slack, Zoom, and email. We designed a flexible curriculum to accommodate the virtual format and our limited access to library resources, mitigate Zoom fatigue, and adjust to differing learning curves for acquiring the necessary digital skills. Using a wide array of information sources and media, the cur- riculum incorporated traditional and nontraditional perspectives and integrated assigned readings, independent research, group discussions, written assignments, tutorials, digital tasks, public speaking, and a daily journal to record productivity, problems, and ideas. In addition, the projection mapping component could not be installed during the program's initial run in the summer of 2020. We realigned our project goals accordingly to include the creation of a website to share information on ancient polychromy and showcase our 3D colorized models of the plaster casts, so that our work could still be displayed in some format despite the set- back. The website, though initially not included in the curriculum,

Figure 1.1: Plaster cast of "Nike adjusting her sandal" (Sandalbinder) from the Temple of Athena Nike in Athens in BMC Special Collections (2016.1.2).

Figure 1.2: Plaster cast of the Borgia Stele in BMC Special Collections (2016.1.1).

became essential to our goal of compiling information in multiple media, allowing the team to outline and document their process and results on both the digital and scholarly fronts.[12] As part of the program, we planned to install the projection video and give a public talk. As part of the exhibit opening in spring 2021, we created a coloring book of ancient sculpture of other plaster casts on display in Carpenter Library that we mailed to participants after the event. We collaborated with Bronwen Densmore, the College's Makerspace Coordinator, to print the coloring books using the RISO printer. Our goal was to provide a tangible and portable representation of the project as a mechanism for continuing the conversation in a fun and interactive way. Since the exhibit is ongoing, in the fall of 2021 we put crayons and individual coloring pages from our coloring book in the "Intellectual Wellness Center" in Carpenter Library for people to take and color. The colored images now decorate space within the library to raise awareness of ancient polychromy. We adopted another augmented reality (AR) tool, QR codes, to help connect the coloring pages with the larger initiative of reimagining these sculptures. Each coloring page had a QR code for our website along with the line "Did you know that ancient sculpture was painted? Scan to learn more!" in order to capture their attention and engage indirectly with the community about ancient polychromy. It was a simple, yet effective XR technology that was easily integrated at no cost and enhanced the accessibility and visibility of Coloring the Past.

The academic content of our curriculum explored various aspects of ancient polychromy from ancient pigments and color combinations to the new technologies for detecting traces of paint as well as exploring the historiography of the discipline, modern reception of antiquity, and social justice issues. The research module was designed thematically to introduce ancient polychromy and its value through a social justice lens. Using popular media, like blog posts and video clips, we examined our understanding of polychromy and how the absence of color on ancient sculpture in museums and in media has shaped our own understanding (or misunderstanding) of the past.[13] The digital module focused on building competencies in data management, critical making and design, and expanding the student's digital skills toolkit. Students learned the practical basics of 3D modeling, animation software, photogrammetry, and website design, and were introduced to concepts such as digital ethics, accessibility, and data stewardship. By combining these pedagogical modules, students took a two-pronged, multidisciplinary path to ultimately present data on polychromy both visually and in writing in an ethical, sustainable, and accessible way. The research module and XR module ran concurrently, alternating each day over the six weeks.

ACADEMIC RESEARCH ON POLYCHROMY AND ANTIRACISM

Ancient polychromy, once seldom discussed beyond a passing reference in public or academic discourse, has begun to be recognized as an integral part of conversations in recent years.[14] Yet we continue to be inundated with images of white bare ancient stone sculpture and architecture in museums, libraries, and popular media despite having indisputable archaeological and textual evidence to the contrary.[15] Thus, white marble sculpture has long been synonymous with idealized representations of beauty. It is important to acknowledge the historiography of valuing the white marble aesthetic for statuary and trace the trajectory of this development.

In the eighteenth century, scholars conformed to the Renaissance vision of ancient sculpture as unpainted and exploited the literal white aesthetic of ancient sculpture by equating racial whiteness with beauty. German scholar Johann Winckelmann, known as one of the fathers of art history, manipulated archaeological evidence of ancient polychromy by attributing painted sculpture to non-Greek and non-Roman cultures, which served to equate Greek and

Roman material culture with emerging ideas about beauty, purity, and whiteness.[16] Although Winckelmann later accepted that Greeks and Romans painted their sculpture, this was only reflected in his scholarship posthumously.[17] Despite evidence that ancient sculptures were painted, statues are still frequently presented without reference to their painted surfaces, which perpetuates the misconception of these objects as unpainted. Recently, however, there has been a push to address this curatorial practice and the historical narrative it reinforces to revive the study of polychromy in public venues in connection with public history.[18]

Our discussions necessarily focused on the value of seeing ancient objects in color and the ramifications of the perceived homogeneity of ancient Mediterranean societies. We delved deeper into how these practices reinforce concepts of beauty and "whiteness," like Winckelmann's. Such concepts have often been appropriated by radical white supremacist groups, like Identity Evropa (later the American Identity Movement), which used images of ancient statues like the Apollo Belvedere and Nicolas Coustou's *Julius Caesar* to overtly appeal to a supposedly "white" classical tradition linked to white European heritage.[19] The Black Lives Matter movement and the protests following the murder of George Floyd lent an urgency to our project to address the misrepresentation of a homogenous and white ancient society. It is a matter of professional ethics to investigate the historiography of this disciplinary paradigm and its modern reception in order to counter these false and harmful narratives.

Having grappled with the impact of modern reception, we shifted our focus to the archaeological, textual, and art historical evidence for ancient and medieval polychromy and the study of pigments, including new scientific and technological advances for detecting and analyzing traces of paint. Our colleague, Marianne Weldon, Collections Manager for Special Collections, discussed with the students how photographic techniques are used to detect trace amounts of paint and have expanded our understanding of pigments. For example, Egyptian blue, a synthetic pigment once considered rare because it was not detectable by the naked eye, is now known to have been in common use in antiquity, because it can now be identified using visible-induced luminescence imaging.[20] Students each chose a relief sculpture to research its history and context. Neither of the original sculptures had traces of paint preserved; therefore, we relied on comparanda—that is, sculpture chronologically and geographically similar to ours on which paint has been preserved—to choose our color palette. For our color choices, we investigated which pigments were used in different chronological periods in order to avoid anachronistic choices.[21] We chose the colors from natural pigments used in the ancient world: dark red, yellow, and brown from ochres; bright red from madder plant roots; black from burnt organic matter; and Egyptian blue.[22] For coloring our models, we used images of recreated ancient pigment swatches from the ColourLex online encyclopedia project.[23] In reconstructing the paint for skin, we followed the ancient artistic convention of representing men with a darker complexion than women who are represented as fair, yet still painted.[24] Drawing on evidence of skin tone from examples like the Treu Head and the Alexander Sarcophagus, we used layers of different pigments at different opacities to create skin tone.[25] While this process is artificial, the pigment swatches allowed us to imitate the exact tone of ancient pigments and the visual texture of a material like red or brown ochre. Although we guided their research, the final decisions on which colors to use on their respective reliefs was up to the students (See Figures 1.3 and 1.4 for their results).[26] Their colorized reconstructions are hypothetical yet grounded in archaeological evidence.[27]

In the past decade, although displaying colored reconstructions has become more common in museums and other public-facing institutions, the methods of exhibiting these reconstructions have varied. For the international traveling exhibit *Gods in Color*, Vinzenz Brinkmann and Ulrike Koch-Brinkmann painstakingly

Figure 1.3: Polychrome 3D reconstruction of the Borgia Stele by Mira Yuan.

Figure 1.4: Polychrome 3D reconstruction of the Nike relief by Vimbai Mawoneke.

recreated full-size plaster replicas of Greek and Roman sculpture and hand-painted them in bright colors and patterns based on research of the originals.[28] However, this method is time-consuming, permanent, and difficult to change based on new evidence, and costly, not least because it requires specialized material resources and the professional expertise of artists and technicians. These temporary exhibits help raise awareness of ancient polychromy, but in order to affect the wider public perception it is necessary to have permanent displays and ongoing programming on the topic to establish and reinforce polychromy as essential to our understanding of ancient sculpture. Museums and other educational institutions should be prioritizing color as a permanent part of their ancient collections both visually and on informational panels.

TECHNOLOGY AND PROJECTION MAPPING

Advancements in digital technologies have addressed the complexities of displaying the colorful nature of the original objects. The simplest method, juxtaposing 2D or 3D digital video or image reconstruction with the original object, is a common practice because it can be easily incorporated into preexisting exhibits and requires little modification to the physical space or display. Often these reconstructions are simple images and do not consider the finish, texture, or dimensionality of the original object because recreating these experiential aspects can be difficult on a screen or plaque. While these digital displays raise awareness of the incomplete nature of unpainted objects, we believe in the sensory importance of seeing saturated, intense colors on the object itself as they provide a scaled visual representation of the original. One of the greatest strengths of projection mapping is the ease with which it can be scaled to display on any item, so that objects only a few inches in height to entire buildings can become canvases. A video or image is limited to the size of a screen or its designated wall space, while a projection mapping is meant to fit the object perfectly, which magnifies its impact in terms of color, texture, and scale.

Projection mapping has not been neglected as a form of display in historical exhibits. For the past decade or so, some museums have integrated projection onto 2D and 3D surfaces into exhibits to enhance sensory experience, and because it is noninvasive, nondamaging, easily modified, and requires limited, affordable hardware.[29] Recent technological advances have made powerful projectors smaller and more financially accessible, creating opportunities for more versatile and smaller-scale exhibits using projectors. Projection can be programmed to change automatically as part of a narrative or to be interactive and further engage the public in the reception of history. Along with the *Medieval Color Comes to Light* exhibit, the *Color the Temple* exhibit at the Metropolitan Museum of Art in New York City was an early adopter of an interactive element, where the audience used a tablet to manipulate the color of the projected output.[30] This temporary exhibit had a low technological requirement for projection mapping, as the low-relief sculpture on the Egyptian Temple of Dendur did not require "mapping" or manipulation of the projection to correct for warping that occurs when aligning a 2D image to a 3D object. Sculpture in high relief and in the round are more complex subjects, but software has been designed explicitly to account for the difference between the 2D projection output and the 3D surface of the sculpture, such as MadMapper used in *Coloring the Past*.

Despite the existence of past projects using projection mapping, embarking on curricular development for the digital and technical side of the project frequently felt like exploring uncharted territory. Other projects on polychromy reconstruction focused more on the scientific analysis of pigments and showcasing of the final products than the methodology.[31] Few projects document or publish details on the hardware, software, methods used, or on the decision-making process. As a result, projection mapping is frequently seen as an impressive yet out-of-reach and costly method for displaying reconstructions. Many larger institutions tend to hire professional firms who use proprietary methodology and expensive graphics software to create digital reconstructions.[32] While the end products are striking, it obscures the availability of cheaper, more accessible methods for XR reconstructions. When a project does publish its methodology, it is often difficult to replicate the technical details because of advancements in software and technology.[33] As a result, thorough documentation of process and rationale was integrated into our project's goals and methods, as we wanted our project to be easily replicated or serve as a framework for others. To build our methodology, we started from the desired product, a projection mapping, and worked backwards to identify the necessary steps, skills, and software needed in order to establish learning benchmarks for the students. The result was an academic program that taught the undergraduates valuable skills such as basics of specific software (see below), website design, and the ethics of digital open-source resources, while simultaneously asking them to apply their academic research to their models. Even if this technology becomes obsolete, our hope is that our methodology will provide a pedagogical and practical framework to assist other projects of any scale or scope.

TECHNOLOGY: MODELING AND PROJECTION SOFTWARE

The pandemic proved to be a test of open-access principles, because we had to rely extensively on free and accessible digital resources. We had intended to use photogrammetry to capture the reliefs digitally, but we were not allowed on campus to take our own photographs. A colleague had used the Borgia Stele as a practice subject in a previous photogrammetry workshop at Bryn Mawr College and gave us these photographs to use.[34] Using photogrammetry software Agisoft Metashape, we created the necessary stereolithography or standard triangle language (STL) file from the photographs by mapping the exterior of the object in virtual space. STL files describe the 3D geometry of an object in space using lines and points in triangular panels without any other descriptors (such as size, texture, or color). The well-known

Sandalbinder relief had been uploaded to MyMiniFactory by the Scan the World project, which houses free scans of cultural heritage objects.[35]

Using 3D digital models allowed us to imitate the play of light and shadow on the figures. The photogrammetric process provided us with a "point cloud," or a map of the 3D object using thousands of dots. The point cloud was then simplified into a digital "mesh" in STL format, which in turn formed the basis of our models. The STL files we created contain mapped "vertex" and "edge" data of 3D objects and are commonly used for 3D printing, as they are easier to work with than point clouds. The number of vertices and faces (also called polygons) present in a mesh makes the model more accurate but also makes it more difficult for a computer to process. After editing the initial models, our face count went from 150,000 faces to 90,000 for the Sandalbinder (the more complicated of the two, see Figures 1.5 and 1.6) and

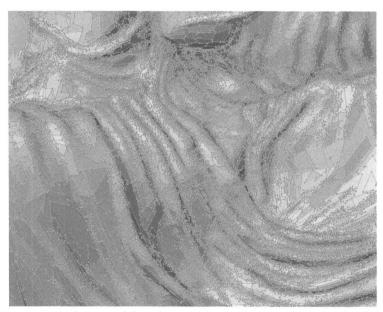

Figure 1.5: A close-up of the edges and facets that create the details of the Sandalbinder's chiton in the 3D model.

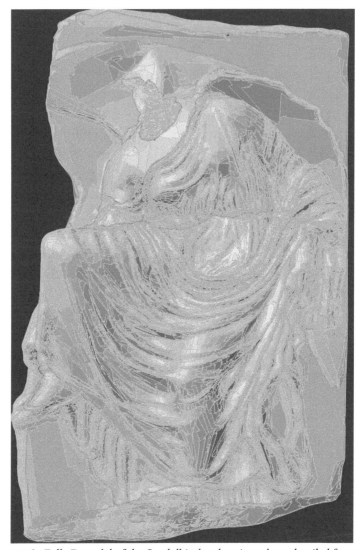

Figure 1.6: Full 3D model of the Sandalbinder showing where detailed facet and edge data was preserved most to retain realistic detailing.

90,000 to 70,000 for the Borgia Stele. These adjustments allowed us to more easily identify seams for UV unwrapping (see below) and lessened both the file size and the rendering time (how long it took the computer to generate the final images of our models).

For both mesh reduction and for coloring the models we used Blender, an open-source 3D animation and design software.[36] The program allows the creation of anything from feature film-quality animations to relatively straightforward projects like our own. The learning curve is steep, however, and the sheer number of features and technical jargon can be overwhelming, especially for students with no prior knowledge of digital modeling. To build the students' digital toolkit, we created a curriculum based on learning from tutorials and self-teaching resources websites such as YouTube.[37] From there, a learning path comprised of asynchronous online tutorials, exercises, and Zoom demonstrations was developed, which the students completed concurrently with the application of their skills to their respective models. The runtime of the two basics courses for Blender (Blender Guru's Donut Tutorial and Donut Tutorial Series) is approximately 12 hours; however, the time commitment can more than double when taking into account the learning curves, troubleshooting, and creative process. In the end, learning both the basics and the selected intermediate skills necessary for our project in Blender took 4 weeks of our 6-week program, with students working about 20 hours a week on digital tools and 20 hours on research each week. Specialized tools in Blender simplified the coloring process and allowed us to play around with paint, light, texture, and finish in order to create realistic models. After importing our STL file into Blender and reducing the number of faces on our models, the next step was creating a canvas on which to "paint" the color. To begin, we had to UV-unwrap the model.[38] UV unwrapping can be visualized by thinking of a 3D cube taken apart at the seams to create a 2D shape, which creates a flat surface to be painted with color. It allows for precise coloring of specific facets of an object, such as clothing (Figure 1.7). We colored the resultant UV maps using the texture painting feature. Texture paint works like a can of spray paint and a stencil, where the stencil is an image file that can be "sprayed" onto the UV with varying opacity. The students simulated the layering techniques uncovered by visible-induced

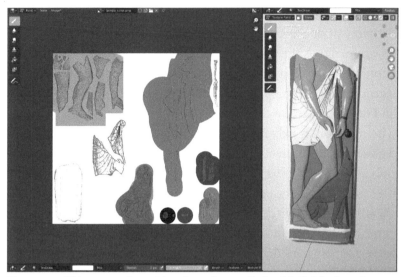

Figure 1.7: UV unwrapping with paint color applied, with finished product on the right.

luminescence imaging by layering different pigments in varying opacities to create custom shades of paint for their reconstructions.

The true flexibility of 3D reconstruction and the power of Blender shines through in the use of texture nodes and the materials shader. Texture nodes are difficult to work with but, when used and combined with tools like the physics engine in Blender, can simulate how light interacts with various types of materials to produce a realistic surface appearance. In our reconstructions, we were able to imitate the use of shiny or matte sealant on painted marble by changing the reflective and refractive properties of the reliefs' surfaces in varying places.[39] We controlled how light would "hit" the reliefs by deciding its color, angle, and strength. The resulting effects are realistic, plausible hypothetical reconstructions that can be modified as new research or technologies develop. In order to highlight the contrast between the painted and unpainted versions, the students learned basic Blender animation capabilities through their tutorials and created an animation of the reconstruction fading in and out.

PROJECTION MAPPING AND INSTALLATION

The final step was to import our completed videos into MadMapper for projection. We used this projection mapping software to scale our projected images and videos and manipulate them as necessary to map onto 3D surfaces and control the looped video playback. In spring 2021, we were able to access the library to install the projection mapping. We repurposed a desktop computer to run the MadMapper software. Our installation was semi-permanent and so we needed the ability to manipulate the video freely and in real time to realign the image and canvas because the projectors would be moved periodically. While one could use a free trial of MadMapper to remain budget-friendly, we licensed this software in order to use advanced features, like the ability to project from one computer through two projectors simultaneously. We placed two standard classroom projectors on a rollaway cart that could be easily moved when the space was needed for other purposes, such as classes or workshops. We marked on the floor the location of the cart enabling it to be easily repositioned to minimize the digital realignment that would be necessary on restoring the exhibit. Using MadMapper, we aligned the features of our digital reconstructions to their physical counterparts on the wall and finally brought our work to life.

CONCLUSION

Screens in multiple countries and across the Bryn Mawr College community flashed in vibrant colors during the virtual opening.[40] The opening exhibit was temporary because COVID-19 restrictions closed the lab until fall 2021. *Coloring the Past* has been reinstalled, and the digital animated images are now projected onto the plaster casts throughout the day. The project stemmed from an interest in using digital technologies to tell a more complete story of the ancient world and reach a wider audience. We felt an obligation to debunk racist narratives of antiquity, address their implications for our students and members of the college community, and provide an alternative method of displaying these objects in full color to foster belonging and learning within the library and on campus. The plaster casts on display in Carpenter Library provided a canvas for promoting polychromy. We used XR technologies grounded in archaeological research to provide an immersive sensory experience that highlights the validity of polychromy as a field of research and the importance of seeing the ancient world in color.

College campuses are ripe with potential collaborations both in and outside the classroom. XR technologies and other digital tools often seem expensive and out of reach to academics, which is why cross-departmental collaboration is key and mutually beneficial, particularly in higher education. Working collaboratively made the workload and various learning curves manageable. *Coloring the Past* exemplifies the value of collaborative partnerships, and it capitalized on the expertise from multiple departments within Library and Information Technology Services (LITS) such as Research and Instructional Services, Digital Scholarship, Special Collections, and the Makerspace. Our interdisciplinary collaboration extended to the students who brought diverse perspectives to our discussions as they engaged with new scholarship and technology. We kept our expenses low by capitalizing on the availability of free online software and tutorials and by reusing available computers and projectors that were sufficient for our purposes. Our largest expense was paying the students full-time for six weeks. Student engagement was central to this project. We wanted to provide a learning opportunity for students to acquire digital skills and knowledge that could be transferable to their own studies. While an emphasis has been placed on integrating digital tools into classes, particularly in the humanities, we also saw firsthand the value of extending beyond the classroom. Its placement within the library extended the reach of *Coloring the Past* to the college community. As learning centers and hubs on college campuses, libraries provide another venue for the dissemination of knowledge to the public who may not have been exposed to these ideas or history in their academic studies. As an immersive visual experience, it showcases the value and capabilities of digital tools and serves as an introduction to the world of ancient polychromy for the Bryn Mawr College community at large, thereby shifting modern perspectives to take on a more inclusive and accurate view of ancient Mediterranean art.

For a complete guide to the project, please visit our website at https://digitalscholarship.brynmawr.edu/coloringthepast/.

NOTES

1. Rose-Greenland, "Color Perception in Sociology"; Lloyd Lee, "Deconstructing Monochromism."
2. Throughout this project, our methodology has been guided by the principles of scholarship of teaching and learning (SoTL). The students were integral in the process and outcomes. We want to acknowledge and credit their work. They have given their permission to include their names and their scholarship in this chapter.
3. "Apps, Maps & Models: Digital Pedagogy and Research in Art History, Archaeology & Visual Studies," updated March 4, 2016, https://aahvs.duke.edu/articles/apps-maps-models-symposium-digital-pedagogy-and-research-art-history-archaeology-and-visual.
4. Dodson, "Rock, Paper, Chisel, 3D Printer"; Duke Digital Art History and Visual Culture (DAHVC) Research Lab, "Medieval Color Comes to Light"; Duke University, "Medieval Art Gets a Modern Twist."
5. Examples of exhibits that integrate XR technologies and were inspiration include: DAHVC, "Medieval Color Comes to Light"; Felsen and Peters, "Color the Temple"; Franklin Institute, "Terracotta Warriors of the First Emperor"; Cleveland Museum of Art, "ARTLens Exhibition"; The Roman Baths at Bath, "Walkthrough," https://www.romanbaths.co.uk/.
6. Dozier, "Pharos"; Bond, "Classical World in Color"; Bond, "Whitewashing Ancient Statues"; Bond, "The Argument Made by the Absence"; Artforum International, "Classicist Receives Death Threats"; Talbot, "The Myth of Whiteness in Classical Sculpture."
7. Private conversation between Laura Surtees and a Bryn Mawr College undergraduate student, included with permission, February 2019.

8. We are grateful for the financial support of a Digital Bryn Mawr Grant as well as the investment of time and knowledge by our colleagues in Library and Information Technology Services at Bryn Mawr College.

9. "The Borgia Stele, late 19th or early 20th century plaster cast after a later 6th to early 5th century BCE original," M. Carey Thomas Collection, 2016.1.1, Bryn Mawr College Special Collections; "Nike adjusting her sandal" from the Temple of Athena Nike in Athens, late 19th or early 20th century plaster cast after original of 5th century BCE." M. Carey Thomas Collection, 2016.2, Bryn Mawr College Special Collections.

10. In our planning phase, we had initially selected plaster relief casts in the atrium because of their prominent location in the library. However, this space was too expansive to project an image across while adjusting for natural light without the permanent hardwired installation of a high-quality, expensive projector which would require a large investment. The space and lighting are important considerations when using a projector, as even moderately powerful projectors will be easily washed out in very bright sunlit rooms.

11. For a discussion of their research, color selections, and process see the projects' website, "Coloring the Past: Restoring Color to Ancient Sculpture Through 3D Modeling and Projection Mapping," https://digitalscholarship. brynmawr.edu/coloringthepast/.

12. "Coloring the Past," https://digitalscholarship.brynmawr.edu/coloring thepast/.

13. Lucas and Lucas, "White at the Museum" is one of many examples.

14. Bond, "Whitewashing Ancient Statues"; Lucas and Lucas, "White at the Museum"; Talbot, "The Myth of Whiteness in Classical Sculpture"; Frischer, "Introduction"; Hedegaard and Brøns, "Lost in Translation"; Østergaard, "Polychromy of Ancient Sculpture"; Østergaard, "Copenhagen Polychromy Network"; Østergaard, "Challenge to Western Ideals?"; Bradley, "The Importance of Colour on Ancient Marble Sculpture"; Brøns, "Ancient Colours"; Warburton and Thavapalan, *The Value of Colour*; Østergaard and Nielsen, *Transformations*.

15. Video games, such as the critically acclaimed *Assassin's Creed: Odyssey*, are increasingly presenting a more accurate colorful representation of antiquity where architecture, sculpture, and clothing were painted.

16. Brinkmann, "Polychromy of Ancient Greek Sculpture."

17. Hüfler, "Geschichte der Kunst des Alterthums."

18. Previous scholarship acknowledges and highlights the ubiquitous nature of ancient polychromy, but it is often disconnected from the analysis and interpretation of these objects/sculpture, resulting in the perpetual false experience

and sensation of seeing these objects as white unpainted objects. Public talks, such as Frischer's "Recovering Polychromy in the Statues of Hadrian's Villa," raise awareness. Recent efforts, such as the Metropolitan Museum of Art's *Chroma* exhibit (2022–2023), spread examples of polychromatic sculpture throughout the existing bare artifacts to reinforce the ubiquity of paint and the fragmentary nature of the archaeological material, rather than relegating them to a single gallery or isolated exhibit. Frischer's Digital Sculpture Project website (http://www.digitalsculpture.org) and the Ny Carlsberg Glyptotek's online database "Tracking Color: Polychromy of ancient world" (https://trackingcolour.com) are other examples of collaborative projects aimed at investigating polychromy with a public online presence.

19. McCoskey, "Beware of Greeks"; Morse, "Classics and the Alt-Right"; Kennedy, "Being 'American', Sophocles' Intentions, and the Debates over 'Western Civ'"; Kennedy, "We Condone It by Our Silence."

20. Webb, Summerour, and Giaccai, "NMAI Archaeological Peruvian Textiles"; Dyer and Sotiropoulou, "A Technical Step Forward"; Verri, Opper, and Deviese, "The 'Treu Head'."

21. Ridgway, "Role of Color," in *Prayers in Stone*, 103–107; Walter-Karydi, "Color in Classical Painting"; Papapostolou, "Color in Archaic Painting"; Richter, "Polychromy in Greek Sculpture."

22. Lipscher, "ColourLex"; Person and Roberts, "Ancient Color"; Feller, Roy, and FitzHugh, *Artists' Pigments*; Douma, "Pigments through the Ages."

23. Lipscher, "ColourLex."

24. Most often seen in Greek wall paintings, but evidence for this convention extends into evidence from painted sculpture as seen in the Treu Head and throughout the *Gods in Color* exhibit; Verri, Opper, and Deviese, "The 'Treu Head'"; Brinkmann, Dreyfus, Koch-Brinkmann, *Gods in Color*; Eaverly, *Tan Men/Pale Women*; Brøns, Hedegaard, and Sargent, "Painted Faces."

25. Koch-Brinkmann, Piening, and Brinkmann. "Rendering of Human Skin"; Verri, Opper, and Deviese, "The 'Treu Head'"; Skovmøller, "Where Marble Meets Colour"; Brøns, Hedegaard, and Sargent, "Painted Faces."

26. These reconstructions are credited to Mira Yuan and Vimbai Mawoneke and are reproduced with permission from the students. For more details, see their work at https://digitalscholarship.brynmawr.edu/coloringthepast/.

27. These reconstructions relied on archaeological comparanda. When the evidence was inconclusive or ambiguous, students made their selections based on visual appeal and aesthetics.

28. Brinkmann et al., *Gods in Color: Polychromy*; Brinkmann et al., *Gods in Color: Painted Sculpture*.

29. The compactness of projectors coupled with their increased affordability expands the possibility of implementing this technology. A simple projection on a blank wall could be executed for the cost of the projection, which could be as little as a couple hundred dollars.

30. *Color the Temple*, initially installed as a temporary exhibit in 2015, remains on display as a looped video without the interactive element. Installed in 2014–2015, *Medieval Color Comes to Light* is still on exhibit today.

31. *Gods in Color* (Brinkmann et al., *Gods in Color: Polychromy*; Brinkmann et al., *Gods in Color: Painted Sculpture*) extensively covers their methodology and research; however, they did not use digital imaging for their reconstructions. The Treu Head reconstruction video (Verri, "Roman Sculpture and Colour") was a companion to the article Verri, Opper, and Deviese, "The 'Treu Head'." However, the methodology for virtual reconstruction was not covered in the video or the publication, which focused on technical imaging research. The *Color the Temple* project also documented their methodology (Felsen and Peters, "Color the Temple"), but their approach was not directly applicable to our project.

32. At the Museum of Fine Arts, Boston's Greek sculpture gallery, a color reconstruction video has been placed next to a Roman copy of the Athena Parthenos statue (dating to the 2nd or 3rd century CE). The video and reconstruction on display were commissioned from experiential exhibit agency Black Math, which has done work for major corporations and sports teams (Black Math, "Athena Reveals Her True Colors"). Bluecadet is responsible for the augmented reality web app experience implemented for the Metropolitan Museum of Art's "Chroma" exhibit, accessible through the exhibit website.

33. Siotto et al., "Ancient Polychromy" at the time noted the need for improvements for a more accurate rendering of the paint and materials; features, namely the layering of texture shaders in Blender, are now available. See also Frischer, "New Digital Tools."

34. With thanks to Matthew Jameson who provided the images.

35. https://www.myminifactory.com/scantheworld. Had the means for obtaining both models not been accessible, two other methods were available. The first is used in the exhibit *Nike is Now* (Schultz and Goodinson, "Nike is Now"), which involved digital sculpting to recreate the sculpture from scratch. This method can be used to create a hyper-accurate mesh that has limited complexity to reduce computer processing power. However, the *Nike is Now* project was developed by a professional artist and intended for virtual display only. The second alternative method was used by the "Color the Temple" project (Felsen and Peters, "Color the Temple"). In this project, an outline was

created by tracing a picture of the temple and coloring it in Adobe Illustrator and then projecting it onto the Temple of Dendur itself. This method is suitable for objects in low relief like the Borgia Stele but would have been difficult to adapt to the high relief of the Sandalbinder.

36. "Open source" means that Blender is run entirely on donations (or the "pay what you can" model), and that the code for the software is available to anyone who wants it. As a result, anyone with an understanding of the code can build extensions and new features and likewise make them publicly available. Artists who need certain tools can create them rather than wait for them to be made by official developers.

37. Social media sites Reddit and Blender's StackExchange host large communities of Blender users to answer questions and share projects. Particularly useful for our purposes was the in-depth introductory tutorials of YouTuber "Blender Guru" (Andrew Price) https://www.youtube.com/channel/UCOKH wx1VCdgnxwbjyb9lu1g

38. UV mapping and UV unwrapping is the process of mapping the surface of a 3D object into 2D space so that an image or coloring can be applied to the surface. U and V refer to the axes of the two dimensions of this flattened surface, as X, Y, and Z are the axes used for the object in 3D space. Using points marked on the XYZ coordinate system that translate to points on the UV plane, the computer is able to flatten the sides of an object into a flat shape or multiple flat shapes. This tool allows us to apply color and images while avoiding the issues normally faced when imposing 2D textures or images on an irregular shape, since it is difficult, for example, to wrap a map onto a sphere to create a globe.

39. Koch-Brinkmann, Piening, and Brinkmann "Rendering of Human Skin"; Siotto et al., "Digital Study."

40. We advertised our Friday Finds talk to the Bryn Mawr Community; however, it was shared widely online and so our audience included people in the United States, Canada, and Europe.

WORKS CITED

Artforum International. "Classicist Receives Death Threats from Alt-Right over Art Historical Essay." Artforum, June 15, 2017. Accessed May 26, 2020. https://www.artforum.com/news/classicist-receives-death-threats-from-alt-right-over-art-historical-essay-68963

Black Math. "Athena Reveals Her True Colors." Museum of Fine Arts, Boston. December 20, 2021. Video, 2 min. 52 sec. https://www.mfa.org/video/athena-reveals-her-true-colors.

Blender Guru (Price, Andrew). YouTube. https://www.youtube.com/channel/UCOKHwxIVCdgnxwbjyb9luIg

Bond, Sarah. "Whitewashing Ancient Statues: Whiteness, Racism and Color in the Ancient World." Forbes, April 27, 2017. Accessed June 11, 2020. https://www.forbes.com/sites/drsarahbond/2017/04/27/whitewashing-ancient-statues-whiteness-racism-and-color-in-the-ancient-world/

Bond, Sarah. "The Argument Made by the Absence: On Whiteness, Polychromy, and Diversity in Classics." History From Below (blog). April 30, 2017. https://sarahemilybond.com/2017/04/30/the-argument-made-by-the-absence-on-whiteness-polychromy-and-diversity-in-classics/

Bond, Sarah E. "Why We Need to Start Seeing the Classical World in Color." Hyperallergic, June 7, 2017. https://hyperallergic.com/383776/why-we-need-to-start-seeing-the-classical-world-in-color/

Bradley, Mark. "The Importance of Colour on Ancient Marble Sculpture." *Art History* 32, no. 3 (2009): 427–57. https://doi.org/10.1111/j.1467-8365.2009.00666.x

Brinkmann, Vinzenz, "The Polychromy of Ancient Greek Sculpture." In *The Color of Life: Polychromy in Sculpture from Antiquity to the Present*, edited by Roberta Panzanelli, Eike D. Schmidt, and Kenneth D.S. Lapatin, 18–39. Los Angeles: J. Paul Getty Museum and The Getty Research Institute, 2008.

Brinkmann, Vinzenz, Oliver Primavesi, and Max Hollein, eds. *Circumlitio: The Polychromy of Antique and Mediaeval Sculpture*. Proceedings of the Johann David Passavant Colloquium, December 10–12, 2008. Frankfurt am Main: Liebieghaus Skulpturnsammlung, 2010.

Brinkmann, Vinzenz, Renée Dreyfus, Ulrike Koch-Brinkmann, eds. *Gods in Color: Polychromy in the Ancient World*. San Francisco: Fine Arts Museums of San Francisco, Legion of Honor, DelMonico and Prestel, 2017.

Brinkmann, Vinzenz, Raimund Wünsche, Ulrike Koch-Brinkmann, Sylvia Kellner, Joseph Köttl, Olaf Herzog. *Gods in Color: Painted Sculpture of Classical Antiquity*. Translated by Rodney Batstone. Munich: Stiftung Archäologie Glyptothek, 2007.

Brøns, Cecilie. "Ancient Colours: Perspectives and Methodological Challenges." In *The Value of Colour: Material and Economic Aspects in the Ancient World*, edited by David Warburton and Shiyanthi Thavapalan, 311–32. Berlin Studies of the Ancient World 70. Berlin: Edition Topoi, 2019.

Brøns, Cecilie, Signe Skriver Hedegaard, and Maria Louise Sargent, "Painted Faces: Investigations of Polychromy on Etruscan Antefixes in the Ny Carlsberg Glyptotek." *Etruscan Studies* 19, no. 1 (2016): 23–65. https://doi.org/10.1515/etst-2015-0012

Cleveland Museum of Art. "ARTLens Exhibition." June 2019. https://www.clevelandart.org/artlens-gallery/artlens-exhibition

Dodson, Alexandra. "Rock, Paper, Chisel, 3D Printer: Teaching Medieval Art with Technology." *Peregrinations: Journal of Medieval Art and Architecture* 6, no. 2 (2017): 13–29. https://digital.kenyon.edu/perejournal/vol6/iss2/4

Douma, Michael, curator. "Pigments through the Ages." (2008) http://www.webexhibits.org/pigments/

Dozier, Curtis. "Pharos: Doing Justice to the Classics." Updated July 21, 2021. https://pharos.vassarspaces.net/

Duke Digital Art History and Visual Culture Research Lab. "Medieval Color Comes to Light." Updated March 28, 2021. Accessed January 28, 2022. https://dahvc.org/project/medieval-color/

Duke University. "Medieval Art Gets a Modern Twist." Duke Today, December 8, 2015. https://today.duke.edu/2015/12/medieval-art-gets-a-modern-twist

Dyer, Joanne, and Sophia Sotiropoulou. "A Technical Step Forward in the Integration of Visible-Induced Luminescence Imaging Methods for the Study of Ancient Polychromy." *Heritage Science* 5:24 (June 19, 2017). https://doi.org/10.1186/s40494-017-0137-2

Eaverly, Mary Ann. *Tan Men/Pale Women: Color and Gender in Archaic Greece and Egypt, a Comparative Approach.* Ann Arbor: The University of Michigan Press, 2013.

Feller, Robert L., Ashok Roy, and Elisabeth West FitzHugh, eds. *Artists' Pigments: A Handbook of Their History and Characteristics, volumes 1–3.* Washington: National Gallery of Art, 1986.

Felsen, Matt, and Erin Peters. "Color the Temple: Using Projected Light to Restore Color." The Metropolitan Museum of Art, December 24, 2014. https://www.metmuseum.org/blogs/digital-underground/2015/color-the-temple

Franklin Institute. "Terracotta Warriors of the First Emperor." September 30, 2017–March 4, 2018. https://www.fi.edu/exhibit/terracotta-warriors

Frischer, Bernard. "Introduction with Remarks on the Methodological Implications of the Digital Restoration of the Richmond Caligula." In *New Studies on the Portrait of Caligula in the Virginia Museum of Fine Arts*, edited by Peter J.M. Schertz and Bernard Frischer. Leiden: Brill, 2020.

Frischer, Bernard. "Recovering Polychromy in the Statues of Hadrian's Villa." Public talk given as part of the Wolf Humanities Center's Forum on Color, October 8, 2014, Penn Museum, Philadelphia, PA. Audio, 1 hour, 32 min.

Frischer, Bernard D. "New Digital Tools for Restoring Polychromy to 3D Digital Models of Sculpture," January 7, 2012. https://hcommons.org/deposits/item/hc:12019/

Hedegaard, Signe Buccarella, and Cecilie Brøns. "Lost in Translation: An Introduction to the Challenging Task of Communicating Long-Lost Polychromy on Graeco-Roman Marble Sculptures." *Analecta Romana Instituti Danici* 44 (2020): 7–28.

Hüfler, Almut. "Adolf h. Borbein, Thomas W. Gaethgens, Johannes Irmscher (†) und Max Kunze (hrsg.), Johann Joachim Winckelmann: Geschichte der Kunst des Alterthums." *Bonner Jahrbücher* 209 (2009): 480–4.

Kennedy, Rebecca Futo. "Being 'American', Sophocles' Intentions, and the Debates over 'Western Civ.'" Classics at the Intersections (blog), May 8, 2020. Accessed June 14, 2020. https://rfkclassics.blogspot.com/2020/05/being-american-sophocles-intentions-and.html

Kennedy, Rebecca Futo. "We Condone It by Our Silence." Medium, May 11, 2017. Accessed August 10, 2019. https://eidolon.pub/we-condone-it-by-our-silence-bea76fb59b21

Koch-Brinkmann, Ulrike, Heinrich Piening, and Vinzenz Brinkmann. "On the Rendering of Human Skin in Ancient Marble Sculpture." In *Transformations: Classical Sculpture in Color*, edited by Jan Stubbe Østergaard, Anne Marie Nielsen, translated by Neil Martin Stanford, 140–51. Copenhagen: Ny Carlsberg Glyptotek, 2014.

Lee, Lloyd. "Deconstructing Monochromism in 'Gods in Color: Polychromy in the Ancient World.'" The Daily Californian, October 30, 2017. https://www.dailycal.org/2017/10/30/gods-color-polychromy-ancient-world-legion-of-honor/

Lipscher, Juraj. ColourLex. Accessed June 2020. https://colourlex.com

Lucas, Kenny, and Keith Lucas. "White at the Museum." Segment from TV show *Full Frontal on TBS*. Aired April 3, 2019. YouTube. Video, 6 min. 32 sec. Accessed May 26, 2020. https://www.youtube.com/watch?v=TkwUCUwt3Rs.

McCoskey, Denise. "Beware of Greeks Bearing Gifts: How Neo-Nazis and Ancient Greeks Met in Charlottesville." Origins: Current Events in Historical Perspective, May, 2018. Accessed June 14, 2020. http://origins.osu.edu/article/beware-greeks-bearing-gifts-how-neo-nazis-and-ancient-greeks-met-charlottesville

Metropolitan Museum of Art. "Chroma: Ancient Sculpture in Color." Metropolitan Museum of Art, July 5, 2022–March 26, 2023. Accessed February 2023. https://www.metmuseum.org/exhibitions/listings/2022/chroma

Morse, Heidi. "Classics and the Alt-Right: Historicizing Visual Rhetorics of White Supremacy." LearnSpeakAct: Liberal Arts in the Moment, February 15, 2018. Accessed June 15, 2020. https://sites.lsa.umich.edu/learn-speak-act/2018/02/15/classics-and-the-alt-right/

Østergaard, Jan Stubbe. "The Copenhagen Polychromy Network. A Research Project on Ancient Greek and Roman Sculptural Polychromy in the Ny Carlsberg Glyptotek." In *Circumlitio: The Polychromy of Antique and*

Mediaeval Sculpture, Proceedings of the Johann David Passavant Colloquium, December 10–12, 2008, edited by Vinzenz Brinkmann, Oliver Primavesi, and Max Hollein, 324–35. Frankfurt am Main: Schriftenreihe der Liebieghaus Skulpturensammlung, 2010.

Østergaard, Jan Stubbe. "The Polychromy of Antique Sculpture: A Challenge to Western Ideals?" In *Circumlitio: The Polychromy of Antique and Mediaeval Sculpture*, Proceedings of the Johann David Passavant Colloquium, December 10–12, 2008, edited by Vinzenz Brinkmann, Oliver Primavesi, and Max Hollein, 78–105. Frankfurt am Main: Schriftenreihe der Liebieghaus Skulpturensammlung, 2010.

Østergaard, Jan Stubbe. "The Polychromy of Ancient Sculpture: Experimental Reconstructions in Permanent Museum Displays." In *Restituer les couleurs: Reconstruction of Polychromy*, Actes du colloque Virtual Retrospect 2017, edited by Maud Mulliez, 187–96. Archéovision 8. Bordeaux: Éditions Ausonius, 2019.

Østergaard, Jan Stubbe, and Anne Marie Nielsen, eds. *Transformations: Classical Sculpture in Colour*. translated by Neil Martin Stanford. Copenhagen: Ny Carlsberg Glyptotek, 2014.

Papapostolou, J.A. "Color in Archaic Painting." In *Color in Ancient Greece: The Role of Color in Ancient Greek Art and Architecture, 700–31 B.C.* Proceedings of the conference held in Thessaloniki, April 12–16, 2000, edited by M.A. Tiverios and Despoina Tsiafakis, 53–64. Thessaloniki: Aristoteleio Panepistemio, 2002.

Person, Catherine and Caroline Roberts, curators. "Ancient Color." Kelsey Museum of Archaeology. Accessed June 19, 2020. https://exhibitions.kelsey.lsa.umich.edu/ancient-color

Richter, Gisela M.A. "Polychromy in Greek Sculpture with Special Reference to the Archaic Attic Gravestones in the Metropolitan Museum." *American Journal of Archaeology* 48, no. 4 (1944): 321–33. https://doi.org/10.2307/499897.

Ridgway, Brunilde Sismondo. *Prayers in Stone: Greek Architectural Sculpture (ca. 600–100 B.C.E.)*. Berkeley: University of California Press, 1999.

The Roman Baths at Bath. "Walkthrough." The Roman Baths, Bath, (n.d.). https://www.romanbaths.co.uk/walkthrough

Rose-Greenland, Fiona. "Color Perception in Sociology: Materiality and Authenticity at the 'Gods in Color' Show." *Sociological Theory* 34, no. 2 (2016): 81–105.

Schultz, Peter, and John Goodinson. "Nike is Now." Anasynthesis, January 29, 2020. https://www.anasynthesis.co.uk/index.php/nike/nike-is-now

Siotto, Eliana, Marco Callieri, Matteo Dellepiane, and Roberto Scopigno. "Ancient Polychromy: Study and Virtual Reconstruction Using Open Source Tools."

Journal on Computing and Cultural Heritage 8, no. 3 (May 7, 2015), Article 16. https://doi.org/10.1145/2739049

Siotto, Eliana, Gianpaolo Palma, Marco Potenziani, and Roberto Scopigno. "Digital Study and Web-Based Documentation of the Colour and Gilding on Ancient Marble Artworks." In *Proceedings of 2015 Digital Heritage International Congress, volume 1*, edited by Gabriele Guidi, Roberto Scopigno, Juan Carlos Torres, and Holger Graf, 239–46. IEEE, 2015. https://doi.org/10.1109/DigitalHeritage.2015.7413877.

Skovmøller, Amalie. "Where Marble Meets Colour: Surface Texturing of Hair, Skin and Dress on Roman Marble Portraits as Support for Painted Polychromy." In *Greek and Roman Textiles and Dress: An Interdisciplinary Anthology*, edited by Mary Harlow and Marie-Louise Nosch, 279–97. Philadelphia: Oxbow Books, 2014. https://www.jstor.org/stable/j.ctvh1dh8b.17

Talbot, Margaret. "The Myth of Whiteness in Classical Sculpture." The New Yorker, October 22, 2018. https://www.newyorker.com/magazine/2018/10/29/the-myth-of-whiteness-in-classical-sculpture

Verri, Giovanni. "Roman Sculpture and Colour: The 'Treu Head' (Ancient Greek and Roman Color / Polychromy)." YouTube, November 25, 2014. Video, 9 min. 6 sec. https://www.youtube.com/watch?v=gRMPYh2QdSM

Verri, Giovanni, Thorsten Opper, and Thibaut Deviese. "The 'Treu Head': A Case Study in Roman Sculptural Polychromy." *British Museum Technical Research Bulletin* 4 (2010): 39–54.

Walter-Karydi, E. "Color in Classical Painting." In *Color in Ancient Greece: The Role of Color in Ancient Greek Art and Architecture, 700–31 B.C.* Proceedings of the conference held in Thessaloniki, April 12–16, 2000, edited by M.A. Tiverios and Despoina Tsiafakis, 75–88. Thessaloniki: Aristoteleio Panepistemio, 2002.

Warburton, David, and Shiyanthi Thavapalan, eds. *The Value of Colour: Material and Economic Aspects in the Ancient World.* Berlin Studies of the Ancient World 70. Berlin: Edition Topoi, 2019.

Webb, E. Keats, Rebecca Summerour, and Jennifer Giaccai. "NMAI Archaeological Peruvian Textiles: Imaging and Analysis for Pigment Identification and Elucidation of Manufacture." Smithsonian Museum Conservation Institute, (n.d.). https://mci.si.edu/nmai-archaeological-peruvian-textiles

CHAPTER 2

BEYOND RECONSTRUCTION: ALTERNATIVE REALITIES AND BREAKING BARRIERS IN CLASSICAL ARCHAEOLOGICAL PEDAGOGY

Elizabeth Wolfram Thill, Matthew Brennan, and Ryan Knapp

Classical archaeology, the study of the material culture of ancient Greece and Rome, began as a branch of art history, concerned with the documentation and analysis of the artistic achievements of past societies.[1] As a result, the academic discipline developed as a pursuit for those sufficiently wealthy and connected to gain access to royal galleries and reception halls across Europe, where elites housed the personal collections of artifacts that would eventually form the seedbed of public museums. Centuries later, there can still be significant barriers to entry for undergraduate students interested in classical archaeology, particularly in the United States, where in-person access to classical archaeological sites and the most prominent museums requires a passport and significant travel costs. Virtual reality (VR) and augmented reality (AR) have emerged as powerful pedagogical tools that can be leveraged to remove (or at least reduce) some of the traditional barriers to entry that can make classical archaeology less accessible to many students. By presenting an expedient to travel, and by visually translating academic representative conventions and discourse into a medium that is more easily understood, VR/AR simplifies students' approach to the material. This allows more students to engage with material at a complex level, which in turn encourages higher-level critical thinking about engaging, universal ideas that transcend disciplines.

This essay presents several case studies of VR exercises for the classical archaeology classroom, which were designed specifically to level the playing field for students with little background in the classical world. These exercises arose out of situational circumstances peculiar to a particular campus and curriculum, and are certainly not intended to serve as best-practice models applicable to the entire field. Nor are they suggested as sweeping solutions for the problematic disparities in access to knowledge that plague classical studies, as well as many other academic fields. Rather, these exercises are offered as informal experiments, a select sample demonstrating the great breadth of both potential pedagogical approaches using extended reality technology, and the complex problems they can help address.

VIRTUAL REALITY IN THE CLASSICAL ARCHAEOLOGICAL CLASSROOM

Given VR's ability to produce a simulation of alternative realities, it is no surprise that the possibilities of virtual reality were immediately seized upon by archaeologists, historians, and other academics whose field of study involved the recreation of vanished realities. As early as 1984, computer-aided design (CAD) modeling was being used to create digital 3D models of historic buildings based on archaeological findings,[2] and in 1989 Reilly suggested the possibilities of applying 3D digital technologies to archaeological visualization and analysis.[3] Nevertheless, early applications of VR technologies to cultural heritage were primarily commercial in nature, due to the high cost of VR systems and attendant computing power.[4]

In response, academic institutions entered the field seeking to create high-quality and historically accurate VR experiences. Labs such as the UCLA Cultural Virtual Reality Laboratory (CVRL) and the CINECA Reality Center formed at academic institutions with the express mission of "creating scientifically authenticated 3D computer models of cultural heritage sites."[5] Founded in 1997, the UCLA CVRL aimed to create 3D models specifically for cultural virtual reality use. In contrast to the organization and approach of early commercial cultural VR projects, the CVRL adopted a methodology that emphasized collaboration with content experts and scholars.

Dissemination of academically rigorous VR materials, however, continued to be hampered by technological limitations and expense. Fully VR experiences typically were located at universities rather than at the museums or archaeological sites that might have been the subject of the cultural virtual reality experience. In order to make the projects accessible to a greater audience, they were often converted to "pseudo-VR" formats and displayed as interactive 3D models running at a kiosk in a museum,[6] on a personal computer,[7] or as noninteractive video sequences of the model or environment.[8] With the launch of YouTube in 2005, pre-rendered video visualizations of highly detailed cultural heritage 3D models could be shared with a vastly greater audience. But it was not until 2012, with the release of the first Oculus Rift developer's kit (DK1), that cultural VR applications were able to shift to an inexpensive, portable, and commercially available headset.

This important shift towards wide (or wider) access to VR applications has opened the doors towards further integration of VR experiences into a classical archaeology curriculum. As the cost and difficulty of creating VR experiences continue to fall, the world will see increasing, and immense, possibilities in the more targeted application of VR to an instructor's specific curriculum goals. One such important goal is easing access to complex archaeological material within a diverse classroom.

The exercises described here were all developed as part of the curriculum at Indiana University-Purdue University Indianapolis (IUPUI), and arose out of the need to adapt conventional classical studies pedagogy to a nontraditional institution and student body. A relatively young institution,[9] IUPUI supports a student population whose demographics fall outside the historic audience for classical studies as a field.[10] IUPUI is an urban university with a reputation for success in science, technology, engineering, and mathematics (STEM) fields, and a substantial majority of the institution's credit hours are earned within STEM-related programs.[11] Unsurprisingly, the classical studies program is small in scale. Established in 1996 and housed within the world languages and cultures department, the program has included only two (sequential) tenure-line professors. The program does not grant degrees, and no nonlanguage courses carry any prerequisites for enrollment. The result of these various factors is that for any given class in classical studies at IUPUI, from the introductory survey to the advanced seminar, the instructor can expect a wide spectrum of student exposure to classical cultures, with most students having little to no previous experience in the field at all.

While these particular factors are situational to IUPUI, the larger challenge of serving students who have never heard of Cicero is one that transcends a single campus. Long gone are the practices of earlier centuries, when a university education consisted primarily in reading the masterpieces of ancient Greece and Rome in the original languages.[12] In response to these considerations, the IUPUI classical studies program has revised its curriculum with an eye to emphasizing the larger conceptual questions the modern discipline is meant to address, such as social organization, the development of a multicultural metropolis, or the experiences of marginalized populations (rather than, say, preparing students for graduate school courses on Augustan Rome). Student learning outcomes (SLOs) based on conceptual analysis are difficult to achieve, however, when students are unfamiliar with the material and data upon which such conceptual questions are based. The VR exercises in this paper have proven exceptionally helpful in bridging the gap between introducing foundational material and practicing critical analysis.

LOGISTICS: DELIVERING CONTENT

Implementing technology that relies on expensive headsets may seem counterintuitive when the goal is to reduce inequality of access to information. While the expense of VR/AR equipment is plummeting, at present an instructor cannot assume ubiquitous access to such equipment for incoming students (as one now can, say, for a computer). Nevertheless, there are numerous solutions that can be implemented currently to provide easy student access to VR.

The first and easiest solution is to rely strictly on browser-based experiences, such as 3D models or "walkthroughs" posted on Sketchfab, an online 3D viewer.[13] The primary advantage of such a presentation format is that most are easily navigable by students. Many platforms themselves are free, and there are numerous varieties of pre-existing open-access resources that can be customized relatively easily for a given curriculum. A disadvantage, however, is the loss of a sense of experiential scale, one of the primary pedagogical advantages of VR.

A second approach is for the institution to make VR equipment available for classroom use. One model is to purchase enough headsets for all students to join the instructor in a VR build (or, more economically, to at least take turns). Another model is to leverage campus assets such as bespoke VR facilities, which can provide equipment and assistance to students outside of classroom hours. As with any pedagogy involving student group work, the practice of having multiple students engage directly in VR lends itself better to small class sizes: a considerable problem given the common American practice of emphasizing large lecture formats for introductory classical studies courses. Even for small classes, any situation where numerous students join simultaneously requires designing a build structure that students can navigate easily in groups.

Without regular practice, furthermore, bringing students into VR can quickly become focused on the technology itself, at the expense of course learning goals. With time these challenges should recede, as VR technology becomes more accessible and mainstream. At the moment, however, they remain significant.

A third approach, and the one used most often at IUPUI, is to have only the instructor wear a VR headset and navigate the VR build. By sharing the VR headset view on the primary screen, as one would a PowerPoint presentation, the students can see what the instructor sees. While this does not capture the same personal immersive experience that wearing the headset would deliver, it does allow students to benefit from other important assets of VR, as outlined below.[14] One advantage of this delivery method is its ability to transfer seamlessly to remote learning platforms such as Zoom, given that the basic principle of screen-sharing remains the same (as discovered unintentionally during the COVID-19 pandemic). It can also be recorded easily for asynchronous delivery.

LOGISTICS: DESIGNING CONTENT

Once a delivery strategy (or combination of strategies) has been decided, the instructor seeking to integrate VR/AR into their classical archaeology classroom has abundant options for content. One approach is to use commercially available experiences, such as *Rome Reborn* or *Assassin's Creed: Odyssey*.[15] While of inestimable pedagogical value in their own right, these come packaged with their own limits and pre-chosen content that may or may not conform to an instructor's standards or needs.

In contrast, designing or assembling bespoke VR/AR curriculum materials provides the freedom to create a wide range of scenarios and simulations, which can be tailored to demonstrate intended SLOs very precisely. Such materials can range widely in scope, from a lesson including the URLs of a series of previously posted models to full VR builds. Although the latter option requires more technological expertise, the process of creating VR builds will most likely become easier, as more instinctive platforms become available, as has been the case for website design.[16] Customized builds need not be overly complicated, furthermore. The IUPUI team found success with a simple structure: a series of rooms leading off of a central "lobby," with each room dedicated to a particular topic for the lesson. For example, the VR build for a lecture on Augustan Rome might include a room with 3D models of Augustan imperial portrait sculpture, with another room leading to a reconstruction of the Forum of Augustus. This basic layout allows an instructor to follow the scaffolding of a traditional lecture, marking the type of clear transitions from topic to topic that facilitate student learning.[17] In order to move between virtual settings, the instructor performs an action—such as dropping a labeled object—that triggers the corresponding new scene to load.[18]

Populating VR builds with 3D assets can be a surprisingly approachable endeavor, as well. Numerous high-quality 3D assets are available for this purpose, having been published online through open-access creative commons licensing.[19] Sketchfab.com is the leading depository for models produced through 3D scanning, especially for professional organizations such as museums, since the platform allows for viewing high-resolution, rotatable, and even annotated models.[20] 3D Warehouse, a model publishing arm of SketchUp, is the best source for detailed CAD renderings of ancient structures.[21] Scan the World, the cultural heritage arm of MyMiniFactory, is popular for posting lower-resolution, downloadable models, often made by avocational contributors (not necessarily with the relevant museum's knowledge or permissions).[22] Although not available for download, Google Earth's VR platform can be used independently in lectures to provide 3D satellite images and 360-degree views of archaeological sites and structures.[23]

VR assets available for the ancient world fall into two main categories: reproduction and reconstruction. Reproduction assets reflect an ancient artifact or building's current preserved state. In most cases they seek to represent or document the contemporary physical world directly, without intentional alteration. When users view the Colosseum in Google Earth, for example, they are meant to see the building as it exists today. Similarly, 3D models of buildings and artifacts as extant are available online, with or without color textures. Increasingly, artists are posting models of classical sculpture in pairs, with one model representing the original scan of the extant piece and the other a polychrome reconstruction.[24]

The most obvious and common use of VR in teaching about the past is reconstruction. Buildings can be rebuilt virtually, sculpture can be restored and placed back in context, and entire landscapes or city spaces can be built up around now isolated ruins, or stripped away in the case of modern additions. The advantages of such an approach in terms of audience engagement are instinctive, and accordingly will not see much discussion here. The limitations of virtual reconstruction may be less manifest to those outside of academia, and warrant some acknowledgment in this context.

Any attempt to create an immersive experience, as many VR experiences do, inevitably runs up against the limits of our knowledge about the past. All reconstructions of the ancient world rely on data for physical entities or situations that are now only preserved in part, decontextualized, or lost entirely. When considering a reconstruction for a given context, different scholars and artists set their own tolerance levels for informed speculation.[25] VR, however, can obscure this process, given its touted advantages in creating an experience that feels real.[26] Broad, immersive, detailed experiences are also expensive, in terms of time, talent, treasure, and processing power. And immersive reconstruction for engagement's sake, while valuable, may suffer from diminishing returns when repeated, particularly for smaller builds. As this article will seek to show, however, the pedagogical value of VR reproduction or reconstruction can be more complex and nuanced than presenting material to students in a more engaging way.

OPENING THE TEMPLE: TRANSCENDING INEQUALITIES IN INFORMATION ACCESS THROUGH VR

One common student learning objective in classical studies courses is for students to understand how monumental architecture directly affected Roman politics. A prevalent example is the design of the Temple of Venus Genetrix, constructed in the first century BCE under Julius Caesar in Rome. Caesar's contemporaries saw the temple's offset staircases as demonstrating his increasing political inaccessibility, since the podium provided him with a divine-like setting from which to address the crowds. The architectural design, therefore, had implications in the eventual assassination of Caesar and the escalation of civil wars at the end of the Roman Republic.

Students' understanding of this concept, however, requires considerable pedagogical investment. Like many academic professionals, classical archaeologists follow long-established representative conventions to mentally process two-dimensional architectural plans as illustrations of three-dimensional structures. Teaching this skill to students can be complex, time-consuming, and uncertain. In a traditional lecture, an instructor might show the plan view of a temple and explain to the students what the various symbols indicate. Then, ideally, the students would see multiple reconstructed views, since a single two-dimensional rendering cannot show the complete exterior of a building, let alone the interior as well. An instructor moving between reconstructions would need to relate them to each other, and to the original plan. After expending considerable time on this process, it is difficult for an instructor to test its results in real time before moving on to more ideational learning objectives. In other words, there are no easy means of checking whether the building forming in the students' minds bears close resemblance to the intended one.

With practice, a student can look at a plan of the Temple of Venus Genetrix (Figure 2.1) and understand circles and squares as indicating columns on large bases. Closely spaced parallel lines became stairs of a high podium; rectangles abutting these lines, circles, and squares reconstruct themselves into flanking plinths bearing water basins. Such a mental process, however, privileges students who have had exposure to a wide range of neoclassical architecture. Familiarity with Monticello, and its inspiration in the Roman temple in Nimes, for example, may help a student recognize a pedimental colonnaded facade on a diagram. This is an advantage over students whose architectural and educational experiences do not include many buildings based on Roman precedents. Thus, even without assuming the prerequisite familiarity with the history, personalities, and temple architecture of Republican Rome that one could expect in a traditional Roman architecture seminar, the logistics of introducing the temple to students can favor those with a certain cultural and educational background.

VR sidesteps this process. Encountering the Temple of Venus Genetrix in VR, a student does not need an explanation of what image represents a column (Figure 2.2).[27] When they walk to the edge of the temple podium, what they see is not a series of parallel lines, but flights of marble stairs winding several meters to the porch level (Figure 2.3). Through a first-person viewpoint, a student can anticipate instinctively whether the stairs are steep or shallow, accessible or imposing. Looking back at the temple facade, a student can recognize its basic shape and visual effect without

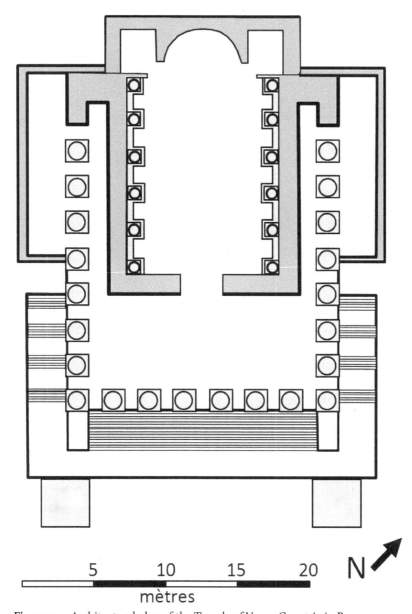

Figure 2.1: Architectural plan of the Temple of Venus Genetrix in Rome.

(After original image by user Cassius Ahenobarbus on Wikimedia Commons https://commons.wikimedia. org/wiki/File:Temple_venus_genitrix_plan.png. Accessed 24 Feb 2022.)

Figure 2.2: Virtual reality reconstruction of Temple of Venus Genetrix.
(Photo by R. Knapp; model by R. Knapp after Tskhondia 2014.)

needing to understand or mentally reconstruct terms such as "pediment" or "Corinthian colonnade." Furthermore, the instructor can presume that all students viewing the model are seeing the same facade structure. Put simply, looking at a VR projection requires substantially reduced investments in time and specific cultural capital, in comparison to deciphering architectural plans. Rather than devoting time to explaining esoteric representative conventions, an instructor can say merely, "Here we are on the temple porch," and everyone is ready to explore.

The considerable lecture time recovered by VR's pedagogical efficiencies can be devoted to other more complex material and SLOs, which themselves can be augmented by VR. In the case of the Temple of Venus Genetrix, presenting the temple reconstructed in VR goes further than allowing students to understand the design of the temple quickly and easily. Moving through the reconstruction enables them to gain some sense of how this podium would have been experienced from the top (Caesar's position, Figure 2.4) and below (his audience's position, Figure 2.5). This facilitates a more visceral but at the same time nuanced discussion of the

Figure 2.3: Detail of podium stairs of Temple of Venus Genetrix reconstruction. *(Photo by R. Knapp; model by R. Knapp after Tskhondia 2014.)*

Figure 2.4: Detail of podium of Temple of Venus Genetrix reconstruction.
(Photo by R. Knapp; model by R. Knapp after Tskhondia 2014.)

Figure 2.5: Detail of podium of Temple of Venus Genetrix reconstruction.
(Photo by R. Knapp; model by R. Knapp after Tskhondia 2014.)

phenomenology of Roman architecture, as well as the political forces it both reflected and affected. The time recovered from explaining all of this through two-dimensional diagrams also can be repurposed to students' asking and answering questions, proposing new ideas, and drawing conclusions.

Going further, VR can facilitate considerations of phenomena that are inherently three-dimensional, such as sightlines and relative scale. Julius Caesar's heir, Augustus, apparently learned from the unfortunate end of his adopted father. The Temple of Mars Ultor that Augustus built nearby exceeded the scale of that built by his predecessor, but notably returned to a more traditional, more accessible direct podium (Figure 2.6). Students experiencing the reconstructed temples in VR can quickly grasp the location of the temples relative to each other, including the sightlines between them. This understanding of relative location, so critical in Roman architectural design, can be augmented by viewing the preserved archaeological remains in Google Earth. Within the reconstruction, students can digest the experiential consequences of the two podiums' different access patterns. With this information firmly in hand, they then can debate the wisdom of Augustus' architectural choice, or how different social classes may have appreciated the monument. These sorts of questions, which explore how archaeological material informs our understanding of the nature of power in Rome's transition from republic to empire, can prove interesting, informative, and relevant for students, regardless of

Figure 2.6: Virtual reality reconstruction of Temple of Mars Ultor.
(Photo by R. Knapp; model by R. Knapp after Tskhondia 2014.)

what previous knowledge they bring to a class, or their intended educational trajectory after it.

REMOVABLE RUINS: MODIFIED RECONSTRUCTIONS AND HYPOTHESIS TESTING

Virtual reality is not just a means of reconstructing a particular reality: it is also a means of manipulating or surpassing that reality. The possibility of changing reconstructions within a build allows students to experiment with multiple reconstructed realities, and in so doing test competing research hypotheses. This can be particularly useful for topics such as topography, the study of the ancient landscape and relationships between manmade structures. In addition to relying on interwoven, heterogeneous lines of fragmentary evidence, topography as a discipline trades in competing reconstructions of three-dimensional spaces. As a result, the field has developed a reputation for dense arguments requiring a wealth of specialized knowledge to parse, let alone evaluate. This is a shame, since the issues topography addresses can be of great relevance to modern society: issues such as the development of urban landscapes and the lived experience of architecture.

An important SLO in classical studies courses is for students to understand how cities change in appearance and use over time, with new structures and plans interacting with preexisting buildings. Such phenomena underpin the famous debate over the identity and location of the Archaic Temple of Athena Polias on the Athenian Acropolis sanctuary.[28] According to the most prevalent theory, this critical temple once stood on a set of foundations now known as the Dörpfeld Foundations (Figure 2.7). Burnt to those foundations in the Persian sack of the sanctuary in 490 BCE, the temple was never rebuilt. Instead, the foundations were left exposed, as an eternal reminder of the Persian devastation. The singular building now known as the Erechtheion, with its famous "Caryatid Porch" still visible today, was built near the foundations

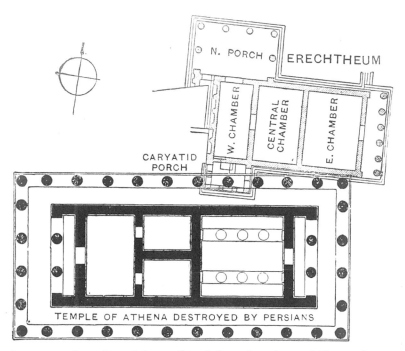

Figure 2.7: Plan of Erechtheion ("Erechtheum") and Dörpfeld Foundations ("Temple of Athena Destroyed by Persians"). Note overlap of the Caryatid Porch with the foundations.

(After Frazier, J.G. 1898 Pausanias's Description of Greece vol. 2; permission British Library @ Flickr Commons, https://commons.wikimedia.org/wiki/File:359_of_%27Pausanias%27s_Description_of_Greece._ Translated_with_a_commentary_by_J._G.Frazer%27_(11292278876).png. Accessed 24 Feb 2022.)

around 420 BCE to house the archaic cult statue, while the building known as the Parthenon was erected on the other side of the foundations. Thus, by the late 5th century BCE the monumental vista of the Acropolis resembled that which a modern visitor encounters today.

This theory, however, has been challenged in an article by G. Ferrari, who proposes a new interpretation of the Acropolis building program.[29] Ferrari argues that major segments of the Archaic Temple remained standing on their original (Dörpfeld) foundations, and that it was this broken but still functional structure that served as the memorial to the Persian horrors (Figure 2.8).

Figure 2.8: G. Ferrari's reconstruction of remains of Temple of Athena Polias between Erechtheion and Parthenon.

(Ferrari 2002: Figure 4.)

The Caryatid Porch, which juts awkwardly and cryptically from the side of the Erechtheion, was designed to obscure a rift that ran through the damaged temple. Ferrari connects these broader concepts to modern examples of memorialization through ruined architecture, a tradition that includes the Kaiser Wilhelm Memorial Church in Berlin and (subsequent to Ferrari's article's publication) the National September 11 Memorial and Museum in New York City.

Comprehension of Ferrari's argument requires students to understand multiple plans of the Acropolis, the architectural remains those plans represent, the possible structures those remains imply, the varying reconstructions of those structures, and the significance of the potential visual effects that would result for each reconstruction. Explaining all this material in a traditional lecture format, while dependent on two-dimensional imaging, poses a considerable challenge, as well as demanding a substantial block of time. This challenge is heightened for students who may not be able to even recognize the Parthenon, let alone its setting within the general tableau of the Acropolis.

Once again, VR can cut through these intermediate steps and create time for a more thorough discussion of significance. The IUPUI team designed and piloted a VR build of the Athenian Acropolis that presented numerous features tailored to the lesson learning objectives.[30] These go beyond the critical but basic contribution of enabling students to experience the ancient buildings, and their relationships to each other, at scale. In addition to the normal human-scale viewpoint, the build makes possible an overhead viewpoint that presents numerous buildings from above (Figure 2.9). From this viewpoint, students can observe several different ground-level overlays: a generic texture; a Google Earth satellite image of the Acropolis; or an architectural plan color-coded to highlight the different architectural remains. These overlays

Figure 2.9: Virtual reality reconstruction of Athenian Acropolis, with removable Parthenon roof serving as control panel for toggling on or off various features, including Google Earth satellite view (left button, toggled on) and architectural plan (right button; see also Figures 2.10a and 2.10b). Note Ferrari's hypothesized Temple of Athena Polias superimposed over Dörpfeld Foundations in lower right corner.

(Photo by R. Knapp; model by R. Knapp after Vasilis 2019.)

can be toggled on or off using a series of virtual buttons, while clearly maintaining the locations of various features. Similarly, an instructor can choose to display various buildings above and aligned to these overlays, creating dozens of possible combinations of plans and reconstructions that can be adjusted in real time to follow student discussions. In addition, the roofs can be picked up to reveal the buildings' interior layouts, to demonstrate more clearly the correspondence between reconstruction and the architectural plans virtually underlying them (Figures 2.10a and 2.10b).

The ability to toggle easily through combinations of features can go beyond reconstructing consensus theories, to the more complex process of hypothesis testing for those reconstructions. In the Athenian Acropolis build, one of the features that can be toggled on is a rough model following Ferrari's hypothesis. With the virtual building in place, students can explore how the presence of the hypothesized building would have affected building accessibility, sightlines, and viewer experience within the Acropolis (Figure 2.11).

While admittedly the finer points of Ferrari's reconstruction are relevant primarily to archaeologists, the broader implications have wider significance. If the traditional reconstruction of the Acropolis is correct, at the height of Athenian power visitors to the sanctuary would have encountered a vista of gleaming new constructions. Only once they reached the heart of the sanctuary would they see an open clearing with the enigmatic bare foundations, and thus be reminded of a past tragedy. If Ferrari's reconstruction is correct, in contrast, the ancient visitor would experience the Erechtheion and Parthenon as new constructions flanking a damaged archaic structure dominating the sanctuary center (Figure 2.12). The implications of this visceral experience, of architecture and memory and cultural identity, are important to understand; for example, as it relates to current debates about the retention or removal of monuments to contested historical

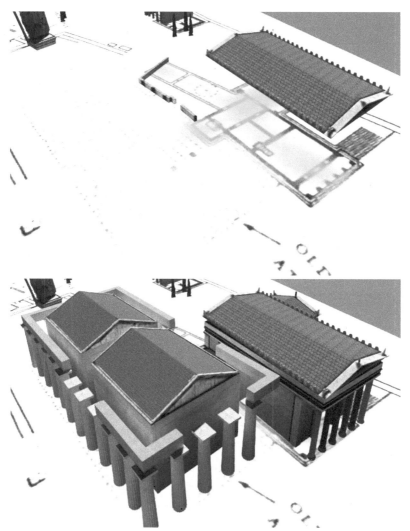

Figures 2.10a and 2.10b: Virtual reality reconstruction of Athenian Acropolis. Figure 2.10a shows an architectural plan layout with Ferrari's hypothesized Temple of Athena Polias toggled off; the Erechtheion is also toggled off, with the roof remaining to remind students of the exterior configuration. Figure 2.10b shows the same scene with both buildings toggled on.

(Photo by R. Knapp; model by R. Knapp after Vasilis 2019.)

Figure 2.11: Virtual reality reconstruction of Athenian Acropolis, showing view of Erechtheion (left), Caryatid Porch (center) and Ferrari's hypothesized Temple of Athena Polias (right).

(Photo by R. Knapp; model by R. Knapp after Vasilis 2019.)

Figure 2.12: Virtual reality reconstruction of Athenian Acropolis, showing view from sanctuary entrance of Ferrari's hypothesized Temple of Athena Polias (left) and Parthenon (right).

(Photo by R. Knapp; model by R. Knapp after Vasilis 2019.)

events, such as the American Civil War. VR allows students to weigh the different reconstructions and contemplate their implications, without becoming confused or inhibited by plans and discussions of architectural membra.

BEYOND RECONSTRUCTION: ADVANTAGES
OF A VIRTUAL REALITY

For some situations, there can be considerable advantages in not even attempting to recreate or reconstruct the physical world. The process of archaeological excavation is one topic that is a particular challenge to teach in a traditional classroom. Real-world excavation experience is expensive and, in the case of classical archaeology, requires an excavation season spent abroad.[31] The challenge for an instructor is to deliver the necessary content to students, without in-person access to a real archaeological excavation.

An important SLO is for students to understand how the combination of past site formation processes and modern research questions determine what information we recover from the past. In the paradigmatic example of site formation processes, a site is occupied for an initial period, resulting in artifact accumulation. A hiatus in occupation allows the buildup of sediment, which covers and seals any evidence of the first occupation. The site is then reoccupied, and artifacts from this second period accumulate on top of the sediment that covers the first. This process is repeated, resulting in a series of distinct stratigraphic layers marking periods of occupation and hiatus, with the lowest, oldest layers underlying those of subsequent periods.

In this particular case, the conventional means of rendering this three-dimensional concept through two-dimensional imagery can obfuscate important aspects of the excavation process. Traditional two-dimensional stratigraphic diagrams take the form of a cutaway view in order to show that later layers lie on top of earlier layers. This misses a key component of field excavation: although guided by scholarship and experience, archaeologists do not know ahead of time what they actually will find as they dig, at least at the detailed level. Influenced by popular representations of archaeology such as Indiana Jones, where the hero is in search of a particular artifact and destroys everything in the path to get it, students tend to imagine that archaeologists dig knowing what is there and how to get it. This wildly distorts the actual excavation process, which is characterized by experiment, flexibility, and discovery.

In modern archaeology, excavation is never a matter of peeling back stratigraphic layers in their entirety to fully expose the ancient occupation layers. One reason is ethical: excavation is an inherently destructive process, given that an artifact's original context is the sediment surrounding it, yet an archaeologist must disturb and remove that sediment to recover the artifact. Best practice, therefore, mandates that archaeologists leave the majority of a site undisturbed, and thus preserved for future generations (who hopefully will employ better, less destructive tools and methodologies in any recovery). More prosaic considerations that limit the scale of excavation derive from issues such as financial constraints and the slow pace of excavation, which force archaeologists to make choices in how to allocate scarce resources when digging.

How an archaeological team will choose to allocate those resources will depend in large part on the research questions asked. For a primary research question involving change in the site over time, a corresponding excavation strategy would call for deep trenches that can extend vertically through the stratigraphy to the earliest buried occupation layers. If the majority of resources are devoted to achieving this sufficient depth, then the resulting trench will be deep but narrow. The archaeologists' view of the site will be akin to looking down a well: the different sequence of stratigraphic layers, and thus the record of chronological change in the site, will be apparent, but at the expense of an understanding of the broader site layout at any given time.

Correspondingly, if the archaeologists wish to understand the broader site layout, they will need to devote resources to widening the trench, at the expense of depth and an understanding of the site development. While this process may seem at first glance to be a technical matter of archaeological methodology, it has critical theoretical implications: we cannot know everything about the past; in fact, we often know very little, and what we do know is shaped by the questions we ask, the methods we use, and the choices we make.

In order to demonstrate these considerations to students, the IUPUI team designed an excavation VR build consisting of three stacked stratigraphic layers (Figure 2.13). Unlike in actual excavation, layers are flat and even, each with its own distinctive color (purple, orange, and cream), in order to facilitate student understanding. Each layer is divided into 9 blocks, or "excavation units" (akin to trenches), each labeled on an alphanumeric grid. Corresponding virtual buttons allow a student to toggle off a given unit, but in this case, they can do so only if the overlying units have been toggled off, or "excavated," first. This recreates the dilemma faced by archaeologists in the field, who are limited in what they can see without strategic excavation. Concealing the lower two layers of the virtual build represents this aspect to students and encourages them to think through the sort of decisions that archaeologists face. Some units conceal columns (representing

Figure 2.13: Virtual reality reconstruction of archaeological excavation. Plates represent domestic occupation, columns religious constructions.
(Photo by E. Thill; model by R. Knapp.)

monumental architecture) and some units conceal plates (representing domestic architecture). Most units, as in an actual archaeological site, conceal no artifacts.

In class, a student is allowed to direct the "excavation" (the sequence of blocks/units removed), either by wearing the headset themselves or by instructing another wearer. A predetermined limit to the number of units they can remove simulates a "resource budget." Based on what they uncover, the student can decide to look for deeper layers, or to expand horizontally and find out more about one layer. Once all chances to remove units have been exhausted, the class can discuss what they have learned about the occupation of the site. Resetting the build restores all the blocks, and allows students to experiment with different strategies, and analyze and compare the results thereof. Finally, removing all units reveals the complete site (an impossibility in real excavations), demonstrating the discrepancy between what each excavation strategy divulged, and the total information possible. Students thus reckon with the fact that any information gained from excavation is based on restricted glimpses into an archaeological site, created by physical and conceptual limitations.

It should be noted that this exercise does not strive to recreate the experience of a real archaeological dig. Indeed, it purposefully includes several design features that would be impossible in an excavation. The structure of the "site" is regular in shape and depth, without aspects of the physical world (disturbed or unclear stratigraphy, impediments like rocks or trees, inconvenient lighting or weather) that would overly complicate teaching purposes. Excavation units can be removed with the effort of pushing a virtual button, and can be preprogrammed to deliver the exact combination of artifacts the instructor needs. Most importantly, the site can be returned to a pristine state, eliminating the primary disadvantage of excavation, namely its destructive, permanent nature, and allowing for experimental repetition. This last aspect sets the VR build approach apart from other methods of teaching these concepts, which tend to preclude easy repetition.[32]

FUTURE VIRTUAL REALITIES

The use of VR/AR in the classroom need not be limited to instructor-led lecture material but can be extended to more student-driven activities as well. In one IUPUI group project, students were asked to create, curate, and present their own sculptural gallery of Roman portraits. Working from a dozen preselected 3D models of Roman portrait busts, students were asked to select five of those busts and create a VR exhibit around whatever interpretive theme they chose. Students used the IUPUI University Library VR Lab to record a brief presentation of their exhibit, which needed to take into account the artifacts as three-dimensional objects that can be rotated, moved, and compared with each other.[33] This ability to arrange and directly manipulate famous examples of sculpture from numerous world museums, all in the same view, went beyond even the more passive experiences of a student able to travel to visit the museums in person.

In another exercise, the intended SLO was to appreciate the revolutionary architectural advantages of poured concrete—a Roman invention—over traditional cut-stone construction. Each student group was presented with a set of small plastic blocks that had been 3D printed from a virtual model.[34] The groups worked together to physically assemble the blocks into a "cut-stone" arch, a complex process that leveraged experiential learning to help students understand the challenges faced and surmounted by Roman architects. The use of a virtual model as the basis for the exercise means that the exercise could potentially be held in VR as well, with students joining groups remotely. The advantages to such assignments include allowing for student experimentation, as well as the chance to build confidence in using new technology.

As VR/AR becomes a more frequent tool in the classical archaeology classroom, it is our hope that it continues to become more flexible and adaptable to the particular needs of specific institutions, instructors, courses, and SLOs. Through creative design, instructors can leverage inherent pedagogical advantages of VR/AR to broaden the experiences of more, and more diverse, student populations. VR, AR, and related technologies give students the chance to see not only the future of technology but also the future of understanding the past.

NOTES

1. This essay uses the term "classical" in the strictly academic sense, in reference to the professional study of past cultures around the Mediterranean Basin, typically between the fluorescence of the Mycenaean kingdoms in the second millennium BCE, to the rise of Constantinople in the fourth century CE. For an introductory exploration of the problematic terminology and history of the academic discipline, see Osborne and Alcock, "Introduction."

2. Messemer, "Beginnings of Digital," 24.

3. Reilly, "Data Visualization in Archaeology."

4. Frischer et al., "From CVR to CVRO."

5. Frischer, "Mission and Recent Projects."

6. Helling et. al.,"The Port Royal Project."

7. Harvard University, "Digital Giza."

8. Frischer, "Mission and Recent Projects."

9. IUPUI (Indiana University-Purdue University Indianapolis) was established as recently as 1969 through a merging of Indianapolis satellite campuses of Indiana and Purdue Universities (https://www.iupui.edu/about/history.html). It should be noted that as of July 2024, IUPUI will be realigning to IU Indianapolis and Purdue in Indianapolis.

10. Traditionally, the stereotypical student of classical studies is white, highly educated, and has access to significant financial support. The examination and critique of the implications of this stereotype represent a growing and complex area of research within the field: for those unfamiliar with the discussion, Bracey's "A Response" (2021) provides a very brief but cogent point of entry. In contrast to these stereotypes of classical studies, nearly 35% of the over 24,000 students enrolled at IUPUI in 2020 identified as people of color (IU Newsroom, "Diversity, academic success"). From 2011 to 2019, the

percentage of beginning students receiving Pell Grant funding (a common shorthand for students with high financial need; https://studentaid.gov/understand-aid/types/grants/pell) was consistently between 39–44% of the student population (Institutional Research and Decision Support, "IUPUI Campus Enrollment Summary," compared to the national average of only 34–40% over the same period (National Center for Education Statistics, "Trend Generator").

11. Institutional Research and Decision Support, "IUPUI Campus Enrollment Summary."

12. A telling example can be found in the 1795 founding "Laws and Regulations" for students and faculty of the University of North Carolina, the first public university in the United States. These rules included a provision for entrance examinations on Latin literature and Greek grammar, the only examinations so mandated. The same document proscribed a curriculum made up almost entirely of classical history and literature for the first two years of study. See University of North Carolina Board of Trustees, "Laws and Regulations."

13. https://sketchfab.com/

14. The experiential difference between wearing a headset in VR and watching another's headset view on screen (either in person or virtually) is broadly comparable to that for other types of interactive content. The popularity of platforms such as Twitch and YouTube, where consumers watch other people do everything from play videogames to crochet, demonstrates our ability to derive meaning from watching someone else's experience, even at multiple degrees of removal. In anecdotal feedback, IUPUI students have expressed great appreciation for VR/AR assets: specifically, they recognize those assets as improvements over traditional delivery methods (two-dimensional images) rather than assuming the assets represent an equivalent experience of seeing the modeled objects in real life, or even of wearing the headset personally.

15. While not technically a VR asset, the video game *Assassin's Creed: Odyssey* nevertheless seeks to provide an experience that is immersive, interactive, three-dimensional, and (primarily) from a first-person view. The game also represents a current highwater mark, in terms of detail and accuracy, in reconstructing the ancient Greek world.

16. In the particular case of IUPUI, the VR curriculum team combined participants from multiple disciplines, with the two primary leads being a classical archaeologist, Dr. Elizabeth Thill, and an information technology specialist, Ryan Knapp. Designing bespoke VR builds is another process made easier by focusing on a single primary user (see main text).

17. Essentially, this approach gives virtual form to the ancient tradition of so-called "memory palaces," exemplified in the Roman philosopher Cicero's first-century BCE rhetorical treatise *De Oratore* (2.86–88). Often known in cognitive studies as "method of *loci*," the technique works by associating a memorized datum with a specific location or object within a well-known space, so that the mind can recall the datum by mentally navigating through the space to the associated location. More practically, the virtual structure also segments the large file size of 3D data and high demand for computational power to render it, thus avoiding computer overloading and maintaining a smooth frame rate.

18. By relying on a simple, direct, and purposeful motion, this technique proved easier to execute quickly and consistently, relative to more complex gestures such as navigating virtual buttons.

19. All discussions of online resources in this article are current as of the time of its writing, with recognition that the suite of available resources can change rapidly.

20. https://sketchfab.com/ Sketchfab devotes a substantial section of its platform specifically to cultural heritage models.

21. https://3dwarehouse.sketchup.com/ Of particular note in this context is the impressive work of L. Tskhondia: see https://www.lviic.net/

22. https://www.myminifactory.com/users/Scan%20The%20World

23. At present, image quality within Google Earth can vary widely. Conveniently for current purposes, Google chose modern Rome and its dramatic architecture as one of its first showcases for a Google Earth experience, so the resolution from satellite data is particularly impressive for that city. The remote archaeological site of Delphi, Greece, in contrast, currently appears even in Google Earth as a low-resolution 2D image. Athens and Pompeii, two other critical cities for classical archaeology, fall between these two extremes. Like all static images, Google Earth views capture a particular moment in time. Accordingly, they are subject to variables such as lighting conditions or the presence of construction scaffolding. These views are updated periodically according to Google's corporate decisions.

24. Although traditionally presented as gleaming white in post-antique displays, most ancient marble decoration (and a good deal of bronze) was painted in bright hues, for both architecture and sculpture. For more on this topic, see Surtees and Kuchler in this volume.

25. For methodological discussion of best practices in constructing historical models, and marking their sources and limitations for an audience, see Frischer, "Mission and Recent Projects."

26. Shapiro and McDonald, "I'm Not a Real Doctor."
27. The team's VR build of the Imperial Fora is indebted to the models of Lasha Tskhondia, "Forum of Caesar" and "Forum of Augustus."
28. For an in-depth discussion of this debate, and an example of the complexities of topographical arguments, see Ferrari, "The Ancient Temple."
29. Ferrari, "The Ancient Temple," n. 98.
30. For the team's VR build of the Athenian Acropolis, we are indebted to the models of Vasilis Iakovidis, "Acropolis of Athens/Ακρόπολη Αθηνών."
31. The costs of a summer field school, even a domestic experience, need to take into account the opportunity costs of lost summer employment. For many low-income students this can prove the decisive factor against field school participation, especially since opportunity costs are rarely covered by scholarships.
32. One perennial favorite in archaeological pedagogy is constructing a miniature "site" in a shoebox, layering various materials such as sand or ground coffee over "artifacts." This or similar approaches do have certain advantages over a virtual excavation, especially tactile aspects that reproduce the physics of digging. But any exercise that involves physical "dirt" can be messy and time-consuming, both in preparation and practice, and cannot be reset easily.
33. Minor adjustments to the assignment can remove the need for headsets entirely. The same open access models that are used in the VR assignment can be loaded into a browser platform such as Sketchfab and rotated with a mouse, approximating the experiences in VR.
34. The 3D model, "Arch Builder Puzzle Blocks," by Devin Montes can be viewed online at: https://www.myminifactory.com/object/3d-print-arch-builder-puzzle-blocks-60374

WORKS CITED

Bracey, John. "A Response to the ACL Affiliated Group Panel at SCS 'Race, Classics, and the Latin Classroom.'" *The Classical Outlook* 96, no. 1 (2021): 25–7.

Federal Student Aid. "Federal Pell Grants." Federal Student Aid, (n.d.). https://studentaid.gov/understand-aid/types/grants/pell

Ferrari, Gloria. "The Ancient Temple on the Acropolis at Athens." *American Journal of Archaeology* 106, no. 1 (2002): 11–35. https://doi.org/10.2307/507187

Frischer, Bernard. "Mission and Recent Projects of the UCLA Cultural Virtual Reality Laboratory." In *Actes du colloque Virtual Retrospect 2003, Biarritz, France 6–7 November 2003*, edited by Robert Vergnieux and Caroline Delevoie, 65–76. Bordeaux: Ausonius, 2003.

Frischer, Bernard, Franco Niccolucci, Nick Ryan, and Juan A. Barceló. "From CVR to CVRO: The Past, Present, and Future of Cultural Virtual Reality." In *Virtual Archaeology. Proceedings of the VAST Euroconference, Arezzo 24–25 November 2000*, edited by Franco Niccolucci, 7–18. British Archaeological Reports S1075. Oxford: ArchaeoPress, 2002.

Harvard University. "Digital Giza: The Giza Project at Harvard University." Harvard University, (n.d.). giza.fas.harvard.edu/ Accessed June 21, 2023.

Helling, Harry, Charlie Steinmetz, Eric Solomon, and Bernard Frischer. "The Port Royal Project. A Case Study in the Use of VR Technology for the Recontextualization of Archaeological Artifacts and Building Remains in a Museum Setting." In *On the Road to Reconstructing the Past. Proceedings of CAA 2008, Budapest, April 2–6 2008*, edited by Erzsébet Jerem, Ferenc Redő, and Vajk Szeverényi, 413–19. Budapest: Archaeolingua Foundation, 2011.

Iakovidis, Vasilis. "Acropolis of Athens/Ακρόπολη Αθηνών." 3D Warehouse, June 23, 2019. https://3dwarehouse.sketchup.com/model/u5dc7fd58-c38c-4860-bf11-a746a9a01e46/Acropolis-of-AthensΑκρόπολη-Αθηνών Accessed October 7, 2020.

IU Newsroom. "Diversity, academic success key themes in IU's fall 2022 class." News at IU, August 31, 2022. https://news.iu.edu/live/news/28007-diversity-academic-success-key-themes-in-ius-fall

IUPUI Institutional Research and Decision Support. "IUPUI Campus Enrollment Summary, Fall Semester 2020." IUPUI Institutional Effectiveness, (n.d.). https://irds.iupui.edu/enrollment-management/census-report.html

Messemer, Heike. "The Beginnings of Digital Visualization of Historical Architecture in the Academic Field." In *Virtual Palaces, Part 2: Lost Palaces and their Afterlife: Virtual Reconstruction between Science and Media*, edited by Stephan Hoppe and Stefan Breitling, 21–54. München: Palatium, 2016.

Montes, Devin. "Arch Builder Puzzle Blocks." MyMiniFactory, March 22, 2018. https://www.myminifactory.com/object/3d-print-arch-builder-puzzle-blocks-60374 Accessed August 1, 2023.

National Center for Education Statistics. "Trend Generator: Percent of Undergraduate Students Awarded Pell Grants." Institute of Education Sciences, (n.d.). https://nces.ed.gov/ipeds/TrendGenerator/app/answer/8/35

Osborne, Robin, and Susan E. Alcock. "Introduction." In *Classical Archaeology*, 2nd edition, edited by Susan E. Alcock and Robin Osborne, 1–10. Blackwell Studies in Global Archaeology. Oxford: Wiley-Blackwell, 2012.

Reilly, Paul. "Data Visualization in Archaeology." *IBM Systems Journal* 28, no. 4 (1989): 569–79.

Shapiro, Michael A., and Daniel G. McDonald. "I'm Not a Real Doctor, but I Play One in Virtual Reality: Implications of Virtual Reality for Judgments about Reality." *Journal of Communication* 42, no. 4 (1992): 94–114.

Tskhondia, Lasha. "3D Reconstructions." LVIIC, (n.d.) https://www.lviic.net (Archived at https://web.archive.org/web/20220218202420/https://www. lviic.net/)

Tskhondia, Lasha. "Models." 3D Warehouse, March 21, 2014. https://3dwarehouse. sketchup.com/user/05779279631156607035122287/LVIIC Accessed May 21, 2020.

University of North Carolina Board of Trustees. "Laws and Regulations for the University of North Carolina, August 2, 1795." Transcribed and edited by E. Lindemann (2005). Chapel Hill, NC: The University Library, University of North Carolina at Chapel Hill. https://docsouth.unc.edu/true/mss01-02/mss01-02.html.

CHAPTER 3

LINGUA VITAE: TEACHING THE LATIN LANGUAGE IN VIRTUAL REALITY

Brian Beams and Lissa Crofton-Sleigh[1]

Ancient languages, such as Greek and Latin, have long suffered from being deemed "dead languages." Due in part to a perceived distance (whether chronological, geographical, or metaphorical) between ancient and modern culture and a lack of native speakers today, some students claim that they do not think classical Greek and Latin apply to their own lives. The unfamiliarity and lack of relatability for students have contributed to declining enrollments in ancient languages at many universities.

Traditional methods of learning these languages can also make it difficult to attract and retain students, because they often present limited opportunities for student engagement and creativity. For example, several well-established textbooks, such as *Wheelock's Latin*, tend to emphasize the memorization of vocabulary and grammar.[2] While utilizing these skills may be beneficial to students' improvement of their English vocabulary and writing abilities, students also can find the experience dry and often become frustrated with the little-to-no emphasis on speaking and creative/narrative writing skills, tools highly emphasized in modern languages.[3] However, shifts in second language acquisition (SLA) and classroom diversity have coincided with new approaches in the teaching of ancient Greek and Latin, especially at the secondary and postsecondary levels. In particular, spoken or "active" Latin movements have begun to take hold across the United States and globally, incorporating comprehensible input (CI), communicative language teaching (CLT), and comprehension-based communicative language teaching (CCLT) strategies within the academic year classroom and into summer Latin immersion camps.[4] These newer approaches include more oral communicative and cultural components as well as narrative- or reading-based and task-based learning.[5] Speaking, reading, and writing/creating in an ancient language can help students to more directly connect themselves to cultures of the past and see a deeper relevance between those who lived thousands of years ago and today. Understanding the past can then enable a more informed view of the present.

In addition to new and enhanced teaching strategies, technology similarly is playing an essential role in language acquisition and cultural awareness. With the advent of the internet, smartphones, apps, and social media, educators are investigating ways to combine formal education with interactive, immersive technology. Websites including Latinitium and apps such as Babbel and Duolingo (the latter of which offers Latin) have changed how users interact with language, bringing a classroom experience of speaking, reading, writing, listening, and comprehending to one's PC or smartphone.[6] Language education through technology, and in particular virtual technology, offers many benefits to students. Immersive environments can increase motivation to learn language through its gamification.[7] Exposure to virtual reality (VR) narratives can increase student awareness and comprehension of the culture producing the foreign language.[8] Furthermore, these virtual experiences facilitate an immersion in real-life contexts, which allows students to interact more concretely with typically abstract concepts and develop more complex levels of thinking.[9] Switching between multiple modes of communication, particularly verbal and visual, within these immersive experiences also helps students to achieve a better understanding of communication within the foreign language and within the environment itself.[10] Finally, engagement with language in a virtual setting enables self-directed exploration or experimentation, which can lead to decreased anxiety and further motivation and engagement with the material.[11] Though these findings stem from modern language research, they are also important for learning an ancient language such as Latin, where the distance between modern and ancient cultures can produce anxiety and/or disinterest. Like all languages, Latin, with the sheer number and difficulty of grammar concepts, can be difficult for students to learn thoroughly in a year (or less). Reaching a comfort level with any concept takes time as well as different types of activities to reinforce the material. Oral and auditory communicative components, as well as interaction with cultural concepts, can greatly assist students in achieving more long-term understanding and comprehension of Latin.

The combination of declining enrollments, evolving teaching strategies, and emergent technologies helped to spur our project in combining Latin language acquisition with virtual reality. We are applying the concept of language immersion to a virtual immersive space, recreating the Roman Forum in 3D as it was when Latin was a spoken language. The goal is not necessarily to replace traditional textbooks, but to supplement and enhance their teachings using more modern and innovative learning strategies and tools. Through the creation of an interactive, virtual ancient environment we seek to eliminate the distance students often feel when studying cultures which thrived several millennia ago by making them feel that they have been transported to ancient Rome. We have crafted a narrative where the player takes on the role of a young poet, named Titus, documenting a Roman "triumph," or military victory ceremony and procession. The player holds small conversations with a variety of characters as the narrative of the story unfolds. Using narrative and interactive design we immerse the player in Latin as a spoken language. Through this project we thus hope to demonstrate that Latin is more appropriately a "language of life" (*lingua vitae*).

In the following chapter, we will discuss the development of the project; challenges we have faced along the way; the (promising) results of our preliminary user studies; and future steps.

DEVELOPMENT

We initiated conception and development of *Lingua Vitae* in September 2018 at Santa Clara University, situated within Silicon Valley. Prior to this, proximity to some of the most innovative tech companies in the world had enabled us to attend many workshops and conferences on the combination of emergent technologies, including extended reality (XR) technology, and education at the secondary and postsecondary levels. While these companies and universities had recognized the benefits of these technologies in science, technology, engineering, and mathematics (STEM) research and education, we noticed a lack of emphasis on humanities-related projects. As we saw it, those same advantages and technologies could be utilized to benefit the humanities, and thus *Lingua Vitae* was born as a virtual supplement to *Wheelock's Latin,* the textbook used for Santa Clara's Latin classes. We delivered a proof of concept by the end of June 2019 and completed our first user studies on the alpha version in fall 2019 and winter 2020.

Lingua Vitae was built using the Unity engine and was developed for the Oculus Rift. The project proposal necessitated the reconstruction of the Roman Forum in 3D and implementation of a narrative system for dialogue and branching story scenarios. The 3D reconstruction of the Roman Forum has been completed before, as in Frischer's *Rome Reborn*.[12] While this project has taken some inspiration from *Rome Reborn*, *Lingua Vitae* differs in some key areas. Rather than placing emphasis on the site of Rome (architecture, topography, and so on), *Lingua Vitae* focuses on the people and communication of ancient Rome, highlighted by the interaction with virtual characters in Latin, telling a story as the player advances.[13] Our reconstruction also focuses on an earlier period in history, circa late 1st century BCE, and thus excludes many of the significant structures found in later dated versions of the Roman Forum (for example, *Rome Reborn* is set in 320 CE). Development was accomplished using the Unity game engine with the build in Unity XR toolkit. To navigate the VR space players would "point and click" to various points in the virtual forum using the Oculus Touch controllers, where non-player characters (NPCs) would be standing. Clicking on the characters would begin a conversation where users had the option to choose dialogue. All dialogue was conveyed through text and voiceover, with three actors each voicing a different character.

Figure 3.1: Virtual reconstruction of the Temple of Concord in the Roman Forum in Unity.

VOCABULARY

One of the challenges when developing the narrative for the project was crafting it in such a way that the vocabulary used in the dialogue aligned with the concepts and vocabulary presented in the textbook. For this we had to consider how to expand the dialogue through the chapters as the story unfolds. For instance, the first chapter of *Wheelock's Latin* teaches the five characteristics of most Latin verbs (person, number, tense, mood, voice); how to conjugate a verb in one tense, mood, and voice (present active indicative); the six verb endings, depending on person and number (-o, -s, -t, -mus, -tis, -nt); the first two conjugations (categories) of Latin verbs (out of four total); and how to be able to recognize the first two principal parts of verbs (out of four total) from a dictionary entry. In other words, students study a small portion of a few verbs in the first chapter and do not develop a more functional vocabulary, including common nouns, until later in the textbook. As a result, the first chapter of *Lingua Vitae* covers the first ten chapters of *Wheelock's Latin*, with the eventual goal of six virtual chapters accompanying the forty chapters of the textbook.

NARRATIVE

Users follow the narrative of a (fictional) young poet named Titus, who attends a military triumph (victory parade) in Rome in order to find inspiration to write a poem and perhaps attract a patron for his work. Along the way, he interacts with various other Romans. Using the narrative design tool Yarn Spinner (Figure 3.2) we are able to link in-text dialogue to the voiceover, animations, and story triggers. NPCs give the player tasks in Latin, which they must translate in order to determine how to complete the task. For instance, the first chapter, titled "Titus and the Hungry Centurion," revolves around Titus delivering a loaf of bread (*panis,* in Latin) to a centurion. While most of

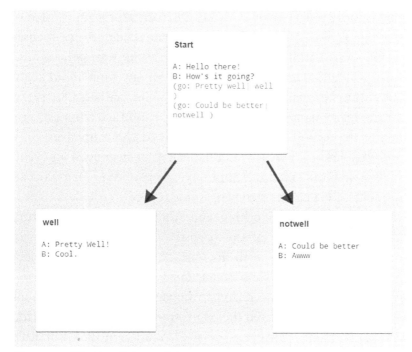

Figure 3.2: The Yarn Spinner dialogue system.

the language in the virtual experience is covered in the first ten chapters of *Wheelock's Latin*, the students at this point of the course, aside from those with previous training in Latin, have not ever heard or learned the word *panis*. Our goal is for the users to learn this word (and others) through understanding the context of the story. Thus, through the verbal interactions and task completion, users have the opportunity to build vocabulary, grammar, and aural comprehension skills, all while learning more about Roman culture.

The use of narrative also provides an opportunity to provide historical contextual information. The characters, scenarios, and locales created for the VR experience are based on archaeological, artistic, and literary evidence, as well as relevant secondary scholarship.[14] In particular, we are interested in creating a story that is more reflective of everyday life in ancient Rome. Much of the digital content created thus far about ancient Rome focuses on the drama and intrigue of the civilization: war, politics, and carnage. Rarely do users or players learn anything about regular, conversational topics like going to the market. Our story, on the other hand, takes place during a military triumph, in a nod to important events of the ancient past, but involves more everyday scenarios that would happen at or near such an event, such as making small talk and buying bread. Like many urban residents, the people of ancient Rome turned to retailers to provide them with food, clothing, and other goods. The 1st century CE Roman poet Martial attests to the prominence of shops in the Roman landscape with his quip, "now it is Rome, but just recently it was a large shop" (*nunc Roma est, nuper magna taberna fuit* [*Epigrams* 7.61]).[15] According to archaeological evidence, shops appear to have dominated the main streets of cities such as Ostia and Rome from their early history.[16] A 3rd-century CE marble relief from Ostia shows a vegetable seller with a large basket and a stall made up of a wooden trestle table, while another relief from Ostia from the second half of the 2nd century CE depicts a woman standing behind cages containing her stock of chickens. On the counter are two bowls of fruit, probably containing figs, and a barrel containing snails. There are even two monkeys on the stall to attract and entertain customers.[17] The artistic evidence not only helped to shape our creation of the shopping area but also encouraged us to include a female shopkeeper in the virtual experience (Figure 3.3). Even more significantly, Vennarucci observes that by the Late Republic in Rome, shops had become part of the social core of Roman life, serving as facilities for gossip and conversation as well as stores.[18] Since these daily retail interactions would have been nearly unavoidable in the ancient world, they thus provide a useful and relatively accurate type of interaction for us to replicate in the VR episode, one that would reflect common life and incorporate more conversational Latin dialogue.

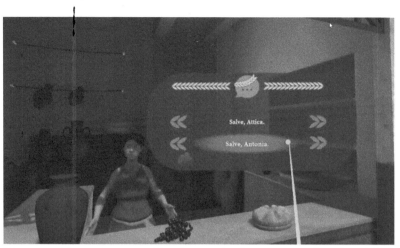

Figure 3.3: Players interact with a Roman shopkeeper to purchase bread for a hungry centurion.

FACULTY/STUDENT COLLABORATION

Lingua Vitae was developed in the Santa Clara University VR Lab (now known as the WAVE+Imaginarium Lab), primarily by student programmers and 3D artists. The collaboration between the student workers and the faculty had several positive effects. First of all, it off-loaded development workload to the students, so that the advising faculty could focus on design, research, and oversight. More specifically, these students were responsible for the actual creation of assets, code, and environments (including a full recreation of the Roman Forum). In doing so, they were able to practice and hone their research, programming, and design skills on a professional project, building skills and reference points, which they could then use as part of their academic CV or résumé postgraduation.

The student workers also contributed to the project beyond implementation, offering suggestions to the design from their perspective as undergraduates, our primary target audience. For instance, the original, admittedly stiff dialogue benefited from student workers suggesting small jokes or transitions to make the interactions smoother and more natural. The students were the first to play-test everything, and were able to communicate feedback to us, which facilitated the revisions and led to a better overall virtual experience.

From a financial perspective, the student workers were managed by the lab director of the Imaginarium, and they were paid out of the lab's operating budget. Prior to this project they were already on payroll assisting with the operation of the lab itself—cleaning VR headsets, installing software updates, and other administrative tasks. This project offered an opportunity for the students, who were previously doing little in terms of practical VR development, to gain the experience while simultaneously fulfilling their duties as lab assistants. However, we also applied for and received an internal grant from Santa Clara (through the Faculty-Student Research Assistant Program, FSRAP), which allowed us to pay for a nontechnical student research assistant. This student compiled much of the research presented above on the benefits of VR technology to foreign language education and also worked with the faculty to create the pre- and post-experiment questionnaires completed by participants in the user study. Finally, we also had high school students reach out to us, looking for volunteer opportunities to help conduct research. One such student assisted us in gathering additional cultural information to ensure the relative accuracy of our builds and interactions between characters.

USER STUDY

In the fall and winter of 2019–2020 we conducted a preliminary study of the effectiveness of *Lingua Vitae* on current and former Latin students at Santa Clara University. The IRB-approved study was designed to test whether a VR supplement might offer students a different perspective and type of learning experience from which to further develop their skills and grow more comfortable with the subject material. It also sought to answer the following questions, in ascending order of scale:

- Can virtual reality aid the acquisition of foreign language, and if so, how?[19]
- Can virtual reality help students to understand cultures and peoples existing thousands of years ago and to recognize the benefit of understanding these concepts and cultures?
- If so, how can virtual reality enrich the humanities and their striving to understand the nature and development of being human?

Obviously, this last question is complex, and by no means did we expect a complete, definitive answer in completing our study, but we do believe the data can help us begin to make these associations and offer potential directions to take in the future.

For this study we targeted students taking introductory Latin at Santa Clara University and randomly placed them into experimental and control groups. There were 19 participants in the experimental group of our study, and 12 in the control group. Both groups participated in the study after learning the first ten chapters of *Wheelock's Latin* in class. Pre- and post-questionnaires (see Appendix) were administered to both groups; the prequestionnaire established demographics and gauged baseline knowledge of Latin in vocabulary and sentence structure based on the following principles:

1. Knowledge (does participant know the words?)
2. Comprehension (can participant understand the words and/or sentence?)
3. Analysis of structure (can participant parse the various words?)
4. Application (can participant apply said knowledge and comprehension to producing their own sentence in Latin?)
5. Synthesis (can participant put together everything which he/she has determined and learned at the end?)

For the experimental group, questions regarding prior VR experience were also placed on the pre-questionnaire. The post-questionnaire, containing many of the same questions as the pre-questionnaire, evaluated how the student's knowledge changed or improved after completing the exercises and, for the experimental group, also asked for participants' reactions towards their experience within VR.[20]

Both groups then engaged with the story of "Titus and the Hungry Centurion," the first chapter of *Lingua Vitae*. The key differences between the experimental VR group and the control group are the roles of interactivity and immersion. In VR the user converses with the characters in real time, and the characters respond differently based on the user's response (Figure 3.4). The control group engaged with the same material through Santa Clara's learning management system Camino (Canvas platform), but instead of the virtual experience, they read and translated dialogue in written form. For the VR group, members of our team were on hand to show students how to use the Oculus Rift VR headset and virtual touch controller in the VR lab and to answer any questions before the participants took part in the virtual experience. The entire

Figure 3.4: Branching dialogue forces users to think critically about their responses to nonplayer characters.

pre- and post-questionnaires and immersive experience lasted approximately 30–45 minutes for each participant. Since students in the control group did not have to answer questions related to their VR experience, they took a slightly shorter range of time (20–35 minutes) to complete their pre- and post-questionnaires and the translations.

RESULTS

Although the small sample size suggests that our findings cannot be considered fully definitive, and some of the participants' answers may prove inconclusive as to the efficacy of VR in Latin sentence structure, there were also some very promising results. The outcomes from the post-survey filled out by participants showed overwhelmingly positive feedback towards the VR experience, as well as some indication of enhanced vocabulary recognition. The following are a sampling of the responses to the short answer question "Do you think VR would be helpful in learning Latin?"

> I do think that interacting with the characters helped increase my active thinking through what the Latin words meant. I also think that repetition of words in different contexts helped me remember or figure out what the words meant when I did not know them before. (Respondent 1)
>
> Because it isn't possible to be immersed in a fully Latin-speaking environment, the VR helps get that immersion and real-time language learning. (Respondent 2)
>
> It is fun being able to hear sentences that we otherwise would not. I also like how it was placed in the Roman Forum, giving us a little bit of culture behind the language. (Respondent 3)

The responses here reflected our own hopes that users would be more engaged with an increased level of immersion from the virtual reality learning experience. When asked in the survey if they had any additional feedback, we continued to receive positive responses from the participants:

> It's fun to see Latin being used in a way that I normally play video games. It's fun to have my knowledge of Latin add to what I am doing in my spare time. Plus it's more practice. I will never forget *panis*! (Respondent 4)
>
> A lot of other foreign languages give the opportunity for others to travel and immerse themselves in the everyday life of the speakers of that language. This is missing with Latin. The simulation really helped me learn. (Respondent 2)
>
> So much fun. I liked using my Latin in a real life situation/conversation. I recognized certain words and I knew what they were going to say, so I could formulate my response. (Respondent 5)

The numerical data appears to support the qualitative responses. On questions related to vocabulary building and identification (for instance, defining the noun denarius, or "coin," and parsing/identifying the first person singular verb *esurio*), we saw a score increase from both the control and experimental groups between the pre- and post-questionnaires. Exposure to the words in the VR experience and translation exercise seems to have led to greater familiarity with what the words mean and how they are formed (an obvious result but still positive towards the learning experience in virtual reality). Where the experimental and control groups differed the most was in defining the noun *panis* ("bread"). In the control group the correct responses went from 42.8% in the pre-questionnaire to 71.4% in the post-questionnaire. By contrast, the experimental group went from 38.8% correct responses in the pre-questionnaire to 100% correct responses in the post-survey. Completing the task of purchasing bread for the centurion in the VR experience was thus effective for the students' retention of this word.

CONCLUSIONS

Owing to the COVID-19 pandemic our user study was cut short. We originally intended to extend the study to more students in future Latin courses to gain more definitive results. Our development was also cut short, due to reduced funding for research programs and the temporary closure of the Imaginarium VR lab. The development of further VR chapters in conjunction with later chapters of *Wheelock's Latin* is only slowly restarting, while we continue to navigate through the COVID-19 consequences. This has given us plenty of time to think about the project retroactively and come to some conclusions about what we might have done differently.

One idea that would have helped early on would have been to narrow the scope for the project. We spent a lot of time and resources trying to recreate the Roman Forum in its entirety. The initial idea was that students would achieve more cultural learning from seeing the Forum in a different perspective from which it is seen today. We wanted to create a Forum that was teeming with the lives of ancient Romans, with the ability to navigate to different story vignettes at will. With the final version we only covered the first ten chapters of *Wheelock's Latin*, and the only interactive location was the *taberna*. Only two characters were interactive, and we had no background characters. We learned that the lack of extra characters did not have a greatly negative impact on the learning experience when we began testing. Scaling back and focusing on individual, self-contained stories would have been a more practical approach.

Challenges with using immersive learning also remain high. Without the use of a dedicated virtual reality laboratory on campus, access becomes a great challenge for users at various universities. Access to the technology due to cost, learning curve, support system, and usability can impact the pace of adoption. Many other XR modern technology solutions that are being developed are faced with similar issues. Especially in the educational technology sector, as departments of education across the United States continue to emphasize, the digital divide cannot truly be bridged until all students not only have access to but also understand how to use the technology.[21] Only a collaborative approach can solve this challenge. With the tech industry, education technology, and school academic affairs closely working together, there are ways to bridge the adoption and the digital divide issue for learners.

Even with these challenges, we believe that the evidence from our study points to a positive affirmation of our hypothesis: interactive immersive learning leads to more natural and retained learning for language acquisition. The subjective feedback from participants also indicates elevated engagement with the subject matter, which we believe makes the study of classics more relatable and exciting to students. Given the small sample size for our study, we cannot conclusively say that the virtual experience is the best way in which to learn Latin, but it is certainly *a* way to learn, and in many ways, learn quite well. While we were pleased with the outcomes in general, we could not help but wonder whether VR is especially important or if we could use another type of technology to drive the narrative aspect of our experience. This is a topic we would like to explore further in future studies by creating a non-VR companion to the VR experience and doing A/B testing between the two to explore differences in effectiveness. Finally, we believe that there needs to be further exploration of interdisciplinary, innovative systems of learning (as facilitated through technology) for Classics and other disciplines.

APPENDIX: PRE- AND POST- QUESTIONNAIRES

A. Pre-Questionnaire

Latin Experience

    1.   Do you have any experience with Latin prior to attending SCU?

2. How much oral practice with Latin do you have? By oral practice, we mean speaking and hearing Latin. (5-point scale, with 1 being none and 5 being a lot of practice.)
3. Explain response to #2.
4. Do you find it more, less, or equally difficult to translate Latin after hearing it vs. after seeing it written down? (More difficult to translate from hearing/More difficult to translate from seeing.)
5. Explain response to #3.
6. Please define the following words (if you don't know, write "n/a"):
   Nomen, nominis (neut.): _____
   Bene (adv.): _____
   Possum, posse, potui (v.): _____
   Panis, panis (masc.): _____
   Denarius, denarii (masc.): _____
7. Parse the word *esurio* (it is a verb: list the five characteristics): _____
8. Translate the sentence: Potesne non nomen meum in corpore meo vidēre?
9. Translate into Latin: I will love this money forever!

VR Experience (Only for Experimental Group)

1. Do you have previous experience with VR? If so, how much? (A lot—some—a little—none)
2. If you have interacted with other virtual reality experiences before, what kind were they?
   a. Games
   b. Educational material
   c. Training for a job
   d. None; no prior experience

B. Post-Questionnaire

Latin experience

1. Please define the following words (if you don't know, write n/a)
   Nomen, nominis (neut.): _____
   Bene (adv.): _____
   Possum, posse, potui (v.): _____
   Panis, panis (masc.): _____
   Denarius, denarii (masc.): _____
2. Parse the word *esurio* (it is a verb: list the five characteristics): _____
3. Translate the sentence: Potesne non nomen meum in corpore meo vidēre?
4. Translate into Latin: I will love this money forever!

VR Experience (Only for Experimental Group)

1. How easy was it to comprehend what the characters were saying? (1–5 scale, with 1 being very difficult and 5 being very easy)
2. Explain your response to #1.
3. Were there any technical difficulties with the experience? For example, were the controllers easy to use?
4. Do you think the immersion helped you to focus on the language more or less? (scale of 1–4, with 1 being no focus at all and 4 being fully focused)
5. Did you have fun in the experience? (A lot; some; a little; none).
6. Explain your response to #5.
7. Do you think VR would be helpful in learning Latin? Please explain your response.
8. Is there anything (type of question/interaction) you would add or like to see in future modules?

NOTES

1. With special acknowledgement to Alexis Miller for her help in compiling research.

2. *Wheelock's Latin*, one of the standard post-secondary Latin textbooks, first appeared in 1956 as F. Wheelock's *Latin: An Introductory Course Based on Ancient Authors*. Its most recent edition, the seventh, was published in 2011 and is the text we are using in conjunction with our project.

3. Additionally, there are flaws in a strictly grammar-translation type of instruction, suggesting that it does not lead to long-term language learning, as emphasized by Adair-Hauck, Donato, and Cumo-Johansen, "Using a story-based approach."

4. For more on the benefits of active Latin (for students, teachers, and enrollments), see, e.g., Keeline, "*Aut Latine aut nihil?*"; Shirley, "Day in the Life"; and Stringer, "What Can Active Latin Accomplish?" (all of which comprise part of a special edition of *The Classical Outlook* on active learning); Ancona, "College Professors"; and Carlon, "Implications of SLA Research." Keeline and Shirley also discuss the benefits of comprehensible input (and output) instruction.

5. While the push for more oral communication, especially in Latin, has seen a recent increase in popularity, it is not a new endeavor. The Standards for Classical Language Learning, as established in 1997, establish the 5 Cs: communication, culture, connections, comparisons, communities. The communication standard includes an oral conversation component. On how the five Cs have been incorporated into Latin and Greek instruction, see, e.g., Gruber-Miller, ed., *When Dead Tongues Speak*. In 2017, the American Classical League (ACL) and Society for Classical Studies (SCS) updated the Standards, and they continue to stress the primary importance of communication, embracing listening, speaking, and writing as much as reading: see revised 2017 standards at https://www.aclclassics.org/Portals/0/Site%20Documents/Publications/Standards_for_Classical_Language_Learning_2017%20FINAL.pdf. On the benefits of task-based learning for modern language, particularly in virtual environments, see Chen, "Effects of pre-task planning."

6. For further discussion of digital technologies in conjunction with reading ancient languages, see Palladino, "Reading Texts in Digital Environments."

7. Borona, Tambouris, and Tarabanis, "Use of 3D Multi-User Virtual Environments." According to Pinto et al. ("Foreign Language Learning"), the effectiveness of XR gamification strategies in teaching foreign language is still under investigation (since these technologies are so new), so researchers

recommend still using the new technologies as a supplement to traditional methods of language instruction rather than in replacement of or as a substitute for them. Furthermore, since the quality and usability of various commercial off-the-shelf (COTS) virtual experiences may vary, researchers at the Kanda University of International Studies in Japan have created a framework designed to assist educators in finding suitable programs for the classroom. This framework, entitled the *VR Analysis Application Framework*, works to evaluate existing programs through four lenses: cognitive load (recognizing the sensory-rich environment of VR and designing with the limits of a working memory in mind); immersive capacity (sense of presence in the virtual environment); communicative capability (ability to communicate with others in the experience through built-in application tools); and purpose (intended usage and genre). For more on this framework, see Frazier, Lege, and Bonner, "Making Virtual Reality Accessible."

8. For the benefits of VR for US-based university students learning introductory French and about Parisian culture, see Mills et al., "Culture and vision."

9. Yu-Li Chen, "Effects of Virtual Reality Learning." Writing in a foreign language requires similarly complex levels of thinking; on the potential benefits of VR for student writing in a foreign language, see Huang, Hwang, and Chang, "Learning to be a writer."

10. Palomeque and Pujolà, "Managing Multimodal Data."

11. Melchor-Couto, "Virtual World Anonymity." Similarly, a study by James York et al. ("Effect of SCMC") on synchronous computer-mediated communication (SCMC), foreign language anxiety, and learning experience found that many native Japanese speakers who were learning English viewed VR environments as the easiest in which to communicate, the most fun, and the most effective environment for language learning. See also Ou Yang et al., "Facilitating Communicative Ability."

12. Frischer et al., *Rome Reborn*. In her article "Reviving Classical Drama," Eleni Bozia surveys additional 3D models and virtual and gaming environments related to ancient Rome and cultural heritage in her discussion of a mixed-reality ancient theater space.

13. In combining the oral/verbal with the visual components, all while walking around the Roman Forum, *Lingua Vitae* highlights a recent scholarly trend within classics in examining space and movement in cities such as Rome or Pompeii. This new research aims toward a multisensory understanding of how a populace might *move* through and experience an ancient city each day. For more on this approach, see, e.g., Laurence and Newsome, eds., *Rome, Ostia, Pompeii,* and especially Betts' article, "Towards a Multisensory

Experience," within Laurence and Newsome. Of course, scholars have been interested in reconstructing ancient Rome, via paintings, maps, prints, sculptures, gardens, and more, since the Renaissance, in order to "bring the whole ancient city back to life," as observed by Albert Ammerman, "Adding time to Rome's *imago*," 297.

14. For this project, "re-creation" (as defined by Favro, "In the Eyes of the Beholder," 322n6 and discussed *passim*) of parts of the Roman Forum is being completed through the use of a Sketchfab model, adapted and revised for accuracy in space and chronology through consultation with the digital reconstruction and archaeological guide provided in Gorski and Packer, eds., *The Roman Forum*, as well as two additional archaeological guides: Coarelli, *Rome and Environs*; and Claridge, *Rome*. Triumph scenarios have been devised with Beard, *The Roman Triumph* as a guide, and clothing in consultation with Croom, *Roman Clothing and Fashion*.

15. Translation Crofton-Sleigh.

16. Vennarucci, "Marketing an Urban Identity," *passim*. Ellis ("*Pes Dexter*," 160) estimates approximately 600 shops existed in Pompeii and around 800 in Ostia, based on archaeological examinations of doorway types. For more on city planning and the location of shops, particularly in Pompeii, see van Nes, "Measuring Spatial Visibility in Pompeii," 105–107.

17. Both reliefs ("Sign of a Poulterer" and "Sign of a Vegetable Seller") are held at the Museo Ostiense (Ostia Archaeological Museum). They can be viewed in the Scala Archives: https://scalarchives.com/.

18. Vennarucci, "Marketing an Urban Identity," 143.

19. In "Immersive Virtual Reality," Legault et al. suggest that immersive virtual environments can aid in the learning of foreign language vocabulary, particularly for students who struggle with the more traditional methods of learning vocabulary. Similar conclusions for the benefits of vocabulary building within VR environments are offered by Luccioni, Benotti, and Landragin, "Overspecified References." While Legault et al.'s study focuses on the acquisition of Mandarin, and Luccioni's on the acquisition of Russian, we are aiming to investigate the efficacy of VR for learning an ancient language. For the effects of AR on learning vocabulary, see Belda-Medina and Marrahi-Gomez, "Impact of Augmented Reality."

20. See Appendix A for a full set of pre- and post-test questions.

21. For one recent example, in February 2021 California's State Superintendent of Public Instruction, Tony Thurmond, started the initiative "California Digital Divide Innovation Challenge," which offers $1 million to spur innovations towards eliminating the digital divide. For more on this program, see https://www.cde.ca.gov/nr/ne/yr21/yr21rel07.asp.

WORKS CITED

Adair-Hauck, Bonnie, Richard Donato, and P. Cumo-Johanssen. "Using a Story-Based Approach to Teach Grammar." In *Teacher's Handbook: Contextualized Language Instruction*, 3rd edition, edited by Judith L. Shrum and Eileen W. Glisan, 189–213. Boston, MA: Thomson/Heinle, 2005.

American Classical League and Society for Classical Studies. "2017 Standards for Classical Language Learning." American Classical League website, 2017. https://www.aclclassics.org/Portals/0/Site%20Documents/Publications/Standards_for_Classical_Language_Learning_2017%20FINAL.pdf

Ammerman, Albert. "Adding time to Rome's *imago*." In *Imaging Ancient Rome: Documentation—Visualization—Imagination*. Proceedings of the Third Williams Symposium on Classical Architecture, 2004. JRA Supplementary Series 61, edited by Lothar Haselberger and John Humphrey, 297–308. Portsmouth, R.I.: Journal of Roman Archaeology, 2006.

Ancona, Ronnie. "College Professors and the New Standards for Classical Language Learning." *Teaching Classical Languages* 9, no. 1 (2018): 64–73. https://tcl.camws.org/sites/default/files/Ancona%2CTCL9.1_0.pdf

Beard, Mary. *The Roman Triumph.* Cambridge, MA: Belknap Press of Harvard University Press, 2007.

Belda-Medina, Jose, and Victor Marrahi-Gomez. "The Impact of Augmented Reality (AR) on Vocabulary Acquisition and Student Motivation." *Electronics* 12, no. 3 (2023): 749. https://doi.org/10.3390/electronics12030749

Betts, Eleanor. "Towards a Multisensory Experience of Movement in the City of Rome." In *Rome, Ostia, Pompeii: Movement and Space*, edited by Ray Laurence and David J. Newsome, 118–32. Oxford: Oxford University Press, 2011. https://doi.org/10.1093/acprof:osobl/9780199583126.003.0005

Borona, Stefania, Efthimios Tambouris, and Konstantinos Tarabanis. "The Use of 3D Multi-User Virtual Environments in Computer-Assisted Second Language Learning: A Systematic Literature Review." *International Journal of Learning Technology* 13, no. 3 (2018): 249–74. https://doi.org/10.1504/IJLT.2018.095963

Bozia, Eleni. "Reviving Classical Drama: Virtual Reality and Experiential Learning in a Traditional Classroom." *Digital Humanities Quarterly* 12, no. 3 (2018). http://digitalhumanities.org:8081/dhq/vol/12/3/000385/000385.html

Carlon, Jacqueline M. "The Implications of SLA Research for Latin Pedagogy: Modernizing Latin Instruction and Securing its Place in Curricula." *Teaching Classical Languages* 4, no. 2 (2013): 106–22. https://tcl.camws.org/sites/default/files/Carlon_0.pdf

Chen, Julian. "The effects of pre-task planning on EFL learners' oral performance in a 3D multi-user virtual environment." *ReCALL* 32, no. 3 (2020): 232–49. https://doi.org/10.1017/S0958344020000026

Chen, Yu-Li. "The Effects of Virtual Reality Learning Environment on Student Cognitive and Linguistic Development." *Asia-Pacific Education Researcher* 25, no. 4 (2016): 637–46. https://doi.org/10.1007/s40299-016-0293-2

Claridge, Amanda. *Rome: An Oxford Archaeological Guide*, 2nd edition. Oxford: Oxford University Press, 2010.

Coarelli, Filippo. *Rome and Environs: An Archaeological Guide* (first edition, revised). Translated by James Clauss and Daniel Harmon. Berkeley: University of California Press, 2014.

Croom, Alexandra. *Roman Clothing and Fashion.* Stroud: Amberley Publishing, 2010.

Ellis, Steven J.R. *"Pes Dexter: Superstition and the State in the Shaping of Shopfronts and Street Activity in the Roman World."* In *Rome, Ostia, Pompeii: Movement and Space,* edited by Ray Laurence and David J. Newsome, 160–73. Oxford: Oxford University Press, 2011. https://doi.org/10.1093/acprof:osobl/9780199583126.003.0007

Favro, Diane. "In the Eyes of the Beholder: Virtual Reality Re-creations and Academia." In *Imaging Ancient Rome: Documentation—Visualization—Imagination.* Proceedings of the Third Williams Symposium on Classical Architecture, 2004. JRA Supplementary Series 61, edited by Lothar Haselberger and John Humphrey, 321–34. Portsmouth, R.I.: Journal of Roman Archaeology, 2006.

Frazier, Erin, Ryan Lege, and Euan Bonner. "Making Virtual Reality Accessible for Language Learning: Applying the VR Application Analysis Framework." *Teaching English with Technology* 21, no. 1 (2021): 128–40.

Frischer, Bernard et al. *Rome Reborn.* 1996–. https://www.romereborn.org/

Gorski, Gilbert and James E. Packer. *The Roman Forum: A Reconstruction and Architectural Guide.* Cambridge: Cambridge University Press, 2015.

Gruber-Miller, John, ed. *When Dead Tongues Speak: Teaching Beginning Greek and Latin.* Oxford: Oxford University Press, 2006.

Haselberger, Lothar, and John Humphrey, eds. *Imaging Ancient Rome: Documentation—Visualization—Imagination.* Proceedings of the Third Williams Symposium on Classical Architecture, 2004. JRA Supplementary Series 61. Portsmouth, R.I.: Journal of Roman Archaeology, 2006.

Huang, Hsiu-Ling, Gwo-Jen Hwang, and Ching-Yi Chang. "Learning to be a writer: A spherical video-based virtual reality approach to supporting descriptive article writing in high school Chinese courses." *British Journal of Educational Technology* 51, no. 4 (2020): 1386–1405. https://doi.org/10.1111/bjet.12893

Keeline, Tom. "'*Aut Latine aut nihil*'? A Middle Way." *The Classical Outlook* 94, no. 2 (2019): 57–65. https://www.jstor.org/stable/26774722

Laurence, Ray, and David J. Newsome, eds. *Rome, Ostia, Pompeii: Movement and Space.* Oxford: Oxford University Press, 2011.

Legault, Jennifer, Jiayan Zhao, Ying-An Chi, Weitao Chen, Alexander Klippel, and Ping Li. "Immersive Virtual Reality as an Effective Tool for Second Language Vocabulary Learning." *Languages* 4, no. 1 (2019), 13. https://doi.org/10.3390/languages4010013

Luccioni, Alexandra, Luciana Benotti, and Frédéric Landragin. "Overspecified References: An Experiment on Lexical Acquisition in a Virtual Environment." *Computers in Human Behavior* 49 (2015): 94–101. https://doi.org/10.1016/j.chb.2015.02.036

Melchor-Couto, Sabela. "Virtual World Anonymity and Foreign Language Oral Interaction." *ReCALL* 30, no. 2 (2018): 232–49. https://doi.org/10.1017/S0958344017000398

Mills, Nicole, Matthew Courtney, Christopher Dede, Arnaud Dressen, and Rus Gant. "Culture and vision in virtual reality narratives." *Foreign Language Annals* 53, no. 4 (2020): 733–60. https://doi.org/10.1111/flan.12494

Ou Yang, Fang-Chuan, Fang-Ying Riva Lo, Jun Chen Hsieh, and Wen-Chi Vivian Wu. "Facilitating Communicative Ability of EFL Learners via High-Immersion Virtual Reality." *Educational Technology & Society* 23, no. 1 (2020): 30–49. https://doi.org/10.30191/ETS.202001_23(1).0003

Palladino, Chiara. "Reading Texts in Digital Environments: Applications of Translation Alignment for Classical Language Learning." *Journal of Interactive Technology & Pedagogy* 18 (2020). https://jitp.commons.gc.cuny.edu/reading-texts-in-digital-environments-applications-of-translation-alignment-for-classical-language-learning/

Palomeque, Cristina, and Joan-Tomàs Pujolà. "Managing Multimodal Data in Virtual World Research for Language Learning." *ReCALL* 30, no. 2 (2018): 177–95. https://doi.org10.1017/S0958344017000374

Pinto, Rafael Darque, Bruno Peixoto, Miguel Melo, Luciana Cabral, and Maximino Bessa. "Foreign Language Learning Gamification Using Virtual Reality— A Systematic Review of Empirical Research." *Education Sciences* 11, no. 5 (2021), 222. https://doi.org/10.3390/educsci11050222

Shirley, Skye. "A Day in the Life of an Active Latin Teacher." *The Classical Outlook* 94, no. 2 (2019): 66–71. https://www.jstor.org/stable/26774723

Stringer, Gregory P. "What Can Active Latin Accomplish? Well Let Me Just Show You: Some Facts and Figures Illustrating the Benefits of Active Latin Instruction." *The Classical Outlook* 94, no. 2 (2019): 81–93. https://www.jstor.org/stable/26774725

van Nes, Akkelies. "Measuring Spatial Visibility in Pompeii." In *Rome, Ostia, Pompeii: Movement and Space,* edited by Ray Laurence and David J. Newsome, 100–17. Oxford: Oxford University Press, 2011. https://doi.org/10.1093/acprof:osobl/9780199583126.003.0004

Vennarucci, Rhodora G. "Marketing an Urban Identity: The Shops and Shopkeepers of Ancient Rome." In *Crossing Boundaries, Spanning Borders: Voyages Around Marketing's Past*, Proceedings of the 17th Biennial Conference on Historical Analysis and Research in Marketing (CHARM), edited by Richard A. Hawkins, 135–58. Long Beach, CA: CHARM Association, 2015.

Wheelock, Frederic M. and Richard LaFleur. *Wheelock's Latin*, 7th edition. New York: HarperCollins, 2011.

York, James, Koichi Shibata, Hayato Tokutate, and Hiroshi Nakayama. "Effect of SCMC on foreign language anxiety and learning experience: A comparison of voice, video, and VR-based oral interaction." *ReCALL* 33, no. 1 (2021): 49–70. https://doi.org/10.1017/S0958344020000154

PART 2

CONSIDERING AND
QUESTIONING THE PRESENT

CHAPTER 4

DESIGNING AND TEACHING A VIRTUAL FIELD TRIP COURSE IN AMERICAN STUDIES

Tim Gruenewald

The COVID-19 pandemic presented serious challenges to postsecondary education including suspension of face-to-face instruction and the cancellation of extracurricular events. One of those challenges was the suspension of experiential learning outside of campus, especially study field trips requiring international travel as borders shut, quarantines were implemented, and air travel ground to a halt. As program director of an American studies major at the University of Hong Kong, I had always considered our required field trip course to Philadelphia, Washington, DC, and New York City as the cornerstone of the major. Students were able to bring their learning from interdisciplinary electives and core courses on U.S. culture, society, politics, and history to the United States and deepen their learning. We debated at key historical sites in Philadelphia and Washington, DC. We experienced social problems and political conflicts in cities and rural areas. We saw and discussed art in public spaces and museums. Most importantly, the intensive time together was crucial for creating social cohesion and identification with the major. When we had to cancel the course for a second time in 2021, I had to find a viable substitute. Since I had conducted research on narrative virtual reality (VR) since 2016, the solution was obvious.[1] I decided to transform the existing course to a virtual field trip and taught it as a fourteen-day block seminar during the summer of 2021 in Hong Kong and then again as a regular semester course in spring of 2022. In the following, I will present the teaching philosophy underlying the course design, its structure, two detailed discussions of VR learning experiences, and conclude with some key lessons drawn from teaching the course.

To state the obvious up front, virtual travel cannot substitute "in real life" (IRL) travel, just as a Zoom class cannot replace a face-to-face seminar. Yet, at least some technological innovations of teaching implemented during the pandemic are valuable and should stay in place in a postpandemic world (see, for example, Reimers and Marmolejo, 2022). For example, virtual travel presents some opportunities that even IRL field trips cannot offer. It is worth giving VR-enabled field trips serious consideration as a tool of experiential learning in university education, not as a substitute for travel IRL but in addition to conventional field trip courses and as additions to regular classes.

LITERATURE ON VIRTUAL FIELD TRIPS IN EDUCATION

While research on using VR for virtual field trips in postsecondary education is limited, the extant literature is largely encouraging. For example, Mohring and Brendel (2021) designed an assignment, in which students had to produce a VR field trip in a course on sense-based geographic education with the aim of teaching how people "acquire" environments through bodily sensation. They conclude: "VR is in some ways a disruptive technology. It integrates perception into routines of digital communication. Like an augmented image, VR can be perceived atmospherically. Therefore, VR is a powerful geographic visualization that creates felt virtual spaces" (378). They observe that a virtual field trip can mimic how people experience the atmosphere of place through senses in physical reality. While VR in its current form can only provide an approximation, nevertheless this technological affordance was a main motivation for selecting VR experiences in my course, specifically to enable students to experience the atmosphere of a broad range of sites in the United States relevant to the course content and to sense the mood at related events such as a Native American ceremony, a protest march, or a Trump rally.

Fung et al. (2019) describe the positive quantitative and qualitative student evaluation of the use of a virtual field trip in an environmental chemistry class, where the instructor led students through a number of 360° photospheres of environments. Students were then given time to explore the virtual sites on their own. While there were some complaints about "disorientation" and technological limitations (low resolution), 64% rated the experience positively vs. 12% negatively (Fung et al., 385). Markowitz et al. (2018) examined the efficacy of VR field trips in environmental education across four studies and argue:

> We suspect that the strong learning effects in immersive VR reflect the medium's unique ability to fully engage a subject in an experience and surround him or her with the feeling of non-mediation (Slater and Wilbur, 1997), but also believe that it is important to explore how immersive VR compares to other media in its potential to facilitate learning about science.
>
> (Markowitz et al., 17.)

This conclusion applies in my experience to the use of VR in the humanities as well. We should not assume that VR content is automatically superior to equivalent content in conventional media. The decision of whether to implement a specific VR experience has to be made carefully case by case. Markowitz et al. also emphasize that VR should be seen as a supplement to but not a substitute for conventional media of teaching (Markowitz et al., 18). Finally, there is a body of literature discussing the value of virtual field trips without using VR technology: for example, through online media, software, or remote online communication. While those studies also stress that a virtual field trip cannot replace a field trip IRL, they generally see virtual field trips as a very effective educational tool (see, for example, Spicer and Stratford, 2001; Harrington, 2009). In my experience, those benefits also apply to virtual field trips with VR technology and are likely to be enhanced by the immersive technology.

TEACHING PHILOSOPHY AND DESIGN PRINCIPLES

The redesign of the field trip course was guided by two core principles of my teaching philosophy that needed to be adapted to teaching with VR. First, the use of VR should add to the students' *experiential learning*. VR enables embodied experiences with strong physical, emotional, and social impact. Chris Milk (2015) proclaimed in a well-known TED talk the case for VR as "the ultimate empathy machine." He argued that VR has the potential to shift a viewer's perspective and facilitate the experience of the suffering of other people unlike any other medium. Thus, he argued, VR could trigger empathy in the viewer and would therefore present the ideal medium of communication for anyone seeking to mobilize support for humanitarian causes. While such claims regarding empathy of early VR content producers were exaggerated and received much criticism in the literature, few would disagree that VR content has at least the potential to affect the body of the viewer more intensely than conventional screen media.[2]

Second, *interactive learning* is central to my course design, especially for the field trip course. At the same time, interactivity is a potential strength of VR. While I did not use VR games because of a lack of suitable content at the time, I aimed to privilege VR experiences with greater degrees of interactivity whenever possible. All VR content discussed in this paper features at least some interactivity, since even for a 360° film, the viewer collaborates in the production of the experience through choosing the direction of the gaze and attention. Strictly speaking, no two VR experiences of the same VR film are exactly the same.

In addition, I propose a third design principle, which could be described as insisting on a *value-added* use of VR. While this may seem self-evident, it is tempting to use new technology for its own sake. To avoid such overuse of technology, the threshold for employing VR in the classroom should always be that it must achieve specific learning outcomes better than conventional media. Erica Southgate (2020) emphasizes that use of immersive technologies in education should be led by pedagogical considerations, not vice versa (5–6). This implies that other media should be employed whenever their educational value is greater than content available on VR. For the present course, this is evident by my ample use of conventional documentary and fiction film screenings and by the assignment of preparatory readings and various online media. Thus, almost all VR content was extensively prepared before students experienced it.

Finally, I considered several limitations of currently available VR platforms and content for use in the classroom. First, extended use of current VR headsets can cause discomfort especially for users with no or little experience using VR, ranging from mild dizziness and eye fatigue to more severe afflictions such as motion sickness, nausea, and headaches (Park and Lee, 2020; Argyriou et al.,

2020). Over two seminars in 2021–22 with a combined 22 students, no student owned a VR headset and only one had noteworthy experience with the medium. Several students in those courses complained about adverse effects like those described above. Since those tend to be less likely and less severe for shorter VR experiences, I decided to restrict myself to shorter content of no more than twenty minutes, especially for in-class use of VR. This did not pose a significant restriction since the vast majority of non-game content at the time met this requirement. I expect the problem of adverse effects to decrease over time as VR experience among students becomes more common and headset technology is refined.[3] At the same time, some VR experiences are expanding in duration and complexity. I expect the variety and quality of VR content to increase rapidly over the next few years and the educational value of using VR in the humanities classroom to rise accordingly over the situation that I found in 2021.

CHOOSING THE VR PLATFORM

At the time of the course in summer of 2021, the Oculus Quest 2 was without alternative, due to both budget limitations and technical specifications.[4] We were able to purchase headsets for ten students at a cost of USD 249 per student. Since we needed standalone devices for at home and in-class use of the headsets, the only plausible alternatives would have been the HTC Vive Focus or the Lenovo Mirage Solo, which at the time were both already outdated (lower resolution and processor), yet were sold for USD 599 and 399, respectively. Of course, the low price of the Quest 2 could only be explained by significant cross-subsidy from the parent company Meta, which was still called Facebook at the time, as CEO Mark Zuckerberg confirmed in an interview in March of 2021 (Heath and Olson, 2021). The extent of the subsidy became clear with the HTC Vive Focus 3, released at the end of 2021 for a price of USD 1,300 with only slightly improved specifications over the Quest 2.

Unsurprisingly, such a subsidy does not come without a cost, which for the Quest 2 came in the form of a Facebook account requirement for setting up the device. This presented a significant problem for a program invested in critical cultural studies, including topics such as populist nationalism and the role of social media in the rise of Trumpism and the outcome of the 2016 election. I had been teaching critiques of Web 2.0's political economy such as Shoshana Feldman's notion of surveillance capitalism in the program's required core course. To mitigate this downside of the Quest 2, I decided to add a critical investigation of social media as a central part of the course. Outside the Facebook issue, the Quest 2 proved to be a suitable choice thanks to reliable hardware, ease of setup, and a stable operating system, all of which presented no technical problems for a total of fourteen devices used over two classes.

COURSE DESIGN AND STRUCTURE

It was not suitable to adapt our existing IRL field trip course to a virtual field trip, since that course was designed to take advantage of sites available in Philadelphia, Washington, DC, and New York City. Although those sites are among the most prominent historical and cultural sites in the United States, such as Freedom Hall in Philadelphia, Capitol Hill in DC, or the Guggenheim in New York, virtually none of them was well represented in VR at the time. On the other hand, it made no sense to submit to the restrictions of travel IRL such as cost and time. I would assume that this applies to almost all IRL field trip courses and that VR field trip courses should generally be designed from scratch as virtual travel courses.

One significant problem I encountered from the outset was a relative dearth of VR experiences suitable to teaching American studies. I had a fairly complete overview of released VR content since I was working on a database of narrative VR experiences that, in summer of 2021, included circa 800 entries.[5] I decided to design the course in direct response to this lack of selection and implemented a modular structure that would provide a broad overview of important contemporary American studies topics. While students would be likely to have encountered several of those topics in other courses previously, I chose them based on the criterion of whether virtual travel or an available VR narrative experience could enhance learning about the issue at hand. In effect, this produced an American studies overview of contemporary social and cultural issues that allowed for maximum flexibility in selecting from a diverse set of VR experiences and that would benefit from virtual travel of geographic variety throughout the United States. This approach resulted in a series of ten topics, two of which formed larger thematic clusters (1–3 and 5; 6–9). For the introductory session and for each topic one or two VR experiences were viewed together (listed under each topic):

- Introduction
  - *Evolution of Verse* (2015, YouTube)
  - *The People's House - Inside the White House with Barack and Michelle Obama* (2017, YouTube)
- Topic 1. We Are Still Here: Memory and Native American Past
  - *Crow: The Legend* (2019, YouTube)
  - *The Occupation of Alcatraz that Sparked an American Revolution* (2017, YouTube)
- Topic 2. Black Lives Matter: Memory and African American Past
  - *Traveling While Black* (2019, VR App)
- Topic 3. Inequity in the U.S. Legal System: The Prison Industrial Complex
  - *Step to the Line* (2017, YouTube)
  - *Send Me Home* (2018, YouTube)
- Topic 4. Gun Violence
  - *Hard World for Small Things* (2016, YouTube)
  - *12 Seconds of Gunfire* (2019, YouTube)
- Topic 5. Black Culture, Hip-Hop, and Resistance
  - *Marshall from Detroit* (2019, VR App)

- Topic 6. Threat to Democracy I: Populist Nationalism
  - *Donald Trump Rally* (2016, YouTube)
  - *In the Media Pen at a Trump Rally* (2016, YouTube)
- Topic 7. Threat to Democracy II: Social Media
  - *VR Chat* (VR App)
- Topic 8. Threat to Democracy III: Immigration and the Southern Border
  - *The Key* (2019, VR App)
  - *Life and Death at the Mexican Border* (2016, YouTube)
- Topic 9. Threat to Democracy IV: Globalization and White Poverty
  - *We Live Here* (2020, VR App)
- Topic 10. Climate Change and Environmental Protection
  - *The Edgar Mitchell Overview Effect* (2020, VR App)
  - *This Is Climate Change* (2017, YouTube)

The summer course in 2021 was scheduled as a series of ten full-day course meetings, whereby each day was dedicated to one topic. The social group experience of the conventional field trip course was crucial to our program for generating a cohort identity among the majors. Hence, I planned several group dinners, daily lunches, and we concluded the course with an overnight two-day IRL field trip to Disneyland Hong Kong, which focused on the topic "Ideologies of U.S. Popular Culture" and which applied many of the critical theory lenses discussed during the previous ten days. While I will not discuss this part of the course here, I would like to note that it was the most successful module of the entire course both in my estimation and based on anecdotal student feedback. This is not to denigrate the educational value of virtual travel but merely to reiterate that virtual travel can be a valuable educational supplement, not a replacement for IRL field trips.

Each seminar day was prepared by a brief reading and online media selected to introduce the daily topic. Course meetings were scheduled from 10 am until 6 pm and each day featured the same five elements:

1. Topic introduction, including a ten-minute student presentation followed by group Q&A (1 hour)
2. One to two VR experiences, followed by group discussion (1.5 hours)
3. Lunch break
4. Student presentation on visual art (1 hour)
5. Tea break
6. Conventional film screening (1.5-2 hours)
7. Virtual group travel with Oculus Wander

This structure reflects the design principle discussed above that the most effective medium should be chosen to achieve a specific educational outcome. It also recognizes the fact that it would be unrealistic to expect the best-suited material for most purposes to be found in a narrative medium that was just over half a decade old at the time. To achieve most desired learning outcomes, for example, a film, a book chapter, or a piece of visual art would likely be the best choice. Thus, each session introduced a different perspective and method for engaging with the topic of the day, allowing for a well-rounded, varied, and more complete understanding of the issues. In the following, I will focus on the VR experiences in detail and show with two examples how narrative VR and virtual travel were employed to contribute to the learning outcomes on their own merit and in concert with other conventional educational materials.

EXAMPLE 1: MEMORY, NATIVE AMERICAN PAST, AND RESISTANCE

The module on Native American studies focused on memory of traumatic and painful past and the contrasting approaches to public memory found in the contemporary United States. I designed this session around my own documentary film *Sacred Ground* (2015), which I created in response to a visit to the Wounded Knee Massacre mass grave and Mount Rushmore on a single day in 2001. While I have taught this film many times in recent years, VR offered a completely new and unique way of approaching this film centered around two contrasting places. After the screening of the film, I divided the class in two groups and then took each group along a virtual site visit of the film's two main locations through the Oculus application Wander.[6] For the first time, I was able to relate the origin story of the film to my students while virtually standing with them at the exact same spots that I visited back in 2001. My personal experience of that day includes a visceral encounter of contrasting spaces that is impossible to communicate verbally or even with conventional photography. However, being surrounded by 360° imagery afforded the students a vivid approximation of what I had experienced, namely the relative absence of people and a feeling of abandonment at Wounded Knee and the contrasting deluge of tourists and commercial activity at Mount Rushmore. The fact that the 360° cameras had captured these contrasting images randomly only reinforced the argument that I was making about the systemic differences between both memory sites. A small technical detail that some students noticed right away added another confirmation to one of the documentary film's main arguments. The image resolution was significantly lower in the 360° photospheres from the Pine Ridge Reservation in contrast with the surrounding counties and Mount Rushmore. My documentary film details and visually illustrates the severe contrast in infrastructure such as roads, municipal services, or the financial system between the reservation and mainstream America. In addition to experiencing the two sites, virtual travel also plainly demonstrated that the infrastructure inequality between both spaces extended into the digital sphere. In summary, the documentary film and virtual travel ideally complemented each other.

Whereas the film provided detailed information and historical context, the Wander app afforded an embodied experience and the affective impact of visiting both places, one after the other. The VR experience was also very interactive, as communication within the application worked well and students could comment and ask questions while experiencing the sites virtually.

Let me emphasize, however, that a virtual visit of sites of traumatic memory such as Wounded Knee must be carefully prepared, just as it should be IRL. In the present case, this preparation consisted of the viewing and discussion of my documentary film and readings that introduce the history of the site, its role in the U.S. national imagination, as well as the contrasting approaches to public memory at Wounded Knee and Mount Rushmore. Only through such careful preparation are participants able to learn from the experience of the site visit in relation to its historical context and understand its relevance for the present as an important site of national memory. Otherwise, such a virtual visit could risk the danger of superficially exploiting the excitement of visiting places of past death and destruction as has been rightfully critiqued in studies of dark tourism (see, for example, Light, 2017; and Stone et al., 2018).

The session on Native American memory included two additional VR experiences. The first one was the animated 3D narrative *Crow: The Legend* (2018), which was among the first Hollywood level VR productions featuring A-list talent such as Oprah Winfrey and John Legend and was directed by Eric Darnell, who had helmed Disney's *Madagascar* franchise. While most available VR experiences are low-budget productions, I selected *Crow* to show students what the new narrative medium is capable of from a technical perspective with adequate budget. At the same time, it offered a more lighthearted and positive example of Native American mythology during a day that was otherwise dedicated to remembering traumatic and painful history. For most students this was only the second VR experience, as I had started the morning with Chris Milk's historically important VR film *Evolution of Verse* (2015) as an introduction to the medium. The well-produced piece with a familiar approach to storytelling worked well to gradually habituate the students into the novel narrative medium.

The VR session concluded with a more unpolished VR experience, highlighting the documentary potential of 360° video that has become quite common in immersive journalism (see, for example, Nash, 2018; Rose, 2018). The documentary short *The Occupation of Alcatraz that Sparked an American Revolution* (2017) raises several core issues of Native American memory such as displacement and loss of homeland. In the opening, it places the viewer in the midst of a Native American ceremony to honor the indigenous resistance that manifested through the occupation of Alcatraz Island from 1969 to 1971 by a protest group called Indians of All Tribes. The ceremony features drumming and dance. The immersive quality of 360° video allows for a more visceral experience as the viewer is enmeshed in sound and movement. In addition, the video communicates a strong sense of place as the viewer is transported to Alcatraz Island, where the ceremony is taking place, and which was central to the occupation. In the second part, the video takes the viewer to the Standing Rock occupation in protest of the Dakota Access Pipeline and thus links memory of the occupation of Alcatraz to resistance in the contemporary context. Again, the concluding scene presents a very strong sense of place as it documents a ceremonial song held in the midst of the vast grasslands on the Standing Rock Reservation. Thus, *The Occupation* affords an immersive visit to two very distinct and iconic U.S. landscapes—one on an island on the West Coast, and the other in the Great Plains of the Midwest—in addition to presenting two immersive examples of indigenous resistance in the present and memory of a painful past.

EXAMPLE 2: MEMORY, SYSTEMIC RACISM, AND BLACK RESISTANCE

Following the killing of George Floyd in May of 2020, the Black Lives Matter movement (BLM) reverberated around the world, even in places as far away as Hong Kong (Gruenewald, 2021: 1–2). In response, I included a session on the movement, two on systemic racial inequality, and one on resistance in hip-hop. This choice was also motivated by the availability of several related and well-produced VR experiences as well as a large number of amateur and professional 360° short videos documenting BLM protests.

The centerpiece of the first day on BLM was the award-winning VR experience *Traveling While Black* (2019), which remembers how African Americans traveled in the era of segregation with the help of the *Negro Motorist Green Book*. The VR experience presents an innovative narrative structure with a sophisticated blend of visual archival materials, period reenactment, and documentary 3D video. The narrative presents an effective reinforcement and illustration of the preparatory readings assigned on the history of Jim Crow and the trauma it caused to African Americans. Similar to conventional documentary, *Traveling* features historical eyewitnesses as they remember their own experiences. However, listening to Sandra Butler-Truesdale (born 1939) and Virginia Ali (born 1934) remembering their childhood during segregation in this case is markedly more impactful thanks to VR's ability to simulate a sense of copresence (Yoshimura and Borst, 2020; Wang et al., 2020). What is more, the viewer is listening while seated on the *same* table with both women in the iconic Ben's Chili Bowl that Ali had cofounded in 1958 and that was one of the establishments to provide safe harbor to African Americans during Jim Crow. Certainly, this is not the same as it would be to be in that room and interact with them IRL. Yet, to experience them in such close proximity while being immersed in the historic location that they are speaking about is also a much more intimate experience than it would be to merely watch them in a conventional film.

However, the VR experience's strongest moment occurs when it connects past discrimination to traumatic injustice in the present. In the second part, seated on the same table as before, the viewer is now facing Samaria Rice, the mother of Tamir Rice, who was shot by police in November of 2014. In a devastating example of traumatic testimony, Ms. Rice recounts the moments when police told her about the shooting, when she arrived at the scene, and how she was prevented from seeing her son. Certainly, on its own, *Traveling* would not be sufficient to teach the issue of systemic police violence, as it is a short experience, necessarily lacking depth of information, context, and background. At the same time, no academic reading can convey what this VR experience offers, namely an affective experience of the traumatic impact of police violence on the individual, and how such systemic injustice looks and *feels* like from the perspective of the victim (or their family). Admittedly, such an interview could be equally powerful in a conventional film. However, the copresence afforded by VR again increases the affective intensity of the experience. Without affect, a merely academic and quantified presentation of systemic injustice lacks a sense of urgency and is in danger of missing the tragic humanity of the problem. VR experiences such as *Traveling* can help add the human dimension to the conventional historical and social scientific curriculum.

The next day of the course was dedicated to systemic injustice in the U.S. legal system. The session was prepared by selected readings from Michelle Alexander's *The New Jim Crow: Mass Incarceration in the Age of Colorblindness* (2010) and included a screening of Ava DuVernay's documentary film *13th* (2016). Here too, for all their brilliant analysis and depth of historical information, the film and the reading were limited in how they communicated the devastating effects of systemic racism on individuals. To complement both, the selected VR content for this session enabled students to virtually experience a high security prison from the inside via two 360° films. The first film, *After Solitary* (2017), explores the effects of solitary confinement on the prisoner. For six of the film's nine minutes the viewer is placed inside a solitary confinement cell. The freedom to be able to turn around and observe the surrounding walls only adds to the sense of enclosure. In a conventional film, this strategy could not work without the ability to change perspective. Even though the scene only lasts for a few minutes, it creates an uncomfortable embodied experience of claustrophobia that could not be achieved through non-immersive media in a similar way.

Of course, such VR experiences cannot enable true empathy with prisoners and much less simulate the IRL experience of solitary confinement. Indeed, as discussed above, a large body of literature has critiqued the early empathy claims of VR creators. No one said it better than Wendy Chun in her 2016 talk "Ditching the Empathy Story:" "When you walk in someone else's shoes, then you've taken their shoes." Any course that includes such VR experiences should at least discuss the limits to empathy in general and in particular with regard to VR. I would recommend reading and discussing one of the recent critiques of empathy mentioned above. At the same time, it would be an overreaction to reject VR experiences such as *After Solitary*. They are able to complement other ways of learning effectively as long as their use is accompanied by a critical discussion of the limitations and ethical dilemmas of such experiences.

The second 360° film, *Step to the Line* (2017), is a short documentary about an event conducted by a nonprofit that brings together outside volunteers with inmates of a California maximum security prison for a day of group exercises and conversations. During the main group activity that gives the film its name, inmates and visitors are lined up in a hall along a line on the ground facing each other. The facilitator presents scenarios such as "When I was a child, I have experienced violence in my family," "I have earned a four-year college degree," or "I have lost someone I loved to gang violence." If the statement applies, participants step towards the line; if it does not, they step away from it. The viewer stands on the line surrounded by the participants on both sides. Since the inmates are virtually all black and the visitors all white, the exercise proves to be a visual illustration of systemic racial inequality in the United States as both groups respond almost uniformly and in opposite ways to each question. However, the key question yields an unexpected result: "Step to the line if you have ever committed a crime for which you could have been arrested." While naturally all inmates step to the line, it comes as a surprise when most visitors do the same. After the facilitator reminds them that in some states smoking marijuana or driving without a seat belt can lead to arrest, virtually all visitors step towards the line. As the viewer is standing in between two long rows of human beings facing each other, the unequal treatment by the legal system based on skin color becomes painfully obvious. In this scene, the proximity to those standing nearby allows the viewer to see the stunned facial expressions. In combination with the freedom to choose the focus of attention, the scene affords, again, a sense of copresence with the prisoners and visitors during the activity.

Following the large group exercise, the viewer stands in a small circle consisting of two inmates and one visitor for a conversation, who are responding to the question "What is the worst experience of your life?" Through the spatial arrangement of the point of view, the viewer becomes another visitor and feels included as a member of the small group. One of the inmates calmly relates losing his son to violence three years ago. As he explains the pain of feeling responsible for the tragedy because of his absence as a father, the other visitor breaks down in tears. The experience is highly affective and once again illustrates the traumatically contrasting lived experiences between the inmates and the fellow visitors. This scene could not function in a similar way in conventional film. Through the sense of occupying the same space and being present with others, the scene achieves a strong affective impact although we know nothing about the three people of that group other than their race and their state of imprisonment or freedom.

As a caveat, let me point out the importance of taking into account students' identities when selecting emotionally intensive texts such as *Step to the Line* for their potential to retraumatize students who may be affected by the described traumas in their personal lives. This necessity is sound pedagogic practice in any case but applies especially to VR experiences because of their increased affective potential.

In summary, VR enabled us to experience a number of sites and spaces that would be impossible to visit during an IRL field trip either for the distance of travel that would be required or the nature of the site as in the case of a high-security prison. VR added an immersive experience of space and place as well as an affective component to the conventional learning materials about systemic inequity in the United States.

CONCLUSION

My positive impression regarding the contribution of VR experiences to the learning in the course was confirmed by both quantitative and qualitative student evaluations. Ninety percent of students agreed or strongly agreed that the course was effective in achieving its learning outcomes. The course had especially high scores in the category of critical thinking, which were significantly higher than in comparable courses that I taught in recent years, with 75% strongly agreeing and 90% agreeing that the course encouraged critical thinking. While I have no hard evidence that this was related to the use of VR, the discussions following VR experiences were more engaged than usual and might have contributed to the students' positive impression of being encouraged to reflect critically. The teacher scores in the quantitative evaluations were equally positive, with 78% strongly agreeing and 90% agreeing that I helped them learn, which is likely related in part to my extra effort invested in procuring and introducing students to VR technology. Several of the anonymous qualitative comments praised the use of VR in the course, mentioning specifically the innovation to teaching and learning that the medium enabled. There was only one negative comment regarding VR, which complained that the use of it had caused headaches. However, even that student did not suggest eliminating VR from the course, but rather to invest in better head straps, a suggestion that I strongly agree with. Upgrading my personal Quest 2 headset with hard plastic head straps significantly improved the comfort level of the device.

Since this was the first time that I used VR technology in the classroom, I gave close attention to its effectiveness as a tool for teaching and learning throughout the course. While it was obvious throughout that VR could not replace IRL travel, students generally appreciated the immersive experiences in the United States at a time when IRL travel was not possible. Further, the affective potential of the medium was apparent and its ability to complement learning about historical context and critical analysis: for example, in the case of the prison industrial complex. The main downside of using VR technology consisted in my impression of occasional discomfort while using VR headsets. This problem must be taken seriously by instructors and mitigated as much as possible through 1) investing time and material to ensuring a comfortable fit; 2) habituating students gradually into the new medium; 3) keeping the use of VR brief, especially at the beginning; and 4) encouraging students to sit down in the case of discomfort.

Overall, the experience of employing VR as a supplement to teaching materials for a virtual field trip course was very positive. I would call the technology even essential for virtual field trip courses nowadays. Moreover, I believe VR could be beneficial for any course in which experience of places, human interaction, or storytelling are important. Let me conclude by reiterating the two most important contributions of VR to the learning outcomes of our American studies field trip. First, VR enabled us to visit sites across space and time that would be virtually impossible to visit IRL in a single field trip. Experiencing those sites added a different, valuable dimension to the learning prepared by other materials such as virtually visiting the shooting locations of a documentary film or spending some time *inside* a maximum-security prison. Second, the experience of copresence with people in VR and listening to their testimony added a level of humanity and thus urgency to the learning about systemic injustice that a merely theoretical study of social inequity simply cannot achieve.

NOTES

1. In 2019, I was awarded a three-year General Research Fund grant by the University Grants Committee of Hong Kong for the research project "Cinematic Virtual Reality: Defining the Language of a New Medium." I would like to acknowledge this GRF grant (17616519) for the support of the research for this chapter. To date, this research has resulted in the publication of the article "Feeling Good: Humanitarian Virtual Reality Film, Emotional Style and Global Citizenship" (Gruenewald and Witteborn, 2020).

2. For critical discussions of empathy and VR, see Gruenewald and Witteborn, "Feeling Good"; Nash, "Virtual Reality Witness"; Herson, "Empathy Engines"; Andrejevic and Volcic, "Virtual Empathy"; Schlembach and Clewer, "'Forced Empathy.'"

3. Aspects contributing to discomfort include the weight of the device in combination with low-quality head straps and low screen resolution.

4. The device was renamed Meta Quest 2 in 2022. The Quest 3 was released in October of 2023 at the cost of USD 499 for the entry model and the price of the Quest 2 was lowered to USD 299.

5. As of early 2024, this database has grown to over 1,100. This database will be made available to the public after the completion of the above-mentioned research project in 2025.

6. Wander was and remains the Meta application that allows virtual visits to a vast number of places around the globe using data from Google Street View. Those visits can be done alone or in groups. At the time, Wander limited the group size to six participants including the host.

WORKS CITED

Andrejevic, Mark, and Zala Volcic. "Virtual Empathy." *Communication, Culture & Critique* 13, no. 3 (2020): 295–310. https://doi.org/10.1093/ccc/tcz035

Argyriou, Lemonia, Daphne Economou, and Vassiliki Bouki. "Design Methodology for 360° Immersive Video Applications: The Case Study of a Cultural Heritage Virtual Tour." *Personal and Ubiquitous Computing* 24, no. 6 (2020): 843–59. https://doi.org10.1007/s00779-020-01373-8

Chun, Wendy. "Ditching the Empathy Story." Presentation at Weird Reality Conference, Pittsburgh, PA, 2016. Cited in: Ruberg, Bonnie. "Empathy and Its Alternatives: Deconstructing the Rhetoric of 'Empathy' in Video Games." *Communication, Culture & Critique* 13, no. 1 (2020): 54–71. https://doi.org/10.1093/ccc/tcz044

Darnell, Eric, dir. *Crow: The Legend.* 2018; Redwood Shores, CA: Baobab Studios. 20 min, 44 sec. YouTube, Feb 4, 2019. https://www.youtube.com/watch?v=DR1gT36OtJQ

DuVernay, Ava, dir. *13th.* 2016; Los Angeles: Kandoo Films. YouTube, April 17, 2020. 100 min. https://www.youtube.com/watch?v=krfcq5pF8u8

Fung, Fun Man, Wen Yi Choo, Alvita Ardisara, Christoph Dominik Zimmermann, Simon Watts, Thierry Koscielniak, Etienne Blanc, Xavier Coumoul, and Rainer Dumke. "Applying a Virtual Reality Platform in Environmental Chemistry Education to Conduct a Field Trip to an Overseas Site." *Journal of Chemical Education* 96, no. 2 (2019): 382–6. https://doi.org/10.1021/acs.jchemed.8b00728

Gruenewald, Tim. *Curating America's Painful Past: Memory, Museums, and the National Imagination.* University Press of Kansas, 2021.

Gruenewald, Tim and Ludwig Schmidtpeter, dirs. *Sacred Ground.* 2015; Germany, Hong Kong, and United States. 93 min. http://www.sacredgroundfilm.com/

Gruenewald, Tim, and Saskia Witteborn. "Feeling Good: Humanitarian Virtual Reality Film, Emotional Style and Global Citizenship." *Cultural Studies* 36, no. 1 (2022): 141–61. https://doi.org/10.1080/09502386.2020.1761415

Harrington, Maria C. R. "An Ethnographic Comparison of Real and Virtual Reality Field Trips to Trillium Trail: The Salamander Find as a Salient Event." *Children, Youth and Environments* 19, no. 1 (2009): 74–101. https://journals.uc.edu/index.php/cye/article/view/6647

Heath, Alex and Matthew Olson. "Mark Zuckerberg on Mind Reading, Apple and the Race to Mainstream VR." Podcast: "The Information's 411." 47 min. The Information, March 8, 2021. https://www.theinformation.com/articles/mark-zuckerberg-on-mind-reading-apple-and-the-race-to-mainstream-vr

Herrman, Cassandra, and Mucciolo Lauren, dirs. *After Solitary*. 2017; Boston, MA: PBS Frontline. 360° Video. 9 min, 7 sec. YouTube, April 18. https://www.youtube.com/watch?v=G7_YvGDh9Uc

Herson, Ben. "Empathy Engines: How Virtual Reality Films May (or May Not) Revolutionize Education." *Comparative Education Review* 60, no. 4 (2016): 853-62. https://doi.org/10.1086/688582

Laganaro, Ricardo, dir. *Step to the Line*. 2017; California: Oculus Studio and Defy Ventures. 360° Stereoscopic video. 12 min. YouTube, August 2, 2022. https://www.youtube.com/watch?v=ejVVsM9yG3U

Light, Duncan. "Progress in Dark Tourism and Thanatourism Research: An Uneasy Relationship with Heritage Tourism." *Tourism Management* 61 (2017): 275-301. https://doi.org/10.1016/j.tourman.2017.01.011

Markowitz, David M., Rob Laha, Brian P. Perone, Roy D. Pea, and Jeremy N. Bailenson. "Immersive Virtual Reality Field Trips Facilitate Learning about Climate Change." *Frontiers in Psychology* 9 (2018). https://doi.org/10.3389/fpsyg.2018.02364

Milk, Chris, dir. *Evolution of Verse*. 2015; Los Angeles: Within Unlimited, Inc. 360° animation. 4 min. YouTube, August 2, 2022. https://www.youtube.com/watch?v=5GcTaEiRzDo

Milk, Chris. "How virtual reality can create the ultimate empathy machine." Talk given March 18, 2015 at TED2015, Vancouver, Canada. Video. 10 min, 16 sec. https://www.ted.com/talks/chris_milk_how_virtual_reality_can_create_the_ultimate_empathy_machine

Mohring, Katharina, and Nina Brendel. "Producing Virtual Reality (VR) Field Trips—A Concept for a Sense-Based and Mindful Geographic Education." *Geographica Helvetica* 76, no. 3 (2021): 369-80. https://doi.org/10.5194/gh-76-369-2021

Nash, Kate. "Virtual reality witness: Exploring the ethics of mediated presence." *Studies in Documentary Film* 12, no. 2 (2018), 119-31. https://doi.org/10.1080/17503280.2017.1340796

Park, SoHu, and GyuChang Lee. "Full-Immersion Virtual Reality: Adverse Effects Related to Static Balance." *Neuroscience Letters* 733 (2020). https://doi.org/10.1016/j.neulet.2020.134974

Reimers, Fernando M., and Francisco J. Marmolejo. "Leading Learning During a Time of Crisis. Higher Education Responses to the Global Pandemic of 2020." In *University School Collaborations during a Pandemic: Sustaining Educational Opportunity and Reinventing Education*, edited by Fernando M. Reimers and Francisco J. Marmolejo, 1-41. Cham: Springer International Publishing, 2022.

Rose, Mandy. "The Immersive Turn: Hype and Hope in the Emergence of Virtual Reality as a Nonfiction Platform." *Studies in Documentary Film* 12, no. 2 (2018), 132–49. https://doi.org/10.1080/17503280.2018.1496055

Schlembach, Raphael and Nicola Clewer. "'Forced Empathy': Manipulation, Trauma and Affect in Virtual Reality Film." *International Journal of Cultural Studies* 24, no. 5 (2021): 827–43. https://doi.org/10.1177/13678779211007863

Seeker VR. *The Occupation of Alcatraz that Sparked an American Revolution.* 2017; Washington, D.C.: Vox Media. 360° video. 8 min. YouTube, June 15, 2017. https://www.youtube.com/watch?v=TBjuhFOeitE

Southgate, Erica. *Virtual Reality in Curriculum and Pedagogy: Evidence from Secondary Classrooms.* London and NY: Routledge, 2020.

Spicer, John I. and J. Stratford. "Student Perceptions of a Virtual Field Trip to Replace a Real Field Trip." *Journal of Computer Assisted Learning* 17, no. 4 (2001): 345–54. https://doi.org/10.1046/j.0266-4909.2001.00191.x

Stone, Philip R., Rudi Hartmann, Tony Seaton, Richard Sharpley, and Leanne White, eds. *The Palgrave Handbook of Dark Tourism Studies.* Palgrave Macmillan, 2018.

Williams, Roger Ross, dir. *Traveling While Black.* 2019; Montreal: Felix & Paul Studios. 360° stereoscopic video. 20 min. https://www.felixandpaul.com/?travelingwhileblack

Wang, Cheng Yao, Mose Sakashita, Upol Ehsan, Jingjin Li, and Andrea Stevenson Won. "Again, Together: Socially Reliving Virtual Reality Experiences When Separated." *Conference on Human Factors in Computing Systems—Proceedings* (2020). https://doi.org/10.1145/3313831.3376642

Yoshimura, Andrew, and Christoph W. Borst. "Evaluation and Comparison of Desktop Viewing and Headset Viewing of Remote Lectures in VR with Mozilla Hubs." In *ICAT-EGVE 2020—International Conference on Artificial Reality and Telexistence and Eurographics Symposium on Virtual Environments,* edited by Ferran Argelaguet, Ryan McMahan, and Maki Sugimoto, 51–9. Eindhoven: The Eurographics Association, 2020. https://doi.org/10.2312/egve.20201259

CHAPTER 5

DEVELOPING A SITE-SPECIFIC ART AND HUMANITIES PLATFORM

David Lindsay and Ian R. Weaver

In this chapter we discuss the development of a platform for exhibiting site-specific digital artwork, called Popwalk. The initial development and continued use of this technology does not constitute a completely novel approach, but it does serve a technological and artistic niche that, at the point of inception and continuing today, has been found useful by many artists, cultural producers, and arts organizations. Popwalk originated outside the sterile environments of board meetings. The initial concept was not a technological resolution for artists to gain a place in the mobile market. Rather, it was the result of a conversation between an artist and a technical writer on Halloween night in 2013. Pulling a red wagon that contained a one-year-old jester and a three-year-old Robin Hood, our families trick-or-treated the gridlocked streets of Lubbock, Texas while we conversed. "Hey," David said to Ian. "Let me run an idea by you. How can digital artists use mobile technology to make their work site-specific?" From this moment forward, David took on the roles of subject matter expert and creative philanthropist in the development of Popwalk, and Ian took on the roles of analyst and sounding board.

At the time, David's research as a faculty member in the School of Art at Texas Tech University had been investigating site-specific artwork, including the earthworks artists of the 1960s and happenings and performance artworks of the 1970s. In particular, he was interested in Robert Smitherson's earthworks like Spiral Jetty[1] and Amarillo Ramp,[2] site-specific artworks whose characters and interpretations are tied up with the environment in which they are located, so much so that, in Serra's words, "[t]o move the work is to destroy the work" (Serra, 1994, p. 194). David was entranced by the interaction of space and artwork, and his own art explored how the viewer's interaction and movement through and around the space of a work added meaning and new interpretations. He was also interested in the growing body of digital artwork, taking the form of both physical objects which owed their existence to digital technologies and artworks whose existence was mediated by a viewscreen. The scope of the latter group seemed limited by the pedestrian and casual way that internet video is typically experienced. David's goal was to create an intersection between the accessibility of digital artwork and the contextual power of artwork, made for a specific location.

In 2013, to the best of our knowledge, no digital platform took advantage of smartphone app technology for making site specificity an absolute or exclusive requirement for accessing digital artwork outside of physical installations or QR code projects. So we developed Popwalk.

DIGITAL SITE-SPECIFIC ART

Since 2013, a long list of art-oriented and site-related augmented reality (AR) apps have been created, some using overlays like

Artivive[3] to augment already existing pieces of art; some providing audio-guided cultural and history tours, such as Gesso[4] and Geotourist;[5] others documenting public art and connecting viewers to artists, like CANVS;[6] and still others offering more fine art experiences, like the *You Be My Ally*[7] work by Jenny Holzer. These art applications, including Popwalk, fall into a longer tradition of exploring AR and digital art's interaction with space and particular sites. To offer a genealogy of Popwalk, we first define what we mean by site-specific artwork; then, we connect the philosophical underpinnings of the app to applications of site specificity within the world of digital art. We conclude this section with some details of how these traditions contributed to developing Popwalk.

Although many AR art apps have site-related components, we distinguish between "site-related" and "site-specific" implementations. We developed Popwalk with a strict sense of site specificity. Site-specific art has a long tradition, popularized by well-known installations like Smithson's *Spiral Jetty* and Christo and Jeanne-Claude's *Running Fence.*[8] We draw our sense of site specificity from these and other artists and maintain that site-specific works are "grounded" at specific locations and are "obstinate about 'presence,' even if [the works are] materially ephemeral and adamant about mobility."[9] We see the identity of site-specific artwork as bound to location, "focused on establishing an inextricable, indivisible relationship between the work and its site, and demand[ing] the physical presence of the viewer for the work's completion."[10] This sense of site-specificity is different from site-related or site-connected applications. We developed Popwalk to be site-dependent, site-necessary; the art and augmented reality is not present, accessible, nor does it exist, unless you are on site.

We see this devotion to "site" as central to challenging the assumption that the spaces we live and move within are empty, waiting to be filled, and originally devoid of meaning. We view mobile AR art technologies as tools to help people develop the spatial consciousness, as Elise Verzosa Hurley calls it, needed to challenge the "seeming transparency of space," that space is something "static, inevitable, and unchangeable."[11] Referencing the power of site-specific artwork to do just that, Nick Kaye in his book *Site-Specific Art: Performance, Place, and Documentation* writes, "site-specificity presents a challenge to notions of 'original' or 'fixed' location, problematising the relationship between work and site." As such, three philosophical tenets that drive Popwalk are: 1) space is produced;[12] 2) space is produced by spatial stories,[13] which are told discursively and by the movement of bodies; and 3), as Doreen Massey puts it, space is "the existence of multiplicity," "always in the process of being made," and "a simultaneity of stories-so-far."[14] The way Popwalk augments reality is by enabling the artist to reveal the multiplicity of stories in a space. The app gives digital artists a way to attach discursive elements (virtual through visual, aural, and textual) to spatial elements (the movement of bodies through space) to augment the viewer's experience.

Augmented reality works well in site-specific work because the technology is designed to engage the digital with lived space, aiming for the two to interact in ways that augment a viewer's experience and understanding. This interaction has been a point of interest for many. Some interest has considered how the two influence each other: do they build on or negate each other?[15] Others have considered how AR technologies change the role of the traditional art viewer; Jeffrey Shaw, for example, writes that virtual reality takes place within a spatial context that takes the viewer from being merely a consumer to someone who is traveling through and discovering space.[16] Other artists have looked at the potential AR digital art has at interrupting spatial narratives. Simona Lodi, for example, has considered the "interventionist actions" of artists using digital augmented reality tools to alter people's understanding and perceptions of familiar spaces;[17] others such as the ManifestAR group have also demonstrated how AR can be used subversively.[18]

Before mobile phone technology, site-specific digital artwork tended to be either overly expensive or somewhat cumbersome.

One example is the "Breathing_Wall_LAX" video installation in the Los Angeles International Airport.[19] This row of fifty-eight video monitors, installed in an undulating line, makes reference to the history of film and digital art in Los Angeles as well as the history of digital art in that city. The six-million dollar price tag for this artwork also reveals the limitation of such projects. To install a continuously running video screen in any location requires both permission and funding. These are often difficult to acquire, particularly if the artist selects an exhibition space outside the parameters of typical public art installation. Another site-specific digital art project is *Syren*,[20] which was a pilot test of AudioNomad's technology that enabled users to experience soundscapes while they moved through space. The mobile technology in *Syren* was "mounted on the Helipad of the cruise liner 'Opera' and toured the Baltic in 2004." The setup included a surround sound system of speakers in which the audience could sit and listen to layered and rich audio that, in effect, "render[ed] a surround-sound, 3D sound-scape corresponding to proximate physical features."[21] On a cruise liner, they were able to move through space and help listeners re-envision the port. This technology used geolocation to enable the material, ensuring the artwork was site-specific. The work of AudioNomad has since grown more sophisticated, but at the time the technology was limited to extensive technological preparation and expertise. To sidestep these limitations, we were looking for an exhibition format that would allow artists to choose the location of their exhibition for any work that would be appropriate to be displayed on the screen of a smartphone, including performance, sound art, animation, video, and so on.

Our initial solution was to use quick response (QR) codes. QR codes are a well-known method, and what we might call an assistive AR technology, for leading participants to a specific URL.[22] Researchers and artists have used QR codes to display and investigate site-specific work. Richard Rinehart notes the potential for QR codes as "'[h]ardlinks' [...] [that] attempt to bind a virtual link" and corresponding content "to our physical environment."[23] One application and study includes Niclas Dristig's investigation of using QR codes to aid storytelling in cultural heritage contexts.[24] A different project by Goodrich, Templehoff, and Steyn developed a platform for using QR codes to explore "place-bound" literature.[25] These instances and the technology itself suggest that people see value in connecting digital content to specific locations.

David wanted his students to understand this value and potential for artists, so he created a number of class projects in which students used QR codes to connect site-specific animations to specified locations. One exhibition was created for the National Ranching Heritage Center museum in Lubbock, Texas. The animations for this exhibition focused on storytelling, myth-building, and site interpretation of the museum's open air exhibits. Physical signage of the QR codes, placed at the locations of display (Figure 5.1), guided audiences to accessing the works at the appropriate locations.

Although the signs informed the public of the artworks' existence in those locations, the physical installments presented disadvantages for using QR codes. First, for example, despite the promise of convenience and efficiency, how QR codes are placed and presented influence whether people want to engage with them.[26] Published in 2012, articles like "Privacy Concerns in Quick Response Code Mobile Promotion: The Role of Social Anxiety and Situational Involvement" indicated how the success of QR codes providing content for viewers depends on context, both physical and psychological.[27] The rhetorical perceptions users have at a particular time and place require content creators using QR codes to do so strategically, not trusting the simplicity of the technology to do all the work.

Second, complicating the desirability of QR codes were security concerns. Also published in 2012, the authors of "QR Code Security" report their work on how QR codes are used for phishing attacks.[28] QR codes, they detail, are "machine readable," so

Figure 5.1: QR code sign placed at the location of viewing for a site-specific animation at the National Ranching Heritage Museum in Lubbock, Texas.

humans cannot discern the threat associated with the codes. Can the viewer or user trust that these signs were placed by trustworthy sources? Third, the physical installations of QR codes were subjected to weather and vandalism. The National Ranching Heritage Center exhibition signs had to be replaced within the first month owing to both. Fourth, the process of obtaining permissions to place signs offered a hurdle for creating the site-specific work. And fifth, QR codes did not strictly bind the content to the specific site. The user learned of and could access the content on site, but they could also keep and view the URL offsite. While QR codes offered the museum a practical and simple solution for connecting people to information, users' perceptions and the maintenance of the signs presented obstacles for moving forward with this kind of technology indefinitely.

The groundwork and design parameters of the Popwalk platform were guided by the experience of creating and curating exhibitions of site-specific digital art using QR codes. We wanted to create a smartphone app that would tie art to location and present a simple interface for low-skilled users to view and interact with the works. We were motivated by the possibility of developing a platform which was straightforward enough for many kinds of artistic and cultural content makers. Our hope was that artists, well versed in the technological requirements of digital art, would be attracted to the project, as well as dancers, musicians, and other performers whose work is site-specific but who may be deterred by a complex technical interface. We were also interested in the 'cross-pollination' of many audiences that could occur by assembling a broad group of cultural creators.

HOW POPWALK FUNCTIONS

As a type of AR, we locate Popwalk on the reality end of Paul Milgram and colleagues' "Virtuality Continuum."[29] The app simply provides access to and plays video or audio content when an individual proceeds to a specified location. As such, Popwalk might be considered non-immersive: the app does not project overlays like a "window-on-the-world" display. Instead, the app is a site-specific alternative to the space in which it is tied. The space offers the user one version of reality, while the video/audio content offers an alternative or companion version. The dynamics of how the site and the artwork interact depends on the artist. The Popwalk application itself is simply the exhibiting mechanism.

The Popwalk app restricts and offers access to art through the use of geofencing. Geofencing has been applied in a range of instances, such as social networking, marketing, surveillance, security, and audience engagement.[30] Popwalk uses geofencing as a means for the artist to locate the viewer. Artists provide the geocoordinates for their work when they submit to exhibit through the Popwalk website. The technology then uses the geolocation information of the smartphone to locate the user in reference to the artwork. Thus the geofence functions like a virtual barrier around any location established for viewing an artwork. Users must navigate to a specified location to enter the diameter of the geofence. Doing so unlocks the art and enables the user to view and/or listen to the content.

Popwalk uses a map as its primary interface to direct this navigation (Figure 5.2). The technology is flexible enough for artists to specify the size of space they want users to be within to access the

Figure 5.2: The map interface for the Popwalk application.

work, as small of a diameter as 20 meters and as large as 120 meters. For example, if the digital artwork is to be experienced in a wide field, the creator might choose to make the geofence much larger, allowing the user to access the work from many points within the space. If the artwork is to be experienced from a more specific location, the creator might make the access boundary much smaller, requiring the user to move to a specific place to access the work. This flexibility is limited, however, as the app does not restrict access based on elevation, for example. If an artist wants a user to view the art under a bridge or on the 13th story of a high rise, the artist must make use of the text field to provide instructions for the user on where to stand, what to look at, and so on.

EVOLUTION OF POPWALK

Beyond QR codes and geofencing, a range of early experiences with how individuals used Popwalk changed how we see and employ the application today. This section overviews key events, exhibits, concepts, and apps that have evolved our understanding and development of Popwalk.

POPWALK AS DIGITAL DOCENT

Soon after the development of the 1.0 version of the Popwalk app in 2015, David was approached by the Texas Tech University public art program. They wanted to create their own smartphone application to encourage interest and engagement with their art collection. Initially asked to participate as an advisor to the design of their own mobile app, David was later included as a creator of site-specific video content for the artworks in the collection. The university's public art program asked David to contact each public artist (over one hundred at the time) and invite them to create a brief video in which they would speak about their work in relation to the collection. Once edited, these videos would be exhibited via Popwalk and the university's public art app.

Texas Tech University's use of Popwalk caused us to rethink the relationship between digital art and site. Our initial design of Popwalk assumed artists would present original works through the app, but Texas Tech University's public art program instead used Popwalk to inform and lay context for already existing site-specific art. Accordingly, the video content David created positioned the artists as, in essence, "digital docents" of their physically installed artwork. This project, therefore, challenged the very foundation of Popwalk; it changed the way we understood the interaction between the actual space of exhibition, the digital content, and the movement of the user through space. We had assumed that a viewer's primary goal would be to access a location to view digital artwork, making their primary sensory experience the visual and auditory information provided by the artist. This project, however, highlighted how the physical artwork and surrounding space took competing precedence. The video served to lead the user physically to and through the real space. The destination, the location, or the site was an end in itself, and Popwalk was a means of fully experiencing that space. In artistic terms, it encouraged a didactic dance around the sculpture or mural.

POPWALK AND SOUNDSCAPES

Another example of the complexity of intellectual and physical interaction between the real space and the digital artwork came from a student project at Texas State University. A number of educators teaching in university art programs have used Popwalk to create projects intended to teach principles of site-specific art. One of the first of these was Professor Liz Rodda at Texas State University. Professor Rodda is both a thoughtful artist and a gifted educator; one of the student works that came from her assignment introduced us to how soundscapes could be exhibited via the app.[31] This artwork was situated near a historic outdoor amphitheater in the middle of the Texas State University Campus. As an audio-only exhibit, the artists provided thorough spoken instructions for how and where to move around the amphitheater. With the aid of earbuds, the audio format meant the user could ignore their phone and place their attention on the surrounding environment. The audio described a poetic, historical (perhaps a little idealistic) version of the location, moving the listener through the space and inviting them to play the roles of stagehand, performer, and audience member. Professor Rodda's project created what Nigel Helyer, Daniel Woo, and Francesca Veronesi would call a "sound composition [...] performed by the mobile presence of the user traversing real geography."[32] The work employed sound effects: audience clapping and the sounds of a theatrical production going on around the user. The experience was immersive and simple and highlighted how soundscapes can become "sonic" and "narrative cartographies"[33] that transform the location through sound and a user's movement through space. This exhibit helped us appreciate the power of the auditory experience, and it helped us understand that "geospatially located audio needs to be highly sensitive to its environmental and architectural context as well as to the fundamentally nonlinear manner in which the user might interact with the content."[34]

For the projects at Texas State University and Texas Tech University, David functioned as facilitator and advisor. But at the same time, he was learning a great deal about the subtle ways that environment and technology could harmoniously amplify the artistic content. Augmented reality, as a humanistic venture, has this dilemma: it attempts to impose a digital fascia over the world, but the character of interaction between those two elements—our surrounding reality and the augmentations that we are attempting to bring to it—is still a Pandora's box waiting to be opened.[35]

POPWALK AND OTHER AR ART APPS

Other influences on Popwalk have included many of the augmented reality art mobile apps published (see Table 5.1 for examples) since we started our collaboration in 2013. Their design intent, use of AR, and relation to site specificity have each helped hone our vision and purpose for Popwalk. Specifically, a few apps have helped us reflect on what type of viewing and listening experience we hope to create for the users. Some of the apps, for example, use a 3D overlay of photographic, video, or computer-generated content to augment the users' immediate location. Examples of this approach include the 4th Wall and Artivive applications. The 4th Wall app allows artists, who create 3D digital objects, to virtually exhibit those works in a specific location.[36] To use the app, the viewer goes to the indicated location of the artwork and holds up the phone in a specified direction. The screen on the phone displays the space as seen through the phone's camera, and the application stitches a digital 3D model into that space. In comparison, Artivive offers artists a way for users to interact with their already-framed, physical artwork. The application does not use geolocation for accessing the work; rather, users view the animations by placing an artwork in the viewfinder of their phone's camera. Artivive then overlays animation on the work, changing the viewing experience for the user.

Both the 4th Wall and Artivive apps are thoughtful solutions to overcome some of the hurdles which have been mentioned here previously. But such "window-on-the-world" applications constantly mediate space via a mobile device's camera and therefore assert the primacy of the visual experience. We have considered adding an overlay feature, but we pause as we consider these questions: if one of the most important parts of these experiences is the site, is it somehow diminished by being relegated to being viewed through the screen? How does one create such a project that engages a more direct experience of the site? Most art AR apps that we have included in Table 5.1 do not use an overlay feature.

Table 5.1

Name	Content type	AR type	Contributors	Geolocated information-tion/access?	Site-specific	URL
Popwalk	public art, history, culture, fine art	video, audio	open	yes/yes	yes	https://www.popwalkapp.com/
Intermountain Histories	history	image, text	open	yes/no	yes	https://www.intermountainhistories.org/
Story Road Utah	history, culture	video, image, audio, text	open	yes/no	yes	https://play.google.com/store/apps/details?id=com.storyroadutah.android&hl=en_IN&gl=US
NHMU Trailhead	history, culture, tour	video, image, audio, text	open	yes/no	yes	https://download.cnet.com/NHMU-Trailhead/3000-20420_4-78277735.html

Art Around Me	public art, archive	image, text	open, users	yes/no	partially	https://www.artaroundme.com/
ArTTrek (TTU)	public art	video, audio	open	yes/no	partially	https://www.texastech.edu/stories/18_04_public_art_app.php (app discontinued)
You Be My Ally	public art, culture	overlay	specific project	yes/yes	partially	https://www.jennyholzer.uchicago.edu/
CANVS	public art, archive	image, text	open, users	yes	partially	https://www.canvsart.com/
4th Wall	public art	overlay, image, audio	open	yes/yes	partially	https://www.4thwallapp.org/
Autio	culture, tour	image, audio	app developers	yes	yes	https://autio.com/about
HISTORY Here	history, culture, tour	audio	app developers	yes/no	no	https://www.history.com/history-here (app discontinued)

(Continued)

Table 5.1. continued.

Name	Content type	AR type	Contributors	Geolocated information/access?	Site-specific	URL
Explore Here	history, culture, tour	audio	app developers, users			https://www.explorehere.app/
Geotourist	history, culture, tour	audio	open	yes/yes	yes	https://geotourist.com/
Gesso	history, culture, tour	audio	open	yes/yes	yes	https://www.gesso.app/
Bluebrain, National Mall album	music	audio	specific project	yes/yes	yes	https://www.smithsonianmag.com/smithsonian-institution/bluebrains-soundtrack-for-the-national-mall-180386064/
Artivive	animated art	overlay, audio	open	no/no	specific to artwork, not location	https://artivive.com/

Our commitment to site specificity values users interacting fully with the environment of the artwork; we have therefore opted to use video and audio as the primary content modes.

Other apps have helped us consider the benefits and limitations of offering access to content based exclusively on site specificity. Many of the cultural and historical apps listed in Table 5.1 link content to specific sites, but they do not necessarily restrict access based on location. Autio is a current incarnation in this category, which offers "10,000+" historical stories about locations across North America. These are made available in any location, or the user can choose to enable a geolocation function, which makes them automatically available to the user while they are traveling. Autio does not use geolocation as a tool to limit the location of experience; rather, geolocation is used as a service to the listener, to more easily enable access. Other apps in this category include Explore Here, Gesso, GeoTourist, and HISTORY Here (app discontinued). Though their content is associated with specific locations, site specificity is optional. In Gesso, for example, you can play the tour content even if you are not on location. The app will indicate you are far from the start point and will ask if you would like locative directions or to view the tour remotely. Site specificity for apps like Gesso is, in essence, optional; it can be toggled on or off. This limits the types of stories artists can tell on such apps. If place is a necessary component to complete the story, artists will need applications where site specificity cannot be turned off. However, restricting access to content based on site specificity reduces viewership. This is neither an ideal option for business plans nor artists seeking to increase visibility of their work. Content curators of these apps, including ourselves, want art to be seen, listened to, and experienced. The trade-off of site specificity, then, is storytelling vs. viewership. To alleviate this issue, Popwalk offers a preview or snippet of content users can listen to before traveling to a location. This movie-trailer-like access allows us to maintain site specificity while hopefully encouraging more viewers to visit the locations.

Last of all, the diversity of AR art applications has given a range of models in how we can manage Popwalk. Specifically, we have noticed different ways for soliciting and publishing content as well as different ways for how we can choose to engage users. Some applications seem to be run by individuals or small teams, such as Art Around Me.[37] Others, like Gesso, ArTTrek (app discontinued),[38] and HISTORY Here (app discontinued)[39] have corporate, university, or other infrastructural and financial backing that enables a certain polish to storytelling and a competitive advantage in updating the technology needed for sustaining functional mobile apps on ever-changing mobile platforms. We have also noted how some app content is created or managed closely by the app developers. Such content seems to be performed by voice actors and finished by experts in video and audio content. For example, organizations which oversee a collection of artwork have developed applications to make the work more accessible to the public. A specific example of this is the ArTTrek app developed for the Texas Tech University public art collection.[40] Like the history applications, this app controls the production of its content and makes the content available anywhere, using the geolocation function to assist in the experience of the content. Conversely, applications like CANVS[41] and Art Around Me allow individual artists and the app users to help develop their content. Popwalk is designed as a digital exhibition platform and therefore follows a model of soliciting content from artists and jurying their submissions. We are currently considering ways to engage users more in content creation.

CASE STUDIES

The early uses of Popwalk helped us evolve our vision of the technology, but three specific and more recent cases have given us clarity on how site-specific AR can change the types of stories told and change who tells the stories. These projects have developed the scope and potential of sharing site-specific cultural content, including finding methods for community engagement. These projects will be discussed for the challenges and questions that they have introduced into the Popwalk ecosystem: Art History in Rome, Public Art at Brigham Young University, and the *Our Valley Speaks* exhibition in Sanpete County, Utah.

Case 1: Access to Storytelling for Art History in Rome

Our first case examines how making digital art site-specific provided access to students to become storytellers. In 2017, students in a study abroad program visited Rome and used Popwalk to produce a multimodal presentation in lieu of a final paper. The program included a studio art course taught by David and an art history course taught by Professor Janis Elliott, an art historian at Texas Tech University. The art history course, entitled "The Late Medieval City in Italy," was organized in a typical manner: the students participated in daily excursions to historical and artistic sites of interest. The site visits were supplemented with readings from textbooks and articles to contextualize the art and architecture. Popwalk altered this experience, though, as students were required to present their final research papers via Popwalk, giving them opportunity to use the affordances of video, audio, and site specificity. The format of the videos did not deviate drastically from what might be expected from a conventional art history paper, which would include text and supporting images. We asked the students to create this same arrangement in their research paper, the difference being that they would have to record a dictation of the paper and combine the audio with the images they would have used in a conventional paper.

The new method of presenting these final papers did not initially present a complication for the students; however, aspects both empowering and complicating emerged. First, as a genre, a written art history assignment invites students to consolidate information within a self-contained package. A successful paper appropriately addresses a general audience by including contextual clues, background information, external references, and illustrations. In doing so, a traditional academic paper somewhat abstracts the studied subject from its reality. Using Popwalk, though, students were required to create an academic exposition within the context of the historical location itself. In other words, the physical sites became a composing element in their final assignments. The site specificity aspects changed the expectations for the assignment. Students no longer needed to include an illustration of the object or spaces that were being referenced in their paper. Instead, they had to lead the user physically through the space, giving them directions about where to go and what to look at. The subject of most of these videos was an architectural space, or an object within an architectural space. Therefore, the videos needed to create thoughtful arguments about the space while determining a physical path through the space that would best support that reasoning. True to the intent of Popwalk, the student could also include illustrations via the app's AR functionality to clarify the arguments of their paper. Such illustrations needed to be contextualized within the presentation.

These videos existed in a new didactic space. They might have been perceived as analogous to historic tourism, giving an exposition of the historic space as one moves through that location. But the expectations, and therefore the experience, were subtly different. An academic paper requires students to compose arguments that explain diverse viewpoints and interpret artwork to support their claims. Historical context's role in these traditional papers functions as evidence for their arguments. Using Popwalk, however, repositioned the real-time and historical context as evidence in the students' arguments, rather than information offered for its own value. The experience of these videos presents a different way of moving through the historic spaces of Rome. The locations discussed were viewed through the lens of academic evidence and historical argument. This subtle difference in the students' site-specific art histories was important in our developing perceptions of the potential of the Popwalk platform

This project in Rome helped us see how the power of context in site-specific artwork can work for digital artists. It showed how context can become part of a digital artist's palette. We live in a time in which our public and historic spaces are being critically reassessed. Historical narratives told through monuments and historic sites, if seen as communicating cultural absolutes, often leave out many important histories. This is true about antebellum monuments to the Civil War in the southern United States.[42] It is also true about the Spanish missions that run the length of California, New Mexico, Arizona, and Florida. The story of these missions, and their role in the communities in which they existed, has often left out the subjugation, forced conversion, and slavery of native peoples.[43] The dissonance that arises when a historical space or heritage object is presented within a context that disregards, or is at odds with, another cultural belief has been termed "heritage dissonance."[44] This dissonance is often exacerbated by political or cultural institutions that work to support those historical narratives. And it is also exacerbated by the physical finality monuments, sculptures, and other site-specific artworks depend upon. The AR technology of Popwalk shows how populations such as students with little power to place a physical artwork on location can articulate their own interpretation and use the context offered by requiring users to visit a location to make their arguments present.[45] We hope AR technology like Popwalk can be picked up as tools for encouraging social justice. Such technologies can offer access to individuals historically excluded from producing sanctioned spatial stories.[46]

The art history in Rome was not revolutionary in its presentation of art historical material. But the project was important for understanding how a historical location or object may be presented within the lens of a contested space. Those students gave singular academic expositions of the spaces that they wrote about, but they also offered a paradigm in which their own conclusions might be contested or updated. The mission and purpose of Popwalk is to make available a platform that gives artists and other content creators a discussion space; the app's mission is to enable digital artists to call out or bring forth a breadth of cultural interpretations to reflect constantly changing ideas about contested cultural spaces. By allowing a multiplicity of voices, monolithic cultural interpretations may be disarmed. This project was an important part of our understanding of the possibilities of presenting site-specific humanities information.

Case 2: Establishing Provenance for Public Art at Brigham Young University

Rosemary A. Joyce argues that an artwork's provenance is necessarily connected to time and place. Archaeologists use the term "provenience," Joyce notes, to describe a similar concept of originality, an object's "findspot." In other words, Joyce claims, art has a "findspot" and therefore both the history and original place of an artwork contributes to the story we can tell about the work's history. In this section we discuss the way in which Popwalk videos can help audiences discover not just the physical location in which the art resides but also the intellectual and creative origin from which the stories about the artwork can grow.

In 2019, Brigham Young University professor James Swenson and the Art History Club collaborated in creating a Popwalk-guided tour of the university's and nearby pedestrian commercial district's public art.[47] Funded by the Charles Redd Center for Western Studies, this project focused on the interpretation of the works as it related to the space in which they were originally sited. The first step in developing the project was to establish parameters for the videos. The students identified potential works of art for the tour. They discussed the thematic and historical framework for the videos, the ideal length of the videos, and the target audience for the works. Public art has not been a very important part of the development of BYU's campus, and there is no funding to support the creation of new artworks. But there have been a number of significant commissions and gifts of artwork to the university. An undercurrent of the students' discussions about this project was how to move the artworks into a more prominent position before the university community: to create awareness of these artworks in the minds of the student body. Both provenance and provenience help explain how they did so.

The authors of this project made deliberate attempts in the videos to make the artworks' "findspots" a more prominent part of the cultural landscape. An example of this can be seen in a video discussing an innocuous sculpture of a family: mother, father, and child (Figure 5.3). The sculpture seems innocent enough, particularly on a college campus that is often rated as a "campus where you are most likely to find a spouse."[48] Upon inspection, one will see that the patina on the mother's outstretched hand has a different

Figure 5.3: Note the shiny fingers of the woman's outstretched arm.

quality than the rest of the sculpture. There is a subtle tradition among devotees: for the married students of the university, it is tradition to rub the hand of the mother if one is trying to become pregnant. This quirky tradition, invisible to most, became a tool for the art historians to bring attention to the artwork's site as well as its cultural landscape. The authors of this project were thoughtful about their audience, and found characteristics and histories of the artworks which were intentional for making art history, and cultural tradition, an interesting part of the experience of that campus. Drawing attention to the tradition highlighted the authenticity of the sculpture in this particular location.

Through the lens of provenience, an artwork's history is importantly connected to a specific place. But the more commonly understood notion of provenance refers to the history of ownership of an artwork. Curators, museums, and art dealers seek to establish an artwork's path of ownership since its creation. This historical information has increasingly become a part of the authenticity, value, meaning, and understanding of some famous works of art. An example that combines both provenance and provenience can easily be illustrated by the complex circumstances surrounding the Southern Civil War monuments celebrating Confederate leaders.[49] The finances to commission and erect these monuments, and the culturally manipulative motivations behind that patronage, have become an integral part of the meaning of those war monuments. Accordingly, if we commence the record of provenance, not with the first patron of the artwork but with the artist and the interactions of artist and patrons to create the work, we open the concept of provenance to include the location and situation of the artwork's creation. By opening the concept of provenance to include aspects of creation and ownership which may affect the interpretation of the artwork (such as a tradition of rubbing a statue to induce pregnancy), we permit a powerful tool in historians' kit to connect a public work of art to the location and audience that is influenced by it.

As we speak of site specificity as an important aspect of an art-work, we might ask: what are those characteristics of a work of art that help to establish an authentic relationship to the location in which it is exhibited? The Elgin Marbles, a group of ancient Greek sculptures that were removed from Greece to England by Lord Elgin in the early nineteenth century, is an excellent example of artworks whose contemporary exhibition is understood through the lens of history and by the path of arrival to their current loca-tion of exhibition.[50] These were removed from Greece during a time of political unrest, and likely faced destruction. Greece has recently called for the repatriation of the statues. This history and political posturing between these countries informs the tension surrounding their continued exhibition in England.

In this example, a history of ownership informs the understand-ing of the artworks. In our example at BYU, the students also took advantage of a surrounding cultural history from which to frame the discussion of the artworks. In one example, a video addresses an abstract metal work of art next to the university museum of art. The narrator asks, "What do you see? Two triangular forms and a sphere? Is that all that this is, a bunch of shapes, or is it something more?" The university campus and its surrounding community do not have a long history of, or familiarity with, abstract art. This Socratic introduction to this work of art shows a sensitivity to the community of students on campus who may not have con-text for interpreting the work. The narrator speaks in the tone of a college instructor, challenging the students' preconceptions of the art and broadening possibilities of interpretation. We might refer to the ability of the author to connect with their audiences as establishing an intellectual provenance for the artwork. By offer-ing the audience an intellectual means of entering into the lexicon of abstraction, the historian offers a starting point of intellectual discourse from which the audience can situate and grow their understanding. This same strategy can be used through a discus-sion of the work's selection, construction, erection, or many other factors that help the audience to establish an intellectual, cultural, or social origin for the artwork.

Case 3: Issues of Authority: Who Gets to Tell the Story in the *Our Valley Speaks* Exhibition?

In 2020, David initiated a collaboration with Granary Arts, a contemporary arts exhibition space in rural eastern Utah. The collaboration between Granary Arts and Popwalk produced an exhibition that includes 65 artworks, spanning the length of Sanpete Valley, in central Utah.[51] The works in this exhibition come from a number of creators, both living within the valley and without. This sparsely populated corner of Utah, along with the rest of the world, was a victim of the layered effects of Covid, financial uncertainty, and social unrest in 2020. Sanpete County was not a flashpoint for any of those difficulties, but community members, and particularly members of the art community that participated in the creation of this exhibition, were sensitive to the cultural self-reflection that was felt in the zeitgeist of that moment. That self-reflection influenced our perception of authority as it relates to the place-based storytelling that we were engaged in. It caused us to ask: what experience or capacity does the author bring with them which allows them to interpret a specific location? And how could we responsibly curate art content via Popwalk that spoke to the kinds of important truths of the moment while allowing arts both within and without the community to be a part of the exhibition?

As we initiated the collaboration, we established a set of categories for site-specific content that we wanted to develop. The first of these categories was video artworks which were produced by artists from all over the United States. These creators interpreted the valley from many points of view. To facilitate the work of this group of artists, David researched and wrote abstracts focusing on many important aspects of the valley—ecological, historical, and cultural. These were not intended to be used as scripts for the artworks but to inspire the artists into deeper investigation of those parts of the valley that interested them. Most of the artists made a trip to the valley and many of them recorded videos during these trips that would be part of their final artworks.

The second category of video work for the exhibition was a series of oral histories. This portion of the exhibition was supported through a grant from Utah Humanities. We were assisted in this work by David Allred, professor of English and folklore studies at Snow College, in Ephraim, Utah. These oral histories included subjects such as high school basketball, WPA projects, National Historic Landmarks, local religious pageants, and the history of a local hardware store. In contrast to the videos made by artists, these oral histories were hyperlocal, dictated by the people that lived those experiences in the valley.

The third category of works for the exhibition featured video interviews by local experts in many fields, including geology, history, ecology, and more. The experts in these videos were primarily from the valley or had a particular connection to the subject matter in the valley. An example of this can be seen in the interviews of Roger Roper, Deputy State Historic Preservation Officer, who lives in Sanpete county. These videos focus on some of the historic buildings in Spring City, Utah.[52]

As mentioned, David wrote abstracts focusing on various aspects of Sanpete valley, which were sent to the prospective artists. Email conversations that developed from these communications attest to the fact that the artists involved in the *Our Valley Speaks* exhibition, who were living outside the valley, perceived themselves as outsiders and did not wish to claim an authoritative voice in defining the community through their artworks. With this humble attitude, there were many thoughtful interpretations of the valley. On the other hand, the octogenarian basketball coach, whose life was spent in the valley and whose name entitles a local gym, has a greater 'authority' to talk about the character of the valley's inhabitants and history. Because of the broad subject matter in this exhibition, it is possible to categorize the works according to insider and outsider. This categorization can be perceived as a result of a number of different philosophical sources. Edward Said's foundational work in postcolonial studies would suggest that a colonial viewpoint is often an unreliable narrator of the local. And it may be rational to label a site-specific artwork which originates from a 'foreign' artist as 'colonizing' a location through the means of site-specific artwork. Speaking of the relationship between the native 'emic' and the 'etic' foreign perspectives, Mostowlansky and Rota note that "etic, a term often loosely employed to identify a researcher's own analytic framework, has fallen out of fashion."[53] But within the artworld, it is common practice to allow an artist to create site-specific cultural interventions, in the form of public art, performance, or music. As curators, we would not allow a complete disavowal of an outside opinion. Art is often, by its nature, an outside opinion. Both of these viewpoints are valid, but it is an important part of a site-specific work to understand what role the author plays in the community that his or her work inhabits.

In the context of site-specific work, we might call this attribute the 'authority' of the author. The term authority here may be left intentionally vague to allow for the many different types of authority on a subject: academic, personal, moral, local. But this project made clear the need to consider authority of site-specific work. Perhaps the most poignant example of the attribute of authority came from Jane Beckwith, the president of the Topaz Museum board. The Topaz Museum, in Delta, Utah, is tasked with preserving the legacy and remains of the Topaz Japanese Internment Camp and "to interpret the impact of Topaz on the internees, their families, and the citizens of Millard County."[54] Although this camp is situated 60 miles to the east of Sanpete Valley, a number of buildings were relocated from the camp when it was closed in 1945. These buildings are currently being used as student housing for Snow College in Ephraim, Utah. Ms. Beckwith has worked for many years to preserve the history of Topaz, and is very knowledgeable of this history. But in prelude to her participation in the exhibition, she said that those who were interned in the camp, and their relatives, should be the ones to tell the history of that camp. Ms. Beckwith recognized the importance of that authority to speak on certain histories, particularly those connected to specific places. Her statement presents the layers of 'emic' perspectives within the site. But what is the most authoritative perspective for that location? Is it that of the Japanese who lived in those buildings during their use in the internment camp? Is it the museum director who has worked to preserve the legacy of the buildings, or even the current occupants of the structures?

These former internment camp buildings hold histories both contested and sacred, depending on the author and the audience. As curators of this cultural content, we observed this idea of authority of an author to speak about a location surface; it informed our curation of the exhibition. Popwalk, we recognize, plays an influential role in arbitrating how individuals speak about a particular location. We do not see the service as the only way or means to give people space to speak; rather, we hope the app aids in helping people identify the layers of meaning already working within a location.

CONCLUDING THOUGHTS

Each of these projects discussed has had an effect on how we understand site-specific cultural video. At an artistic level, the ability to use any location as a backdrop or interpretive lens for a cultural work is very powerful. There are many practitioners in the visual arts, dance, theater, art history, heritage management, and many other fields who are creating meaningful site-specific work. The ability to democratize information, not through the decontextualization of the web, but through a format which makes it available onsite, both to the content consumer and to the content creator, is a worthy goal.

As a project in the realm of digital humanities, Popwalk goes against the grain of much recent work. Prevailing trends have sought to broaden the accessibility of cultural and artistic production through digital means. Improving accessibility is important and these projects are to be applauded. We recognize that a weakness of Popwalk is accessibility: to experience the works on Popwalk, you need to be on location. But this issue of accessibility is also an important part of our work. There are many stories to be told whose impact can be felt most keenly in a specific location. There are many works of art whose meaning and interpretation should be colored by the lens of a certain place. There are important histories and traditions of our shared human experience that can best be understood in their places of origin. By connecting our stories to place, we hope to encourage an understanding of the human condition that allows for introspection, conversation, and perspective.

NOTES

1. Smithson, "Spiral Jetty."
2. Smithson, "Amarillo Ramp."
3. Artivive app, https://artivive.com/
4. Gesso app, "Audio City Guides," https://www.gesso.app/
5. GeoTourist app, "Experience Your Environment," https://geotourist.com/
6. CANVS, "Bringing Interactivity to Street Art," https://www.canvsart.com/
7. Holzer, "You Be My Ally."
8. Christo and Jeanne-Claude, "Running Fence."
9. Kwon, *One Place after Another*, 11.
10. Kwon, 11–12. Though Miwon Kwon critiques and labels these definitions of site specific as traditional, we find them helpful to theorize how digital art and AR—both fluid and more ethereal than physical installations—connect and depend on space for meaning.
11. Hurley, "Spatial orientations," 100.
12. Lefebvre, *Production of Space*.
13. De Certeau, *Practices of Everyday Life*, 122. De Certeau points to the influential role of spatial stories, writing that they "tell us what one can do in [...] and make out of" space. In a city, for example, "the street geometrically defined by

urban planning is transformed into a space by walkers" (117). Spatial stories, then, are played out in discursive and spatial practices. We see Popwalk as a way for artists to help people become aware of the spatial stories, interact with them, and change them.

14. Massey. *For Space*, 9.
15. Manovich, "Poetics of Augmented Space." For example, Manovich has written, "How is our experience of a spatial form affected when the form is filled in with dynamic and rich multimedia information? Does the form become irrelevant, being reduced to functional and ultimately invisible support for information flows? Or do we end up with a new experience in which the spatial and information layers are equally important?"
16. Shaw, "Modalities of Interactivity."
17. Lodi, "Spatial Art," 12.
18. Freeman, "ManifestAR." "Public space is now truly open, as artworks can be placed anywhere in the world, without prior permission from government or private authorities—with profound implications for art in the public sphere and the discourse that surrounds it."
19. Bravo, Artesur profile.
20. Helyer, Woo, and Rizos, "Syren for Port of Jackson."
21. Helyer, Woo, and Veronesi, "Artful media."
22. Hudson and Hudson, "Marketing for tourism."
23. Rinehart, "Site, Non-site, and Website."
24. Dristig. "Searching for milk hares."
25. Goodrich, Templehoff, and Steyn, "Site-specific Cultural Infrastructure."
26. Nguyen, "Convenient efficiency."
27. Okazaki et al., "Privacy Concerns."
28. Kieseberg et al., "QR code security." More recent discussions are considering how to embed checks for authenticity: Focardi, Luccio, and Wahsheh, "Usable security."
29. Milgram et al., "Augmented Reality."
30. Suganya. "Usage and Perception of Geofencing."
31. Filimowicz. "Mobile Augmented Soundscape." Filimowicz provides an annotated bibliography of 30 examples of mobile-based soundscapes.
32. Helyer, Woo, and Veronesi, "Artful media," 2.
33. Helyer, Woo, and Veronesi, "Artful media," 4.
34. Helyer, Woo, and Veronesi, "Artful media," 4.
35. There have been a number of systems of classification offered for the many approaches of augmented reality; one example was developed by Dubois and Nigay, "Augmented Reality."

36. 4th Wall app/Baker Cahill, "Liberty Bell."
37. Art Around Me app, https://www.artaroundme.com/
38. Lacefield, "Texas Tech Launches ArTTrek App."
39. HISTORY Here app https://www.history.com/history-here.
40. Texas Tech University System, "Public Art Collection."
41. CANVS, "Bringing Interactivity to Street Art."
42. There has been much recent work on the ways in which Confederate monuments have served as tools for political and ethnic suppression. A recent example of scholarship in this area is Cox, *Common Ground* (2021).
43. See Archibald, "Indian Labor."
44. Kisić, *Governing Heritage Dissonance.*
45. Finding ways to represent multiple interpretations of space is important, as Caron Mattingly explains, because "those who control [...] space influence our understanding of the past." Mattingly, "Woman's Temple, Women's Fountains," 135.
46. Ian makes a similar argument and offers a more in-depth analysis of what we mean by access. Weaver, "Access As a Participatory Design Principle," (2022).
47. The project was not a class but was an extracurricular effort hosted by the Art History Club.
48. Martin, "50 colleges."
49. Calame, "Dissonant Heritage." Accessed February 15, 2023, https://jrap. neduet.edu.pk/arch-journal/JRAP_2021(FirstIssue)/JRAP-2021(1stIssue). pdf#page=18. See also Byrne, "Stone Monuments and Flexible Laws."
50. This case has been largely studied and discussed; for the British Museum's response to the marbles' repatriation, see British Museum, "The Parthenon Sculptures."
51. Lindsay, "Our Valley Speaks."
52. Roper, "Interviews with Roger Roper."
53. Mostowlansky and Andrea, "Emic and etic."
54. Topaz Museum, "About the Topaz Museum."

WORKS CITED

4th Wall app/Baker Cahill, Nancy. "Liberty Bell." Art Production Fund, July 4, 2020 Accessed February 2023. https://www.4thwallapp.org/liberty-bell.
Archibald, Robert. "Indian Labor at the California Missions: Slavery or Salvation?" *Journal of San Diego History* 24, no. 2 (1978). https://sandiegohistory.org/journal/1978/april/labor/

Artivive app. "Create with Artivive." Accessed February 3, 2023. https://artivive.com/

Art Around Me app. "Art Around Me." Accessed February 3, 2023. https://www.artaroundme.com/

Bravo, Monika. Artesur profile. Accessed November 17, 2023. http://www.arte-sur.org/artists/monika-bravo

British Museum. "The Parthenon Sculptures," British Museum website, Accessed February 3, 2023. https://www.britishmuseum.org/about-us/british-museum-story/contested-objects-collection/parthenon-sculptures

Byrne, J. Peter. "Stone Monuments and Flexible Laws: Removing Confederate Monuments Through Historic Preservation Laws." Georgetown University Law Center, July 15, 2020. https://papers.ssrn.com/sol3/papers.cfm?abstract_id=3633473

Calame, Jon. "Dissonant Heritage and the Hazards of Retention." *Journal of Research in Architecture and Planning* 30, no. 1 (2021): 10–16.

CANVS. "Bringing Interactivity to Street Art," CANVS Interactive, Inc. website. Accessed February 3, 2023. https://www.canvsart.com/

Christo and Jeanne-Claude. "Running Fence." Christo and Jeanne-Claude Foundation. Accessed February 24, 2023. https://christojeanneclaude.net/artworks/running-fence/

Cox, Karen L. *No Common Ground: Confederate Monuments and the Ongoing Fight for Racial Justice.* Chapel Hill, NC: University of North Carolina Press, 2021.

De Certeau, Michel. *The Practices of Everyday Life.* Translated by Steven Rendall. Los Angeles: University of California Press, 1984.

Dristig, Niclas. "Searching for Milk Hares: Evaluating a Web-Based Tool for Location-Based Storytelling within Cultural Heritage." Master's degree project. Skövde: University of Skövde, 2020. Available from: https://www.diva-portal.org/smash/get/diva2:1450780/FULLTEXT01.pdf

Dubois, Emmanuel, and Laurence Nigay. "Augmented Reality: Which Augmentation for Which Reality?" *Proceedings of DARE 2000 on Designing augmented reality environments.* New York: Association for Computing Machinery, 2000: 165–66. https://doi.org/10.1145/354666.354695

Freeman, John Craig. "ManifestAR: An Augmented Reality Manifesto." John Craig Freeman website, January 24, 2012. Accessed February 21, 2023. https://johncraigfreeman.wordpress.com/manifestar-an-augmented-reality-manifesto/

Filimowicz, Michael. "The Mobile Augmented Soundscape: Defining an Emerged Genre." *Hz 20* (July 2015). Accessed February 24, 2023. https://www.hz-journal.org/n20/filimowicz.html

Focardi, Riccardo, Flaminia L. Luccio, and Heider A.M. Wahsheh. "Usable security for QR code." *Journal of Information Security and Applications* 48 (2019), 102369. https://doi.org/10.1016/j.jisa.2019.102369

GeoTourist app. "Experience Your Environment in a New and Inspiring Way." Accessed February 3, 2023. https://geotourist.com/

Gesso app. "Audio City Guides for Temporary Locals." Accessed February 3, 2023. https://www.gesso.app/

Goodrich, Andre, Gustaf Templehoff, and Juan Steyn. "Site-specific Cultural Infrastructure: Promoting Access and Conquering the Digital Divide." Presentation at Digital Humanities 2017, Montreal, Canada, August 8–11, 2017). Accessed February 16, 2023. https://dh-abstracts.library.virginia.edu/works/4067

Helyer, Nigel, Daniel Woo, and Chris Rizos. "Syren for Port of Jackson," Sonic Objects: The Nature and Culture of Sound, March 31, 2006. Accessed February 24, 2023. http://www.sonicobjects.com/index.php/2006/03/31/syren_for_port_jackson/

Helyer, Nigel, Daniel Woo, and Francesca Veronesi. "Artful Media: The Sonic Nomadic: Exploring Mobile Surround-Sound Interactions." *IEEE MultiMedia* 16, no. 2 (2009): 12–15. https://doi.org/10.1109/MMUL.2009.38

HISTORY Here app (discontinued). A&E Television Networks. Accessed February 3, 2023. https://www.history.com/history-here

Holzer, Jenny. *You Be My Ally*. University of Chicago, October 5, 2020. Accessed February 3, 2023. https://www.jennyholzer.uchicago.edu/project

Hudson, Louise, and Simon Hudson. *Marketing for Tourism, Hospitality & Events: A Global and Digital Approach*. Thousand Oaks, CA: Sage, 2017.

Hurley, Elise Verzosa. "Spatial Orientations: Cultivating Critical Spatial Perspectives in Technical Communication Pedagogy." In *Key Theoretical Frameworks: Teaching Technical Communication in the Twenty-First Century*, edited by Angela M. Haas and Michelle F. Eble, 93–113. Logan, UT: Utah State University, 2018.

Joyce, Rosemary A. "From Place to Place: Provenience, Provenance, and Archaeology." In *Provenance: An Alternate History of Art*, edited by Gail Feigenbaum and Inge Reist, 48–60. Los Angeles: Getty Research Institute, 2012.

Kaye, Nick. *Site-Specific Art: Performance, Place, and Documentation*. New York: Routledge, 2000.

Kieseberg, Peter, Manuel Leithner, Martin Mulazzani, Lindsay Munroe, Sebastian Schrittwieser, Mayank Sinha, and Edgar Weippl. "QR Code Security." In

Proceedings of the 8th International Conference on Advances in Mobile Computing and Multimedia, 430–5. New York: Association for Computing Machinery, 2010. https://doi.org/10.1145/1971519.1971593

Kisić, Višnja. Governing Heritage Dissonance: Promises and Realities of Selected Cultural Policies. Amsterdam: European Cultural Foundation, 2013.

Kwon, Miwon. One Place after Another: Site-Specific Art and Locational Identity. Cambridge, Massachusetts: MIT Press, 2002.

Lacefield, Scott. "Texas Tech University System Public Art Program Launches ArTTrek App." News Stories, Texas Tech University System, April 24, 2018. https://www.texastech.edu/stories/18_04_public_art_app.php

Lefebvre, Henri. The Production of Space. Translated by Donald Nicholson-Smith. Cambridge: Blackwell Press, 1991.

Lindsay, David. "Our Valley Speaks: A Sanpete Experience." Granary Arts, August 22, 2021. Accessed March 1, 2023. https://www.granaryarts.org/our-valley-speaks

Lodi, Simona. "Spatial Art: An Eruption of the Digital into the Physical + Interview." Leonardo Electronic Almanac 19, no. 2 (2013): 12–31. https://www.leoalmanac.org/vol19-no2-spatial-art/

Manovich, Lev. "The Poetics of Augmented Space." Manovich Cultural Analytics Lab, 2002. Accessed February 21, 2023. http://manovich.net/index.php/projects/the-poetics-of-augmented-space

Martin, Emmie. "50 colleges where you're most likely to meet your future spouse." Business Insider, June 1, 2015. https://www.businessinsider.com/colleges-where-youll-meet-your-spouse-2015-5

Massey, Doreen. For Space. London: Sage Publications, 2005.

Mattingly, Caron. "Woman's Temple, Women's Fountains: The Erasure of Public Memory." American Studies 49, no. 3/4 (2008): 133–56.

Milgram, Paul, Haruo Takemura, Akira Utsumi, and Fumio Kishino. "Augmented Reality: A Class of Displays on the Reality-Virtuality Continuum." Telemanipulator and Telepresence Technologies 2351, (1995). https://doi.org/10.1117/12.197321

Mostowlansky, Till and Andrea Rota. "Emic and etic." The Open Encyclopedia of Anthropology, November 29, 2020. Edited by Felix Stein. http://doi.org/10.29164/20emicetic

Nguyen, Dang. "Convenient efficiency: A media genealogy of QR codes." New Media & Society (2022). https://doi.org/10.1177/14614448221141086

Okazaki, Shintaro, María Ángeles Navarro-Bailón, and Francisco-Jose Molina-Castillo. "Privacy Concerns in Quick Response Code Mobile Promotion:

The Role of Social Anxiety and Situational Involvement." *International Journal of Electronic Commerce* 16, no. 4 (2012): 91–120. https://doi.org/10.2753/JEC1086-4415160404

Rinehart, Richard. "Site, Non-site, and Website." *Leonardo Electronic Almanac* 19, no. 2 (2013): 9. https://leonardo.info/sites/default/files/1_leavol19no2-aceti.pdf

Roper, Roger. "Interviews with Roger Roper: The Bishop's Storehouse." YouTube, April 26, 2021. Video, 3 min. 28 sec. https://www.youtube.com/watch?v=E4pTdjp2jcs

Serra, Richard. *Writings/Interviews.* Chicago: University of Chicago Press, 1994.

Shaw, Jeffrey. "Modalities of Interactivity and Virtuality." Jeffrey Shaw Compendium, July 1992. Accessed February 10, 2023. https://www.jeffreyshawcompendium.com/modalities-of-interactivity-and-virtuality/

Smithson, Robert, "Amarillo Ramp (1973)." Holt Smithson Foundation. Accessed February 24, 2023. https://holtsmithsonfoundation.org/amarillo-ramp

Smithson, Robert. "Spiral Jetty (1970)." Holt Smithson Foundation. Accessed February 24, 2023. https://holtsmithsonfoundation.org/spiral-jetty

Suganya, Varadarajan. "Usage and Perception of Geofencing." *EPRA International Journal of Economics, Business and Management Studies (EBMS)* 9, no. 2 (2022): 1–4. http://www.eprajournals.net/index.php/EBMS/article/view/61

Texas Tech University System. "Public Art Collection." Accessed February 3, 2023. https://ttuspublicart.com/

Topaz Museum. "About the Topaz Museum." Topaz Museum website. Accessed February 23, 2023. https://topazmuseum.org/topaz-history/about-topaz-museum/

Weaver, Ian. "Access As a Participatory Design Principle: Grant Writers Moving from Securing Resources to Codesigning with Communities." *Open Words: Access and English Studies* 14, no. 1 (2022): 73–95. https://wac.colostate.edu/docs/openwords/v14n1/weaver.pdf

CHAPTER 6

AN EMBODIED ARTS-BASED RESEARCH METHODOLOGY: AUGMENTED REALITY (AR) PORTRAIT PAINTING IN DIALOGUE

Elham Hajesmaeili

As we embark on this journey of exploration, let us pause to consider the significant impact of the intersection of technology and art on research methodology. The combination of these two fields presents a vast realm of potential and possibilities; it is a place where creativity and innovation come together to push the boundaries of what is possible, where the digital and the physical merge to create something entirely new. Not only does this field help us understand the present, but it holds the power to shape the future and change the way we perceive and interact with the world around us. In this chapter, I will explain how the combination of augmented reality (AR) and portrait painting can be utilized to develop an embodied arts-based research methodology providing novel approaches for analyzing and visualizing data.[1]

The integration of art in research can allow for a more expressive approach that incorporates human emotions and imagination in constructing knowledge. This approach may address "what is potentially 'left out' of discursive analyses."[2] The importance of fostering democratic and subjective knowledge, incorporating artistic activities and human creativity to expand beyond the limits of linguistics, and identifying and filling gaps in conventional academic research, led me to develop "AR portrait painting in dialogue" as an embodied arts-based research methodology.[3] I utilized the potential virtues of AR and portrait painting in analyzing and visualizing data by considering the meaningful relationship between "form of representation and form of understanding"[4] and the "unfinished and endless gap" between what can be seen and what can be heard.[5] By embracing pluralism in my methods, this methodology resists categorical or binary thinking and values diverse interpretations in different social contexts.[6]

In my pursuit of developing AR portrait painting methodology and to understand its main characteristics, identify its potential problems or limitations, and assess its feasibility, I have done a pilot test using AR portrait painting methodology to study the narratives of four Iranian immigrants living in the United States. In the pilot testing of the methodology, I collaborated with these women, whose experiences are the source of subjective knowledge for my inquiry into the suggested methodology. Thus, the embodiment of research participants' subjectivities and narratives is crucial to highlight their critical role in achieving the research findings. Embodying the subjectivity of the subject matter is crucial in constructing knowledge that is inclusive, democratic, and representative of the experiences and perspectives of all involved. By recognizing and highlighting the critical role of research participants in achieving research findings, we can create a more equitable and just understanding of the world. Social scientist Kay Inckle defines embodied research methodology as ways of "conducting and representing research which reflects the embodied nature of the subject matter."[7] The use of portrait painting and AR technology as research strategies provides a unique opportunity to embody the subjectivity of the participants, giving them a platform to present themselves through their own perspectives and voices. By using AR art in disseminating research findings, participants can "come alive" in front of the viewers, allowing them to present themselves in a more dynamic and engaging way compared to more traditional methods such as text or photographs. Additionally, AR can enable viewers to interact with the participants' representation in a more intimate and personal way, which can help to further embody the participants' subjectivities.

Portrait painting as a research strategy allows for an expressive representation of the participants. By painting a portrait, the artist is more likely to convey the emotions, expressions, and individualities of subjects. Through portrait painting, participants can be represented in a manner that transcends linguistic barriers and is accessible to a broader range of audiences, including those who may not be able to read or understand written or spoken language. Together, AR and portrait painting can create an embodied and subjective representation of research participants that can be engaging, immersive, and accessible for viewers, granting participants of study the authority to shape their own representation in the eyes of viewers.[8]

Highlighting subjectivity[9] of research participants in constructing knowledge, I aim to challenge the *power geometry*[10] in the conventional form of research, which can "carry substantial risks for exploitative treatment to participants"[11] and give authority to the researcher as the central figure who influences the collection, selection, and interpretation of data.[12] To resist the power structure in research,[13] I suggest a new form of triangular subjectivity of researcher, participant, and viewer in three phases of research: collecting data through interviewing participants; analyzing and interpreting data through creating AR portrait paintings; and presenting AR portrait paintings for viewers to interpret and generate dialogues. Through the triangular subjectivity model, I highlight the intertwined subjectivities of the researcher, participants, and viewers who are in dialogue with one another in constructing nonhierarchical knowledge. Figure 6.1 shows a diagram of how dialogues emerge from the relationships between all involved in the research process while each one is simultaneously in dialogue with art and technology as methodological facilitators.

The collaboration between artist-researcher and participants in making portrait paintings, as well as the endless interpretations by diverse viewers, clearly manifest the concept of *portraits as dialogue*.[14] This concept is at the core of my arts-based research methodology, as the act of encountering art often leads to multiple ongoing internal and external dialogues that shape

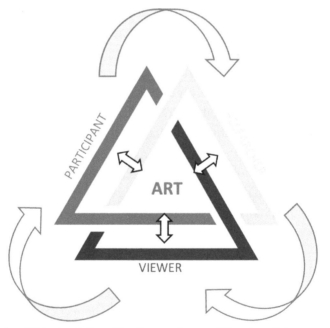

Figure 6.1: Dialogic relationship of researcher, participant, and viewer, 2021.

and reshape viewers' understanding. Utilizing artistic activities like drawings or other forms of artmaking as research techniques can improve communication and mutual understanding between artist-researchers and research participants,[15] resulting in what art education scholar Elliot Eisner calls an "empathic experience."[16] If we take empathy as "the mediation of emotional information between two body consciousnesses"[17] with relational subjectivities, then experiencing "lived differences" challenges the "thematized subject" through intersubjective mediation.[18] In arts-based research, the empathic experience fosters a safe space for participants to express themselves, while also enabling viewers to become active agents generating dialogue with the embodied subjectivity of the participants and create meaningful communications with the research findings by "experiencing, feeling, and associating with the [art]work rather than standing apart from it."[19] Hence, the active involvement of research participants and viewers in constructing knowledge and engaging in dialogue through AR portrait paintings is crucial to the effective implementation of my research methodology.

By connecting viewers' identification with the subject of a portrait painting, I intend to reinforce the concept of world traveling as espoused by Latinx feminist philosopher Maria Lugones, which is to travel to others' worlds not passively and apart from them as others but actively and in connection with their own subjectivities and loving them.[20] The simultaneous position of being "self" and an *other* constructs the nature of an artwork, "which is to be in relation to its 'other' and to exist for an 'other,' with multiple subject positions that provide an echo."[21] Through encountering AR portrait paintings, viewers attain new perspectives on the Iranian women's world and think of their positionality in their oppressive situations, feeling a kind of empathy and understanding of "their own capacities to experience the effective response to life that the arts evoke."[22] The aesthetic experience allows viewers to believe they have the right to engage in critique through dialogue.[23] The concept of *simultaneous subjectivity* truly resonates when viewers encounter a portrait painting in which they seek out their own subjectivities in the subject of the artwork.[24] Here, the "dialogic relation" between a portrait and viewer, in which both are partners in constructing dialogues, creates a coercive occasion in which they not only cooperate in meaning-making but also exchange the authority to grant it to the viewer.[25] In such a process, the "audience might simply identify a turn in the circulation of social meaning."[26]

AR portrait painting in dialogue as a creative analytic practice takes advantage of integrating art and technology in transferring knowledge that potentially creates an affective experience for the viewers and evokes their emotions through deep understanding.[27] Analyzing affect theory as an inseparable element of my arts-based research methodology, I stick to the definition of *affect* as a happening or event, and a dimension of every event.[28] For instance, our desire to talk after watching a movie or sharing a post about it on social media (Facebook or Instagram) could be the embodiment of affects which I interpret as a profound emotional understanding. Artwork is not simply an object but rather an *event site*,[29] where one might "encounter the affect."[30] Inspired by Australian feminist philosopher Teresa Brennan, who defines an affective experience as "the psychological shift accompanying a judgment," the goal of my artwork is to engage viewers' subjectivities toward a psychological shift in perspective.[31] Considering affective experiences as forming judgments means feeling does not just register sensory information but interprets it.[32] Based on prior studies, a premise of my work is that encountering art as an *affective means* can change the subjectivities of viewers by creating a deep emotional understanding, and potentially leads to actions regarding a narrated situation in the portrait paintings.[33]

I am specifically interested in and inspired by feminist aspects of affect theory regarding its power to change human actions and interpretations. British-Australian scholar Sara Ahmed in *The Cultural*

Politics of Emotion emphasizes the importance of what emotions can do rather than what they are.[34] As a viewer encounters an artwork (material of expression), new complex subjectification becomes possible, which can also be interpreted as *resingularisation,* referring to reordering self and its relation to the world.[35] In the pragmatic and aesthetic process of reconfiguration, "one creates new modalities of subjectivity in the same way an artist creates new forms from a palette."[36] Therefore, we need "a concept of subjectivity that is based on relationality with others and with things."[37] In the context of my research, I interpret the new form of subjectification under the affective experience of encountering AR art as the main factor, which enables viewers to reidentify their subjectivities in connection with a portrayed person in the paintings. Furthermore, the affect theory relates to my research regarding the impact of emotions on political and social life, worldviews, perspectives, and actions. Emotional experiences are not isolated from the social environment since, under an affective experience, one transmits the affects to the environment.[38] The potential of AR and portrait painting to elicit social actions is well-recognized; to fully utilize this potential, my research methodology employs a combination of these tools.[39] Exploring the capabilities of portrait painting and AR to bridge the gaps in traditional research methodologies offers innovative potentials and opportunities that provide a fresh perspective on academic research.

PORTRAIT PAINTING AS AN ANALYTICAL METHODOLOGY

Creating portrait paintings as a philosophical form of art to study people presents a complex challenge for artists.[40] On one hand, artists must aim for accuracy and faithfulness to the subject, capturing sitter essence with precision. On the other hand, they must also embrace freedom in artistic expression, allowing their own style and interpretation to influence the portraiture.[41] This delicate balance between accuracy and artistic expression requires skill and nuance as a critical aspect of successful portrait painting. The challenge of capturing a person's subjectivity through portrait painting is what makes it both a fascinating and complex art form. American philosopher of art, Cynthia Freeland suggests four ways to capture the subjectivity and essence of a sitter in a portrait: (a) "accurate likenesses"; (b) "testimonies of presence"; (c) "evocations of personality"; and (d) "presentations of a subject uniqueness."[42] Portraying the subjectivity and essence of a sitter is not a simple achievement, as Freeland emphasizes the tension between artist and subject recurs in the relationship between viewer and the subject of painting and determines whether viewers of a portrait painting interact with the subject of a portrait as another person or more as an object.[43] I have applied the four techniques suggested by Freeland to capture the subjectivity of the first participant of my study, as illustrated in Figure 6.2.

The *accurate likeness* is the first criterion for capturing a person's subjectivity, which holds that it is important for the depicted portrait to be distinguishable and recognizable. The likeness means the artist renders "the key aspects of a person's physiognomy or external appearance."[44] In the portrait painting titled *A Single Mom* (see Figure 6.2), there is a detailed rendering of eyebrows, hair, eyes, lips, and the shape of the face. Accurate likeness requires artists to study the face and appearance of the subject closely. However, Freeland believes simply capturing a figure's likeness does not guarantee to capture a person's subjectivity since photography could capture a sitter's likeness even better; still, the subjectivity and individuality of a person are not captured in every photo of that person. Photo IDs are the best examples to illustrate that facial likeness is merely a façade and represents only a single aspect of a person's identity that usually fails to capture their full personality.

The second factor of capturing a person's subjectivity in a portrait painting is *testimonies of presence*, which, in Freeland's words, means "the actual presence of a person in the sense of bringing a person there into contact with us."[45] As you can see in Figure 6.2,

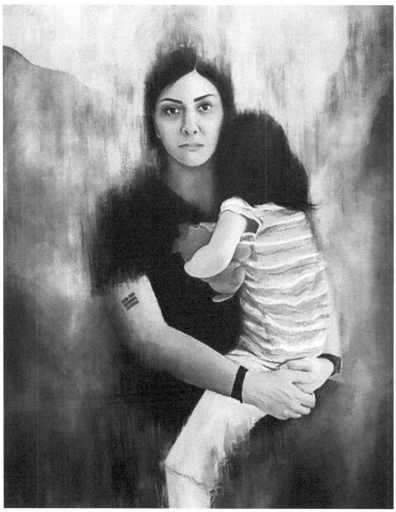

Figure 6.2: Elham Hajesmaeili. *A Single Mom*, 2019. Acrylic on canvas. Penn State University.

the mother seems as though she is emerging from the canvas carrying her baby. Here, the actual resemblance and her facial likeness are not as important as creating a connection with the viewer. In the portrait of the *A Single Mom*, the portrait confronts viewers with a direct gaze. Here, the eye contact with the portraiture is the key to creating a connection with viewers. In an interdisciplinary study, the authors used separate eye-tracking measurements and functional magnetic resonance imaging to investigate the neuronal and behavioral response to painted portraits with direct versus averted gaze.[46] The findings indicate that portraits where the subject is making direct eye contact with the viewer can activate the viewer's brain and prompt them to infer about the subject's mental states, emotions, and even anticipate their communicative intentions.[47] The authors discuss gaze as "an instrument of social communication" which modifies the perception of emotions and enables decoding of mental states, related to the process of theory of mind or mentalizing.[48] Through the recognition of gaze direction and eye contact as a *modulating cognitive process*, portraying research participants with a direct gaze in portrait paintings, enables viewers—whose roles often might not be sincerely considered in research—to more likely perceive the subjectivities of the participants accurately, encouraging them to initiate meaningful dialogue and paving the way for a more empathic and accessible approach to studying human experiences.[49]

The third way an artist can capture the subjectivity of a sitter is through *evocations of personality*.[50] This approach involves portraying the individual's unique characteristics, quirks, and mannerisms that define their personality and set them apart from others. The artist might use various techniques such as body language, clothing choices, or expressions to give the portrait a sense of the sitter's individuality and personality. While I am not a mother but rather an outsider in mothers' world, observing the mother's relationship with her child informs me to portray the child as the fundamental element in the mother's life. I intend to convey various psychological information about single motherhood through dark and gloomy colors in the backgrounds and by rendering the woman unapologetically carrying and protecting her child, giving viewers information about the psychological states of a single mom. For example, the detailed rendering of the hands tightly holding the child conveys the mother's deep concern and care for her daughter. Accordingly, the child's body language freely holding the stuffed doll represents the child understanding her mom is always on her side, watching her, and protecting her from the unknown and blurred world surrounding them; see Figure 6.2.

The last way of capturing subjectivity in portraiture is *presentation of a subject's uniqueness* meaning a person's essence or unique "air," or recognizable energy specified to the depicted person.[51] Citing Roland Barthes' discussion in *Camera Lucida*[52] in which he searches through images of his recently deceased mother to find one that captures her "air," Freeland states:

> In a blurry photograph that shows her as a young girl, he claims to find something that goes beyond resemblance, something he calls her "air" (the expression, the look). He says it is unanalyzable: 'The air is that exorbitant thing which induces from body to soul-animula, little individual soul, good in one person, bad in another.' He also describes the air as a 'kind of intractable supplement of identity.'[53]

Barthes, describing the "air" in the photo, states that "there remained a soul, ageless but not timeless since the air was the person I used to see, consubstantial with her face, each day of her long life."[54] In the portraiture of the single mom, there is a complex 'air' that comes from both the child and the mother, dominating the artwork and highlighting the woman's subjectivity as a mother; however, it is difficult to determine if I have truly captured the essence of the figures in my painting, as our experience of the world, particularly of other humans and artworks, is a complex interplay of both subjectivity and objectivity.[55] This complexity results in a unique perception of artwork for each individual, making it difficult to arrive at a definite answer, but the process of exploring the possibilities and contemplating the perspectives is a thrilling and thought-provoking journey.

AUGMENTED REALITY AS AN ANALYTICAL METHODOLOGY

Augmented reality as an innovative technology has the potential to revolutionize the way we view and analyze information. This technology blends the physical world with virtual elements, creating an environment where the boundaries between the two are blurred. In such environments, viewers are given the unique opportunity to not only observe and understand data, but to actively engage with it in a way that fosters deeper understanding, insights, and dialogue.[56] AR opens a new realm of possibilities for exploration and analysis, bridging the gap between traditional static data visualization and dynamic, immersive interaction with data that provoke emotions, conversations, and questions rather than passively transferring certain data.[57]

In this study, I leverage AR technology developed through *Unity*, a game design app, to create custom AR applications for each portrait painting. These apps are designed to identify the artwork as programmed and provide additional information associated with each portraited woman. To install and access the AR apps, users require an Android device, allowing them to scan the artworks and view the augmented information. All artworks and their corresponding augmented features are accessible to viewers via the following website: https://hajesmaeilielham.wixsite.com/mysite.

There are some technical characteristics in AR that can affect viewers through their expressive power, leading to an emotional experience. As a medium, AR allows viewers to explore the connections between the physical environment and the virtual information presented by the AR app, leading to experience of a potentially affective moment.[58] Simultaneous engagement with time, space, and the interplay of virtual and real elements endows artists with expressive, immersive, and artistic potential to affect people.[59] As part of my research for this project I analyzed the AR portrait painting in dialogue methodology through Ana Javornik's theory of AR characteristics to clarify AR potentials as methodological tools in constructing, analyzing, and visualizing data.[60] With the aim of affecting viewers through my AR artwork, I examined how and to what extent AR characteristics—including but not limited to interactivity, hypertextuality, modality, connectivity, location specificity, mobility, and virtuality—play roles in the context of my research to understand their significance in shaping my research methodology.[61] The left image in Figure 6.3, shows another portrait painting, titled *Harassment*, that I made of the second participant in my study; the picture on the right shows what viewers see when they use the AR app.

Virtuality

The utilization of AR as a form of artistic expression pushes the boundaries of traditional visual arts[62] and gives artists the

Figure 6.3: Elham Hajesmaeili. *Harassment*, 2020. Acrylic on canvas. Penn State University. Image description: Left: the original portrait painting; Right: a screenshot of AR features.

opportunity to tap into something known as *invisible visualities.*[63] Invisible visuality refers to a visual representation that is not immediately apparent but can be experienced through a different mode of perception or interaction. The process of augmentation enables artists to create some virtual elements that are initially imperceptible to viewers, allowing the artist to control viewers' exposure to these elements.[64] As a result, viewers can experience a fleeting moment to consciously recognize the process of perception, their shifts, and affections.[65] Virtuality as a crucial aspect of AR enables artists to overlay multimodal elements on their work without affecting the originality and authenticity of the artwork.[66] In Figure 6.3, the virtual auditory elements that I have augmented on the portraiture include the woman's voice narrating her story and the sound of a phone ringing. I have also augmented some visual elements, like the phone in the background of "Harassment" that blinks while ringing, followed by the subtle "bleeding" of the work by the end. Connecting physical painting with all its expressive marks, textures, and colors with virtual elements within the AR portraiture (Figure 6.3) allows viewers to experience a liminal space between virtuality and reality.

Interactivity

In the realm of AR art, interactivity is indispensable, as it requires viewers to access the entire content of the artwork by engaging with the medium and the message.[67] Viewers need a mediating device (a smartphone or tablet) to access an immaterial, invisible visuality networked to the spatial dimension of the immediate environment.[68] I am specifically interested in the created *flow*[69] as a result of collaboration of body and medium that potentially establishes perceived behavioral control, increases exploratory and participatory behavior, and creates positive subjective experiences.[70] Encountering AR art can lead to various other interactions, such as users being able to interact with AR applications and virtual and physical elements, as well as virtual elements being integrated into the real world.[71]

Effective interactivity in AR art requires responsiveness, partial control, and the avoidance of randomness,[72] which is particularly relevant in AR art where, for instance, the viewers' interactive roles in accessing the content significantly influence their aesthetic experience of the artwork.[73] By elaborating on the importance of interactivity in AR art, we can better analyze the concept of aesthetic interaction[74] and the aesthetic connectedness to the context, use, and instrumentality.[75] Since augmentation involves multisensory systems and crosses time and space dimensions that blur the virtual and physical realm,[76] viewers experience a kind of aesthetic interaction that facilitates the interpretation of meanings and emotional arousal.[77]

Modality

In AR art, modality refers to the use of static and dynamic multimedia elements that artists overlay on the artwork through an augmentation process.[78] For instance, in *A Single Mom* (Figure 6.2) the emergence of scales, along with the subject's voiceover accompanied by the sounds of swinging metal, connects viewers to the balancing act and injustices the subject is facing. Here, the combination of static and dynamic elements creates a new form of subjectivity for viewers affected by the blurred line between static reality and virtual, variable elements.[79] The same process happens in *Harassment* (Figure 6.3), where the sound of a phone ringing in the background abruptly pulls viewers out of the virtual world and into the physical space, emphasizing the trauma endured by the subject.

Hypertextuality

Hypertextuality refers to the relationship between two texts, where one text builds on, imitates, fulfills, or transforms the prior text.[80] In the context of this study, if we take AR art as a document (text), there are different signs and symbols on the painting and its AR app that could potentially create a non-linear, interconnected structure of information in which viewers can freely have their subjective interpretation. For instance, if we take the painting *Harassment* as hypotext (text A), and its AR features as the hypertext (Text B), the semiotic relationship between the painting's content (such as the phone in the background) and the way it transforms (to blinking and ringing in the AR app mimicking the way a phone rings in reality) creates a web of interconnected meanings that have the capacity to link to viewers' personal experiences and ultimately help viewers to deeply understand the traumatic experience portrayed in the artwork.

New media theorist Lev Manovich, in *The Poetics of Augmented Space*, describes augmentation as more than just technology; it is an idea, cultural practice, and aesthetic approach.[81] Augmentation has the capacity to transform a piece of art into a multimedial hypertext object[82] which has the potential to be a meaningful sociopolitical act.[83] From the phenomenological perspective of a human subject, the physical space is prioritized; but from a technological perspective and its social, political, and economic uses, the physical space is not more important than any other added dimensions.[84] This redefinition of space and reality challenges our concept of perception and expands the boundaries of what we consider real.[85] By combining an experimental moment with conscious awareness, augmentation offers a shift in perception and provokes emotional thinking.[86] In AR art, the semiotic connections between static content and dynamic AR features generate a network of meanings that dismantles the rigid view of painting as a purely visual medium and instead deepens viewers' perception and appreciation of the artwork.

Mobility

In the context of my research, mobility is crucial in two senses: the physical portability of devices; and the movement of images and information across different media on local, national, and global levels.[87] This two-fold understanding of mobility is essential to my research, as it allows for the widespread dissemination of research findings and utilizes mobile devices as mediators for engaging with audiences.

Connectivity

As a communication model, connectivity is often associated with social media.[88] While AR technology does not facilitate connectivity with as many parties as social media, it can be shared through social media, allowing for wider outreach. Taking advantage of the instrumental role of new media in political and social change,[89] I aim to reach a global audience through the website that provides interactive access to my research findings, including portrait paintings and downloadable AR apps.[90] By leveraging the potential of this platform, users can negotiate the contents and engage with the research beyond geographic borders.

Location Specificity

Location specificity refers to the Global Positioning System (GPS) that allows the tracking of a user's location through personal devices and delivering location-specific information; consequently, the location specificity could limit the access to AR content to a specific location.[91] My AR app's content is not linked to GPS; instead, the app tracks the portrait paintings so that it is not necessary to be in front of the original paintings. The images of the paintings could thus be displayed on a laptop screen or printed on a piece of paper. The augmented content is delivered as soon as the AR app recognizes the painting's image.

CONCLUSION

This chapter has highlighted the immense potential of AR portrait painting in dialogue as a novel research methodology that combines the efficiency and usability of new technologies with the creative and analytic potentials of art. By utilizing this methodology, it is possible to foster a collaborative and nonhierarchical research environment, where knowledge is constructed through multiple types of dialogue, emotion, and interaction, leading to more authentic and truthful research findings.

Combining art and technology as methodological facilitators equips artist-researchers with the means to represent their research beyond the traditional academic sphere, reaching a wider range of audiences, and potentially evoking social action. By prioritizing authenticity and truthfulness, this embodied arts-based research methodology offers a unique approach to humanities research that emphasizes equal participation and the deconstruction of hierarchical collaboration in academic research. Inspiring researchers to explore the creative and analytic potentials of combining new technologies and art in their work, AR portrait painting in dialogue offers a transformative approach to research that has the potential to break down traditional boundaries and open innovative avenues to overcome the limitations of conventional academic research. It is an exciting time for research, and we look forward to seeing the continued evolution and innovation of research methodologies in the future.

NOTES

1. Before diving into the heart of this chapter, please take a moment to visit the website https://hajesmaeilielham.wixsite.com/mysite to explore the AR artworks that will be discussed in this chapter.
2. Chadwick, "Embodied Methodologies," 55.
3. Eisner, "Art and Knowledge."
4. Eisner, "Promise and Perils," 4.
5. Bochner and Ellis, "Arts and Narrative Research," 511.
6. Kara, *Creative Research Methods*, 14.
7. Inckle, "Telling Tales?" 27.
8. Paakspuu, "Re-Reading the Portrait," 312.
9. Ortner, "Subjectivity and Cultural Critique." Ortner's definition of subjectivity works in the context of my research: "By subjectivity, I will mean the

ensemble of modes of perception, affect, thought, desire, fear, and so forth that animate acting subjects. But I always mean as well the cultural and social formations that shape, organize, and provoke those modes of affect, thought and so on," 31.

10. Massey, "Power-Geometry," 59.
11. Rice, "Imagining the Other?" 249.
12. Finlay, "Outing the Researcher," 531.
13. Riley, Schouten, and Cahill. "Exploring the Dynamics," paragraph 6.
14. Böck, "Whose Portrait is it?" 490.
15. CohenMiller "Visual Arts as a Tool," 22.
16. Eisner, "Art and Knowledge," 7.
17. Schertz, "Empathic Pedagogy," 8.
18. Schertz, "Empathic Pedagogy."
19. Bochner and Ellis, "Arts and Narrative Research," 510.
20. Lugones, "Playfulness," 3.
21. Rayner, "Audience," 21.
22. Eisner, "Art and Knowledge," 11.
23. Baptiste, "Managing Subjectivity," 503.
24. Rayner, "Audience," 13.
25. Rayner, "Audience," 13.
26. Rayner, "Audience," 20.
27. Richardson, "Writing," 375.
28. Massumi, *Politics of Affect*; O'Sullivan, "Aesthetics of Affect," 125.
29. Badiou, *Deleuze*, 84–5.
30. O'Sullivan, "The Aesthetics of Affect," 128.
31. Brennan, *The Transmission of Affect*, 5.
32. Labanyi, "Doing Things," 223.
33. Massumi, *Parables for the Virtual*, 219.
34. Ahmed, *Cultural Politics of Emotion*.
35. Guattari, *Chaosmosis*, 21.
36. Guattari, *Chaosmosis*, 7.
37. Labanyi, "Doing Things," 223.
38. Åhäll, "Affect as Methodology," 40.
39. Longenbach, *The Resistance to Poetry*.
40. Freeland, "Portraits in Painting"; Freeland, *Portraits and Persons*.
41. Freeland, "Portraits in Painting," 95.
42. Freeland, "Portraits in Painting," 100.
43. Freeland, "Portraits in Painting," 108.
44. Freeland, "Portraits in Painting," 100.

45. Freeland, "Portraits in Painting," 101.
46. Kesner et al., "Perception of direct vs. averted gaze," 125.
47. Kesner et al., "Perception of direct vs. averted gaze," 97.
48. Kesner et al., "Perception of direct vs. averted gaze," 88.
49. Kesner et al., "Perception of direct vs. averted gaze."
50. Freeland, "Portraits in Painting," 100.
51. Freeland, "Portraits in Painting," 100.
52. Barthes, *Camera lucida*.
53. Freeland, "Portraits in Painting," 102.
54. Barthes, *Camera lucida*, 110.
55. Freeland, "Portraits in Painting," 108.
56. D'Ignazio, "Feminist Data Visualization," 4.
57. Li, "Data Visualization," 309.
58. Craig, *Understanding Augmented Reality*.
59. Gwilt, "Augmented Reality."
60. Javornik, "Augmented Reality," 254.
61. Javornik, "Augmented Reality," 252.
62. Gould, "Invisible Visualities," 25.
63. Gould, "Invisible Visualities," 25. Invisible visualities implies that "no AR art-works are nakedly visible"; in other words, the body and the media (usually a smartphone) play collaborative roles in accessing invisible visualities.
64. Manovich, "Poetics of Augmented Space," 219.
65. Dolinsky, "Shifting Perceptions," 295.
66. Javornik, "Augmented Reality," 255. Javornik defines virtuality as the capacity of showing virtual elements or virtual worlds.
67. For more information about interactivity in AR see: chapter 6 in Craig, *Understanding Augmented Reality*; Suhr, "Audience and Artist Interactivity"; Liu and Shrum. "What is Interactivity?"
68. Gould, "Invisible Visualities," 27.
69. Csikszentmihalyi, *Finding flow*. Flow means a state of consciousness, concentration, and absorption in an activity.
70. Hoffman and Novak. "Flow Online," 24.
71. Craig, *Understanding Augmented Reality*, 66.
72. Smuts, "What is Interactivity?" 65.
73. Smuts, "What is Interactivity?" 61.
74. Petersen et al., "Aesthetic Interaction," 269. "Aesthetic interaction [...] can be obtained when the human body, intellect and all the senses are used in relation to interactive systems."
75. Petersen et al., "Aesthetic Interaction," 270.

76. Suhr, " Audience and Artist Interactivity," 120; Xiaobo and Yuelin, "Embodiment, Interaction and Experience," 168.
77. Xiaobo and Yuelin. "Embodiment, Interaction and Experience," 168.
78. Javornik, "Augmented Reality," 254. According to Javornik, modality refers to different formats/types of content by which information transfers to audiences, including audio and visual formats to enrich the communication process.
79. Suhr, "Audience and Artist Interactivity," 113.
80. Rosenberg. "Gérard Genette and Hypertextuality," 16.
81. Manovich, "Poetics of Augmented Space," 219.
82. Sergio Cicconi, "Hypertextuality," 26.
83. Lodi, "Spatial Narratives in Art," 277.
84. Manovich, "Poetics of Augmented Space," 219.
85. Lodi, "Spatial Narratives in Art," 283.
86. Dolinsky, "Shifting Perceptions," 295: "A perceptual shift is the cognitive recognition of having experienced something extra-marginal, on the boundaries of normal awareness, outside of conditioned attenuation." Dolinsky, "Visual Navigation Structures."
87. Sheller and Urry. "New Mobilities Paradigm," 212.
88. Javornik, "Augmented Reality," 255.
89. Keifer-Boyd, "(New) Media," 207.
90. https://hajesmaeilielham.wixsite.com/mysite
91. Javornik, "Augmented Reality," 255.

WORKS CITED

Åhäll, Linda. "Affect as Methodology: Feminism and the Politics of Emotion." *International Political Sociology* 12, no. 1 (2018): 36–52.

Ahmed, Sara. *Cultural Politics of Emotion*. Edinburgh: Edinburgh University Press, 2014.

Badiou, Alain. *Deleuze: The Clamor of Being*. Translated by Louise Burchill. Minnesota: University of Minnesota Press, 2000.

Baptiste, Lennise. "Managing Subjectivity in Arts Assessments." In *Reconceptualising the Agenda for Education in the Caribbean*, edited by Lynda Quamina-Aiyejina, 503–9. Washington: School of Education, 2008.

Barthes, Roland. *Camera lucida: Reflections on Photography*. Translated by Richard Howard. New York: Hill and Wang, 1981.

Bochner, Arthur P. and Carolyn Ellis. "An Introduction to the Arts and Narrative Research: Art as Inquiry." *Qualitative Inquiry* 9, no. 4 (2003): 506–14.

Böck, Angelika. "Whose Portrait is it?" *Critical Arts* 27, no. 5 (2013): 490–510.

Brennan, Teresa. *The Transmission of Affect.* Ithaca: Cornell University Press, 2004.

Chadwick, Rachelle. "Embodied Methodologies: Challenges, Reflections and Strategies." *Qualitative Research* 17, no. 1 (2017): 54–74.

Cicconi, Sergio. "Hypertextuality." In *Mediapolis: Aspects of Texts, Hypertexts and Multimedial Communication,* edited by Sam Inkinen, 21–43. Berlin: Walter de Gruyter, 1999.

CohenMiller, Anna S. "Visual Arts as a Tool for Phenomenology." In *Forum Qualitative Sozialforschung/Forum: Qualitative Social Research* 19, no. 1, (2018).

Craig, Alan B. *Understanding Augmented Reality: Concepts and Applications.* Waltham, MA: Elsevier, 2013.

Csikszentmihalyi, Mihaly. *Finding Flow: The Psychology of Engagement with Everyday Life.* New York: Basic Books, 1997.

D'Ignazio, Catherine. "What would Feminist Data Visualization Look Like?" MIT Center for Civic Media, December 1, 2015. https://civic.mit.edu/feminist-data-visualization

Dolinsky, Margaret. "Shifting Perceptions–Shifting Realities." In *Augmented Reality Art: From an Emerging Technology to a Novel Creative Medium*, edited by Vladimir Geroimenko, 295–304. Plymouth: Springer, 2014.

Dolinsky, Margaret. "Visual Navigation Structures in Collaborative Virtual Environments." In *Stereoscopic Displays and Virtual Reality Systems XI*, Proceedings of the International Society of Optical Engineering (SPIE) 5291, 517-24. San Jose, California: SPIE, 2004.

Eisner, Elliot. "Art and Knowledge." in *Handbook of the Arts in Qualitative Research: Perspectives, Methodologies, Examples, and Issues*, edited by J. Gary Knowles and Ardra L. Cole, 3–13. Thousand Oaks, CA: Sage, 2008.

Eisner, Elliot W. "The Promise and Perils of Alternative Forms of Data Representation." *Educational Researcher* 26, no. 6 (1997): 4–10.

Finlay, Linda. "'Outing' the Researcher: The Provenance, Process, and Practice of Reflexivity." *Qualitative Health Research* 12, no. 4 (2002): 531–45.

Freeland, Cynthia. "Portraits in Painting and Photography." *Philosophical Studies* 135, no. 1 (2007): 95–109.

Freeland, Cynthia. *Portraits and Persons.* New York: Oxford University Press, 2010.

Gould, Amanda Starling. "Invisible Visualities: Augmented Reality Art and the Contemporary Media Ecology." *Convergence* 20, no. 1 (2014): 25–32.

Guattari, Félix. *Chaosmosis: An Ethico-Aesthetic Paradigm.* Translated by Paul Bains and Julian Pefanis. Bloomington, IN: Indiana University Press, 1995.

Gwilt, Ian. "Augmented Reality and Mobile Art." In *Handbook of Multimedia for Digital Entertainment and Arts*, edited by Borko Furht, 593–99. Boston: Springer, 2009.

Hoffman, Donna L., and Thomas P. Novak. "Flow Online: Lessons Learned and Future Prospects." *Journal of Interactive Marketing* 23, no. 1 (2009): 23–34.

Inckle, Kay. "Telling Tales? Using Ethnographic Fictions to Speak Embodied 'Truth'." *Qualitative Research* 10, no. 1 (2010): 27–47.

Javornik, Ana. "Augmented Reality: Research Agenda for Studying the Impact of Its Media Characteristics on Consumer Behaviour." *Journal of Retailing and Consumer Services* 30 (2016): 252–61.

Kara, Helen. *Creative Research Methods in the Social Sciences: A Practical Guide*. Bristol: Policy Press, 2015.

Keifer-Boyd, Karen T. "(New) Media." In *Gender: Sources, Perspectives, and Methodologies*, edited by Renée C. Hoogland, 207–20. Farmington Hills, MI: Macmillan, 2016.

Kesner, Ladislav, Dominika Grygarová, Iveta Fajnerová, Jiří Lukavský, Tereza Nekovářová, Jaroslav Tintěra, Yuliya Zaytseva, and Jiří Horáček. "Perception of direct vs. averted gaze in portrait paintings: An fMRI and eye-tracking study." *Brain and Cognition* 125 (2018): 88–99.

Labanyi, Jo. "Doing Things: Emotion, Affect, and Materiality." *Journal of Spanish Cultural Studies* 11, no. 3–4 (2010): 223–33.

Liu, Yuping, and Lawrence J. Shrum. "What is Interactivity and Is It Always Such a Good Thing? Implications of Definition, Person, and Situation for the Influence of Interactivity on Advertising Effectiveness." *Journal of Advertising* 31, no. 4 (2002): 53–64.

Lodi, Simona. "Spatial Narratives in Art." In *Augmented Reality Art: From an Emerging Technology to a Novel Creative Medium*, edited by Vladimir Geroimenko, 277–94. Plymouth: Springer, 2014.

Longenbach, James. *The Resistance to Poetry*. Chicago: University of Chicago Press, 2004.

Lugones, María. "Playfulness, 'World'-Traveling, and Loving Perception." *Hypatia* 2, no. 2 (1987): 3–19.

Manovich, Lev. "The Poetics of Augmented Space." *Visual Communication* 5, no. 2 (2006): 219–240.

Massey, Doreen. "Power-Geometry and a Progressive Sense of Place," in *Mapping the Futures: Local Cultures, Global Change*, edited by Jon Bird, Barry Curtis, Tim Putnam, and George Robertson, 59–69. New York: Routledge, 2004.

Massumi, Brian. *Parables for the Virtual: Movement, Affect, Sensation*. Durham, NC: Duke University Press, 2002.

Massumi, Brian. *Politics of Affect*. Cambridge: Wiley, 2015.

Ortner, Sherry B. "Subjectivity and Cultural Critique." *Anthropological Theory* 5, no. 1 (2005): 31–52.

O'Sullivan, Simon. "The Aesthetics of Affect: Thinking Art Beyond Representation." *Angelaki: Journal of the Theoretical Humanities* 6, no. 3 (2001): 125–35.

Paakspuu, Kalli. "Re-Reading the Portrait and the Archive's Social Memory." *Canadian Review of American Studies* 46, no. 3 (2016): 311–38.

Petersen, Marianne Graves, Ole Sejer Iversen, Peter Gall Krogh, and Martin Ludvigsen. "Aesthetic Interaction: A Pragmatist's Aesthetics of Interactive Systems." In *Proceedings of the 5th Conference on Designing Interactive Systems: Processes, Practices, Methods, and Techniques*, 269–76. New York: ACM Press, 2004.

Rayner, Alice. "The Audience: Subjectivity, Community and the Ethics of Listening." *Journal of Dramatic Theory and Criticism* (1993): 3–24.

Rice, Carla. "Imagining the Other? Ethical Challenges of Researching and Writing Women's Embodied Lives." *Feminism & Psychology* 19, no. 2 (2009): 245–66.

Richardson, Laurel. "Writing: A Method of Inquiry." in *Turning Points in Qualitative Research: Tying Knots in a Handkerchief* 2, edited by Yvonna S. Lincoln and Norman K. Denzin, 379–96. Walnut Creek, CA: Altamira Press, 2003.

Riley, Sarah, Wendy Schouten, and Sharon Cahill. "Exploring the Dynamics of Subjectivity and Power Between Researcher and Researched." *Forum: Qualitative Sozialforschung/Forum: Qualitative Social Research* 4, no. 2 (2003).

Rosenberg, Gil. "Gérard Genette and Hypertextuality." In *Exploring Intertextuality: Diverse Strategies for New Testament Interpretation of Texts*, edited by Brisio J. Oropeza and Steve Moyise, 16–28. Hershey, PA: IGI Global, 2016.

Schertz, Matthew. "Empathic Pedagogy: Community of Inquiry and the Development of Empathy." *Analytic Teaching* 26, no. 1 (2006): 8–14.

Sheller, Mimi, and John Urry. "The New Mobilities Paradigm." *Environment and Planning A: Economy and Space* 38, no. 2 (2006): 207–26.

Smuts, Aaron. "What is Interactivity?" *The Journal of Aesthetic Education* 43, no. 4 (2009): 53–73.

Suhr, H. Cecilia. "The Audience and Artist Interactivity in Augmented Reality Art: The Solo Exhibition on the *Flame* Series." *Critical Arts* 32, no. 3 (2018): 111–25.

Xiaobo, Lu, and Liu Yuelin. "Embodiment, Interaction and Experience: Aesthetic Trends in Interactive Media Arts." *Leonardo* 47, no. 2 (2014): 166–9.

CHAPTER 7

THE IMPERATIVE OF PREPARING LANGUAGE TEACHING PROFESSIONALS FOR VR/XR ENVIRONMENTS

Fabiola P. Ehlers-Zavala and Jay Schnoor

For many language learners around the world, learning English is their primary personal, professional, and academic goal as English is recognized for its key role in global communication and professional advancement. Yet despite the prominent and hegemonic role of English, not all learners, especially those in countries where English is not the dominant language, have opportunities to interact with others through English in authentic situations (Chien et al., 2020). Therefore, especially in contexts where opportunities for authentic interaction are few, the role of technology becomes critically important as technology can help language professionals offer opportunities to language learners that can be meaningful and much more authentic than when technology is not available or present in an educational context.

In today's world, being able to provide language learners with experiential learning in the language class via immersive technologies, such as virtual reality (VR) and extended reality (XR), is increasingly more possible than ever before. Their primary advantage is that, with the use of virtual simulations in 3D environments, they offer language teachers the opportunity to bring the world to their language learners. This experience allows language learners to engage more fully with the teaching and learning process as most, if not all their senses, will become activated or engaged as they interact with simulated worlds. In doing so, they have real chances to develop and acquire language skills, with particular attention to nurturing their intercultural/cross-cultural competence to function as global citizens. In doing so, language learners will be demonstrating proficiency and attainment of one of the main World Readiness Standards for foreign language acquisition put forward by the American Council on the Teaching of Foreign Languages (ACTFL) in their goals document known as the 5Cs (communication, cultures, connections, comparisons, communities). Further, learners can now have an opportunity to truly demonstrate language learning through more real contexts and engage in meaningful autonomous self-directed learning (Ou Yang et al., 2020). Through virtual environments, language learners in all parts of the globe can thus now have the world at their fingertips, without limitations previously experienced, to help them demonstrate how they can effectively function in the world in culturally appropriate ways.

In the literature of language teacher preparation, the topic and discussion of the role of technology in language learning has a long-standing tradition. In the field of teachers of English to speakers of other languages (TESOL), for example, two key comprehensive accounts of the work related to technology and language learning are found in the edited collections by Farr and Murray (2016) and Chapelle and Sauro (2017). However, much of the scholarship is spread across journal venues. Most of it is likely to appear in technology-focused journals (*CALICO Journal, Computers & Education, Language Learning & Technology, Educational Technology & Society, Computer-Assisted Language Learning, ReCALL*, and so on). In TESOL/applied linguistics, as an area of study, most of the research has fallen under computer-assisted language learning (CALL), a subfield of applied linguistics, which Chun (2019) argues should be more "aptly designated as Technology Enhanced Language Learning (TELL)" (14).

Some researchers (for example, Chun, 2019; Wang, 2021) have indicated that the origins of CALL can be traced back to the 1960s while others (for example, Kalyaniwala and Ciekanski, 2021) have noted that CALL was fully introduced in the field of TESOL and applied linguistics in the early 1980s, when it emerged as a professional paper delivered at the TESOL International Annual Meeting. Either way, with more than fifty years in existence, CALL or TELL has certainly evolved in time as our understandings of effective language teaching and learning have also advanced, ranging from behaviorist to more recent ecological perspectives (Chun, 2019). Yet, despite its evolution, in theory and practice, Ziegler et al. (2017) pointed out that few studies have accounted for the use of "intelligent CALL systems to deepen our understanding of the process and products of second language (L2) learning" (219), suggesting the need for more research on this realm to continue to inform pedagogical approaches in language teaching and learning.

It is also worth noting that despite the long history of the role of technology in supporting language instruction, efforts to advocate for its inclusion in the curriculum of language teacher preparation have proven only somewhat effective. The integration of technology in both language instruction and in the preparation of language teachers has typically been explored or enacted by those with a specific and concerted interest in it. As it currently stands, in the United States, where we experience a decentralized approach to education as compared to other countries around the world, programs for language teacher preparation vary outside of the common core that attends to knowledge of language, culture, instruction, assessment, and professionalism, as outlined in TESOL standards for language teacher preparation. Beyond the core courses, and though TESOL developed a separate document that articulates technology standards in TESOL (Kessler, 2016), variation among language teacher preparation programs, to some significant extent, has typically reflected faculty's areas of expertise or specialization. In other words, in language teacher preparation programs that lack faculty with expertise in the use of technology for purposes of language teaching and learning, the development of the technological competence on the part of pre-service or in-service teachers enrolled in those programs is simply not a viable option. When that is the case, the potential development or acquisition of a technological competence on the part of pre-service or in-service language teachers is likely to be mediated by their own interest in or curiosity regarding technology, or what they observe their professors doing during course delivery. Or as Hanson-Smith (2016) more succinctly and bluntly put it: "Past and current practices in language teacher education have often relegated training in technology to elective coursework, or even worse, left student teachers to their own devices" (210).

Consequently, unless teachers in training take individual action to seek professional development related to technology outside their own programs, their skills and knowledge concerning the role of technology to support language instruction, more than likely, will be highly limited. Further, it has been argued that, at times, fear regarding the perceived potential of technology to replace language teachers may also play a role in the desire (or lack thereof) to actively embrace the role of technology in language teacher preparation. Kessler (2016) discusses, for instance, how ACTFL felt the need to issue a position statement that underscored the importance of considering technology as a tool to assist language teaching and learning as opposed to a goal in itself—a goal that, as it was noted, could run the risk of replacing language teachers.

Thus, despite efforts to advocate for the incorporation of technology in the curriculum of language teacher preparation, the reality is that, in the United States (and quite likely around the world), those efforts or actions have remained optional or approached with much caution despite multiple acknowledgments across decades of its benefits when properly implemented. The question we would like to raise at this point in this chapter is: In a world that aims at narrowing the digital divide to achieve social justice (that is, be more inclusive, provide greater access to quality education to those that may face diverse constraints—financial, physical, learning, and so on), should the integration of technology in language teacher preparation increase and expand to include VR/XR as a compulsory element?

With the context just described and being fully cognizant of some of the challenges that must be overcome (fear by teachers for perceived potential to be replaced by technology; limited up-to-date infrastructure; and lack of financial resources, among others), in this chapter we issue a call for expanding language teacher preparation to consider the systematic training in the use of current technologies in the curriculum of language teacher preparation courses. In doing so, we believe in the need to fully engage with VR/XR advances to make the most of what technology can offer. Central to the current conversations among TESOL and applied linguistics professionals is the goal of preparing teachers with the understandings and skills needed to achieve equity and social justice in our professional settings. By increasing access and inclusivity to diverse learners in higher education, domestic or international, through the use of digital learning and teaching, including VR and XR, institutions of higher education are contributing to narrowing the social divide, bringing us closer to achieving social justice goals in education (Ndubuisi et al., 2022). When properly implemented by language teachers, as noted at the start of this chapter, new immersive technologies can help us provide greater access to meaningful language teaching and learning experiences to more learners than ever before, even those who may not have the opportunity or resources to travel to places where English is used for day-to-day communication. Unlike those of us who learned English as another language prior to the advent of the internet, learners from around the world are now being born in a world that was impacted by the COVID-19 pandemic. Chang and Gomes (2022) noted that, due to the COVID-19 pandemic in 2020, "online delivery became the sole mode of education in many education institutions across the world" (119), which is consistent with what others had previously highlighted. Kern (2021), in talking about the impact of COVID-19, pointed out that such an event "put digital literacies at the heart of *all* learning" (134), and language teaching and learning are no exception. In fact, here is what language teachers need to be fully cognizant of: "Digital literacies integrate listening, speaking, viewing, reading, writing, and critical thinking, along with the skills necessary to operate digital devices and navigate their various resources" (Kern, 2021: 143). For this reason, at the very least, it is imperative that language teachers be equipped with the necessary technological knowledge and skills needed to make a difference in their work with language learners in today's classrooms. This effort will require learning about immersive technologies that have the potential to achieve positive outcomes in language teaching and learning.

Further, teachers of English to speakers of other languages in the United States or around the globe are major players in the internationalization of education on university campuses. They are not only responsible for teaching language, but also for helping develop their learners' intercultural competence. This important goal in turn contributes to the cultivation of a global mindset that learners need to effectively interact with others from diverse backgrounds (linguistic, cultural, social, abilities, and so forth). Bringing learners from around the globe together is happening through virtual environments. In fact, international education and campus internationalization are transforming rapidly, embracing what has come to be known as virtual internationalization (VI) (Bruhn-Zass, 2022).

Particularly, in this context, the teaching of English is fundamental for student participation in international higher education, especially at top-ranked institutions situated in the English-speaking countries that attract the highest numbers of international students (United States, United Kingdom, and Australia). While there is still (and will continue to be) a social divide in terms of who can access this type of higher education through VI, it cannot be denied that nowadays there is greater access to it, and VR and XR environments are part of the new normal. As Bruhn-Zass (2022) noted, very quickly the new normal is becoming hybrid internationalization in higher education. Therefore, this reality, exacerbated by the COVID-19 pandemic, offers yet another reason for the imperative of educating teachers of English to speakers of other languages on how to effectively deploy these new technologies so that learners can participate in the new educational opportunities that are becoming increasingly available.

Consequently, this chapter is intended to accomplish four goals. First, keeping in mind key critical questions related to technology and language teaching, it highlights key findings from published research on the topic of the integration of technology in language teaching and learning, focusing on the need to consider immersive technologies and their effectiveness in language learning. This discussion aims at underscoring the value of immersive technologies in the humanities and, particularly, in the field of TESOL/applied linguistics (for example, Lan et al., 2015; Godwin-Jones, 2016; Sánchez Bolado, 2017; Lan et al., 2018; Alfadil, 2020; Lan, 2020; Pegrum, 2021). Second, it acknowledges challenges discussed in the literature. Third, it advocates for building institutional partnerships with the public and private sectors to make immersive technologies increasingly more accessible and affordable to achieve a more socially just society. Finally, it outlines directions for future research, including the need to engage in replication studies to build a robust body of knowledge on the effectiveness of immersive technologies in language teaching and learning.

CRITICAL QUESTIONS IN TECHNOLOGY AND LANGUAGE TEACHING

In the preface of *English Language Learning and Technology*, Chappelle (2003) reminds us that people typically comment on how technologies quickly change. She also notes that, despite the fast-changing environment of the world we live in, there are timeless questions. For Chapelle, these questions include:

> How does technology intersect with language teaching practices in ways that benefit learning? How can research on second language acquisition help to inform the design of technology-based language learning? How can the learning accomplished through technology be evaluated? How do technology-based practices influence and advance applied linguistics? (xi)

While the questions remain a concern for language teaching professionals, the frustration she expresses in her own book probably remains in place, not only for her but for all of us involved in language teacher preparation two decades later. Chapelle (2003) attempts to make a case for the "imperative for applied linguistics and technology" (173), and the questions she once raised for technology in general remain true for its advancements in VR and XR. Therefore, with these questions in mind, we will highlight some key findings from research pertaining to immersive technologies.

WHAT VR AND XR RESEARCH TELLS US

For quite some time now, language teachers and researchers have been interested in virtual environments for their perceived potential as well as for the identified benefits to language teaching and learning (Peterson, 2016; Shadiev et al., 2020). In fact, Peterson notes that positive findings in the research include:

- Learner-centered interaction
- Engagement and participation enhanced
- Target language (TL) output elicited
- Meaning negotiation
- Social interaction involving peer collaboration in the TL
- Exploratory learning
- Risk-taking
- Inhibition and anxiety reduced
- Development of learner autonomy
- Motivation enhanced
- Knowledge of the TL culture increased
- Avatars may support immersion (316)

Thus, it is not surprising to continue to observe, as technology advances, what Lan (2020) notes:

VR is becoming a new favorite of both researchers and educators due to its ability to provide hands-on and being there experiences. It is highly worthwhile to investigate how to effectively and efficiently use VR as a learning environment for enhancing the SLA of FL learners. According to Lan (2016), whenever VR is adopted for pedagogical purposes in the field of language learning, the following elements should be considered: Learners, linguistic knowledge and competence, and the process of acquiring the language. FL researchers and educators must focus on providing each individual with precise suggestions and scaffolding during the VR exploration process. (9)

In fact, in educational research in general, students have noted the following advantages of VR (McClendon and Riggall, 2019: 140):

- Visualization
- In scale

- Extreme reality
- Simulations
- The potential for active design-based learning

Thus, recent accounts give increasing testimony to the positive in the world of VR. For instance, Bucea-Maea-Țoniş et al. (2020) argue that "VR and AR associated with collaborative learning bring about two other advantages: deep comprehensive learning facilitated by the 'learning-by-doing effect,' as well as the engagement of all the senses at the same time during simulated reality" (2). They also note that collaborative learning "can strengthen positive attitudes towards learning, improve performance in academic results, and enhance self-esteem, by promoting interaction and mutual support among young people" (1). These advantages are exactly what language teachers will want to consider to be able to provide an enhanced language experience environment to learners conducive to successful language acquisition/learning. After all, as Lee and Egbert (2016) point out, "when the use of technology makes the language task more engaging or more effective, greater learner achievement can be expected" (187).

The available research on the impact of VR on language learning is more recent (that is, in the last decade or two) and relatively new (Parmaxi, 2023). There is still plenty of work to tackle in this regard. In examining accounts related to VR, what research reveals is that the "various VR applications for language education can be roughly classified into five categories based on different pedagogical purposes: visual experiences, entertainment, social networking, operation, and creation" (Lan 2020, 3). Emerging research in VR offers a positive account of its benefits. Ho et al. (2011) demonstrate the potential of using VR in a language curriculum to improve learners' ability to engage in activities that enable multimodal meaning-making. Chen (2016) shows the positive effects of task-based learning that involves VR, affirming the potential of more fully engaging language learners in their educational journey.

Alfadil (2020) accounts for the positive impact of VR on vocabulary learning for language learners learning English as a foreign language. Chien et al. (2020) also provide evidence for the positive effects on learners' speaking abilities. Further, more than a decade ago, it had already become evident that immersive virtual environments had already enjoyed great popularity due to the expansion of gamification available online (Chen et al., 2011). Similar to research cited above, Bucea-Manea-Țoniș et al.'s (2020) research even accounts for what students find advantageous about VR: the 3D experience itself (clarity, visualization, manipulation, dynamic interaction), attractiveness, motivation, opportunity for the use of creativity, facilitation of learning (comprehension, for instance), joyful learning, and hands-on/experiential learning.

When it comes to XR, the era of XR is here (Hillmann, 2021). Previously, Pomerantz (2019), while acknowledging standing challenges (for example, time, skills, and cost), had noted that XR technologies were being used to optimize learning across various categories or domains. It has been demonstrated that XR and experiential learning constitute a great fit (Pomerantz, 2019). In fact, Bucea-Manea-Țoniș et al. (2020) argue that XR is associated with collaborative learning and it "offers a further advantage by facilitating deep comprehensive learning" (1). VR also has the potential of promoting the development or acquisition of intercultural competence (Shadiev et al., 2020)—a skill that, no doubt, will serve language learners well in a world where it is now possible to connect with someone across the globe instantly.

For decades, language teacher preparation has embraced the concepts of multimodality and recognized the value of embodied learning. Language educators know full well the value of appealing to all sensory modalities on the part of language learners to increase engagement in the classroom. In fact, as any language specialist knows, when language learners are not engaged, language learning is not going to take place effectively. Thus, embodied language learning through the use of XR offers an opportunity to more fully engage learners in the *experience* of language learning. Further, in describing XR, Bucea-Manea-Țoniș et al. (2020) note:

> The XR experience affects all the senses: visual (using hamlets, neurotransmitters, goggles: head-mounted displays (HMD), Oculus Rift), auditory (e.g., audio tools such as Oculus or KAI Tech), tactile (using haptic devices to send vibrations/electrostatic shock: gloves, backpacks, etc.), olfactory (devices that change the smell in the VR environment), and taste (which works more as an autosuggestion facilitated by the visual and auditory senses). These applications use bodysuits and vibration controllers for the kinetic stimulation of the entire body. All these elements have to be considered as part of the new teaching methodologies. (3)

Thus, following their research findings, they conclude that students are excited and prefer XR because of the "high interactivity, the requirement for motivation and enthusiasm, and the opportunities for experimentation and simulation" (15). Thus, they advocate for having universities "adopt these technologies and develop new methodologies of training and teaching in accordance with millennial expectations and the technological revolution (modern mobile technologies, interaction with AI, ubiquitous computing and technology, real-time communication with students, and continuous interactions between universities and companies)" (15).

In sum, research has shown in recent years that VR (immersive or non-immersive) as well as XR technologies are of increasing importance to language professionals and learners themselves. Work in immersive technologies can be very much supported by sociocultural theories of language teaching and learning and up-to-date approaches to theories of second language teaching and learning (Lan, 2020). As Kaplan-Rakowski and Meseberg (2019) note when discussing the role of immersive technologies, telepresence "is the key factor to open a range of opportunities to create and experience presence, empathy, and immersion" (153). Furthermore, it can be argued that such interest has been enhanced by the global pandemic that basically forced educators to venture into unanticipated teaching scenarios resulting from the sudden transition to remote teaching and learning—a challenge met to varying degrees by educators due to their own skills and comfort levels in the use of technologies.

CHALLENGES

When it comes to the utilization of technology for educational purposes, challenges or limitations have been easily identified. In addition to what Peterson (2016) notes as potential challenges (risk of technostress, training, sociocultural concerns, for example), Lee and Egbert (2016) reference previous accounts that highlight how diverse educational contexts were limited in many different regards, including:

- Limited general access to technology
- Limited internet connections
- No software
- Mandated software
- Limited hardware
- Set curriculum
- Limited time
- Large classes
- Limited teacher training
- Limited funding for any aspect of technology
- Limited administrative support
- Lack of culturally relevant electronic resources
- Student lack of strategies for electronic media use (186)

Though Lee and Egbert acknowledge that the causes behind these challenges may differ, and that solutions may vary from context to context, we know that these challenges will remain the reality for many educational settings. It is also not difficult to anticipate that these challenges will, in varying degrees, likely remain barriers to the adoption of technological advances, such as of VR and XR. Finding solutions will take time, but progress (for example, affordable cost) is starting to unfold and the educational adoption (which has historically fallen behind other industries, such as commercial, government, health sectors, and so forth) has been increasing (McClendon and Squires, 2019). We know that this work, in any case, will require much resilience and collaboration with both public and private entities on the part of those working to overcome these significant obstacles.

Thus, it is evident that adoption and effective implementation of immersive technologies will not be without challenges. In line with the list presented earlier, challenges will likely relate to knowledge, skills, implementation, professional support, cost, and infrastructure, to mention a few (see Lan, 2020). Research by Bucea-Manea-Țoniș et al. (2020) shows that students themselves accounted for these challenges:

> Students think that the most notable disadvantages of VR's inclusion in the e-learning process are cost and technical issues. The equipment used for VR is very expensive and increases the cost of studies. Sometimes technical issues, such as low-resolution content, large file sizes, or a slow or unreliable Internet connection can affect the e-learning process. Other disadvantages associated with e-learning platforms are isolation and the lack of hands-on teaching. Students may feel isolated or miss social interaction (before discovering the forum), and the instructor may not always be available on demand, affecting the teaching flow. (13)

Finally, consistent with what Chun et al. (2016) had previously pointed out regarding critics' concerns, Murray et al. (2020) mention the potential of immersive technologies of becoming distractive technologies if not properly deployed or used by learners. Thus, Murray et al. (2020) propose working towards ensuring that teachers engage learners in critical literacy practices for meaningful and productive work. If these challenges are not met or overcome, they will very likely limit our ability to reach the ultimate goals of using technology to bridge the existing and continuously growing digital divide, thus perpetuating social inequalities around the globe. In the end, a healthy approach may be the one articulated by Kern and Malinowski (2016), who view challenges as opportunities to find creative solutions and see the value that technology offers in blurring some of the significant challenges that can impede educational and social advances (such as spatial, temporal, cultural, and material boundaries).

ADVOCACY

With the goal of advancing the work related to technology and language teaching, including its consistent incorporation in teacher preparation, advocacy will be needed at different levels and for different purposes. In fact, what will be needed is a collaborative and concerted effort to achieve equity in the use of technology and language teaching and learning.

Regarding language teacher preparation, greater advocacy in the preparation of language teachers to use technology is required, and such effort must be ongoing. It is imperative that professional organizations continue to play a role in this process. Examples such as the ACTFL (2017) position statement on the "Role of Educators in Technology-Enhanced Language Learning" need to be supported or replicated by all professional organizations that influence language teacher preparation at all levels (international, national, state, and local). Fortunately, though more work is needed to keep them at the center of our conversations and curricular improvements for language teacher preparation, some of these accounts do exist. As Chun (2019) notes:

> The role of technology has been recognized in certain teacher education standards, e.g., in Europe (Kelly, Grenfell, Allan, Kriza,

& McEvoy, 2004) and in the U.S. (ACTFL, 2013), and specific technology-focused standards have been developed, e.g., the TESOL Technology Standards (Healey et al., 2011) and the ISTE Standards (International Society for Technology in Education, 2008)" (17).

Furthermore, accrediting bodies (such as the Commission on English Language Program Accreditation, known as CEA) can also influence the work of language teacher preparation by incorporating clear standards that address the development of technological skills on the part of language teachers. Today's society basically demands the use of technology as a fundamental need. As we work towards a more equitable world, all teachers and learners ought to have meaningful access to technology, including VR/XR. In fact, the new normal is likely to involve being well-versed in all contemporary technologies for which professional development must be ongoing.

Concerning the overcoming and eradication of barriers towards greater equitable advancement of technology in language teaching, partnerships will be needed with those that may be key to deploying resources: governments, private sector, philanthropic entities, and so forth. Experts representing diverse areas are needed to find solutions to already identified areas that merit attention to ensure that immersive technologies are implemented to positively transform language education, and education in general. One example of meaningful and significant collaboration is the work generated by EDUsummIT:

> EduSummIT is a global community of policy-makers, researchers, and educators working together to move education into the digital age. The EDUsummIT community recognizes the need to respond to the challenges of a world transformed by globalization and economic transformation, caused to a large degree by the development of digital networking technologies. The EDUsummIT seeks to engage educational leaders from across the world in conversations framed around issues and challenges facing education today

and through that dialog, develop action items that are based on research evidence.

(Voogt and Knesek, 2019: 1)

Thus, working groups have been formed, and must continue to be formed, to work towards finding solutions to the issues identified, leading to real collaborative practices intended to address the various priorities.

Governments also need to prioritize access to technology. Fortunately, the United States, through the Bipartisan Infrastructure Deal (that is, the Infrastructure Investment and Jobs Act), may now have a unique opportunity to lead the way by ensuring that more Americans have access to a broadband infrastructure, which is *one* important step towards making technology more accessible and equitable, though many other challenges will still need to be addressed as well. These challenges include critical digital literacy, financial resources needed to afford newer technologies, and understanding how to make the most of having the opportunity to connect with others, as noted by Turner Lee (2022)—author of the upcoming book *Digitally Invisible: How the Internet Is Creating the New Underclass*. She points out, "At $65 billion, broadband funding from the now enacted Infrastructure Investment and Jobs Act (IIJA), will be the largest-ever digital infrastructure investment and the first since the 2009 American Recovery and Reinvestment Act (ARRA), which allocated $4.7 billion to close the digital divide" (1).

In other words, as Voogt and Knezek (2016) put it:

> It is increasingly agreed upon that the implementation of digital technologies in education needs a systemic approach in which stakeholders at the micro, meso and macro levels of the education system actively interact with each other to align the needs of learners and the potential of technology with requirements of educational systems" (1).

Indeed, work towards meeting this challenge or narrowing this social gap when it comes to a digital divide will need the combined support of governments and all other entities that have as a goal a more socially just and equitable world. Or as it more commonly said in proverbial terms: "It takes a village to raise a child."

DIRECTIONS FOR FUTURE VR / XR RESEARCH

Eutsler and Long (2021) note, "more research is needed at the intersection of technology, design, and pedagogy when integrating VR" (28). Indeed, given the relative newness of VR and XR in the world of language teaching and learning, more research is needed to move away from the positive or promising, yet limited and provisional findings, as suggested by Peterson (2016), to more robust and definitive findings. Extensive and sound research is what is needed to build the arguments for enlisting support at all levels in society (governments, private sector, philanthropic efforts). This effort will contribute to level the playing field as far as technology in general is concerned, and more specifically, for our purposes, VR/XR research. As we think about the future of VR and XR research and its impact on language teaching, and consistent with what Chapelle observed back in 2007 for language teaching research in general, three fundamental areas continue to be of utmost importance to us in the field of language teaching and learning: "the role of replication, the need for synthesis, and the infelicity of educational research design—are critical for those of us who attempt to draw implications from research in hopes of improving teaching and learning" (405).

Moreover, these areas need to be explored in relation to a variety of contexts: face-to-face, hybrid, and fully online. Hokanson and Norden (2019) note the growth that online learning (synchronous or asynchronous) has consistently experienced, yet Lee (2016) states that "no evidence from L2 research studies has been found regarding the potency of digital technologies on learner autonomy within a fully online context," (82) clearly highlighting one area of much needed research. Therefore, in light of what research suggests, we present a list of areas that we believe merit attention and can serve us well if further addressed in research endeavors. Here is what we believe needs to be prioritized in VR/XR research.

- **Mixed studies.** Given that most of the published research has been quantitative in nature (Chun, 2019), it is imperative that qualitative research be generated to offer deeper insights into the role of technology and language instruction. This work needs to be addressed for fully online, hybrid, and face-to-face learning environments.
- **Replication research.** As Handley (2018) notes, replication research is fundamental to develop valid and reliable accounts for what works in the field of CALL. Understanding the power of research is key to building a solid understanding of evidence-based approaches that can truly inform the future use and applicability of CALL, especially when it comes to VR and XR, to also merit the investment in the infrastructure needed to deploy these emerging technologies to meet the expected levels of satisfaction.
- **Longitudinal studies.** Ultimately, as with other types of educational research, it is necessary to not only examine practices in the short term, but in the long term to fully assess the impact of properly implemented immersive technologies. Longitudinal studies are needed to develop sound practices in the field of language education.
- **Meta-analyses.** Of much importance in building a coherent understanding of proven robust research will be the formulation of meta-analyses. Meta-analyses have the power to provide a sound account of what works and what does not in the incorporation of immersive technologies in language teaching and learning. Such an

account is necessary to inform resource allocation for effective, efficient, and meaningful implementation of immersive technologies in language education and the preparation of language teachers.

As was the case at the turn of the century with Chappelle's call for explicitly studying how technology is changing the practices of applied linguistics, we must continue to work along that path. In addition to indicating and explaining how VR and XR have changed the practices of applied linguists as researchers or language teaching professionals, research is needed to account for what is working or not working with language learners in a variety of contexts to more adequately and accurately inform language teaching practices as well as the development of new technologies and professional development support.

In pandemic times, understanding the potential of VR and XR in language teaching and learning is fundamental to provide access to quality education to language learners around the world. Further research on VR and XR is needed to understand how to redesign or reconfigure learning spaces, as it has been clearly demonstrated that we must prepare to accept the fact that digital natives are not, and do not have to be, confined to the physical space of a traditional classroom to learn. Therefore, we need to understand what is needed to optimize their language learning within the classroom and beyond.

FINAL REMARKS

Consistent with what Lan (2019) has noted, in this era, we (language educators, researchers, and advocates) have witnessed the impressive speed at which technology has evolved. Of course, with new developments skepticism and reticence also emerge. Many will likely question whether all of this innovative work is worth pursuing from many angles (resources, budgets, time, effort, and so forth) (Kaplan-Rakowski and Meseberg, 2019). Different positions will be debated, justifiably so. However, it is incumbent upon us, and our programs, to ensure that our graduates have the necessary opportunities to fully participate in this global economy as they learn to put to practice their critical competencies, one of which is technology. In a world that seems to grow in inequities, technology may provide us with one important key to bring everyone to a better place. If anything, the lockdown we experienced resulting from the COVID-19 pandemic forced us to navigate our worlds virtually. In many places around the world, the need for digital literacies within this pandemic became evident, as even developing economies have expected their citizens to use technologies in order to function in society to meet basic social needs (to buy food, communicate, attend to medical needs, request transportation), and in many of those places, the concern is with those who are not digital natives (such as the elderly and those with special needs) for whom technology becomes a real challenge. Technological advances will continue to unfold, and we will need to understand how this evolution will also shape our own understandings of how language teaching needs to unfold. As Sadler (2017) notes when discussing virtual worlds: "As these environments and their associated technologies continue to advance, they promise to change the ways that we understand both human-to-human interaction and what it means to be a student of language" (199). Therefore, as educational leaders, we must advocate to ensure that future generations are ready to experience a world that continues to become even more highly technological.

ACKNOWLEDGMENTS AND LIMITATIONS

This chapter includes the personal opinions of the authors who embrace VR/XR environments for educational purposes, and who see the potential benefits for its use in language classrooms, recognizing the challenges as noted. Because technology will continue to evolve, as well as the desire of institutions of higher education to keep up with the times, the focus of our chapter has been to advocate for preparing teachers of English on the proper and effective use of VR/XR technologies, making it an integral part of English language teacher preparation, not an option as it currently is.

This work is also influenced by the authors' professional work and understandings of the world, as each of them has traveled extensively and is familiar with a diversity of educational contexts (private and public) worldwide. Both authors are first-generation college graduates, who grew up in contexts of low socioeconomic status. Jay Schnoor grew up in the United States, and Fabiola Ehlers-Zavala in Chile. Both, through their own lived experiences, are well acquainted with the social challenges that characterize our world, and they are working to advocate for ways to address those through their professional and scholarly work.

Finally, this chapter was not intended to focus on an important aspect of education that is integral to discussions related to achieving social justice: the education of exceptional children (that is, individuals with disabilities or those who are high achieving/performing) as English learners or not. Such contribution, the authors believe, is best addressed by those with direct expertise in special education and the intersection with VR and XR.

WORKS CITED

ACTFL. "World-Readiness Standards for Learning Languages: The Roadmap to Language Competence." ACTFL Educator Resources. Updated December 19, 2013. https://www.actfl.org/educator-resources/world-readiness-standards-for-learning-languages

ACTFL. "The Role of Technology in Language Learning." ACTFL position statement, May 19, 2017. https://www.actfl.org/news/the-role-of-technology-in-language-learning

Alfadil, Mohammed. "Effectiveness of Virtual Reality Games in Foreign Language Vocabulary Acquisition." *Computers & Education* 153 (2020). https://doi.org/10.1016/j.compedu.2020.103893

Bruhn-Zass, Elisa. "Virtual internationalization to support comprehensive internationalization in higher education." *Journal of Studies in International Education* 26, no. 2 (2022): 240–58. https://doi.org/10.1177/10283153211052776.

Bucea-Manea-Țoniş, Rocsana, Radu Bucea-Manea-Țoniş, Violeta Elena Simion, Dragan Ilic, Cezar Braicu, and Natalia Manea. "Sustainability in Higher Education: The Relationship between Work-Life Balance and XR E-Learning Facilities." *Sustainability* 12, no. 14 (2020): Article 5872. https://doi.org/10.3390/su12145872

Chapelle, Carol. *English Language Learning and Technology*. Philadelphia: John Benjamins Publishing Company, 2003.

Chapelle, Carol. "Pedagogical implications in *TESOL Quarterly*? Yes, Please!" *TESOL Quarterly* 41, no. 2 (2007): 404–6. https://www.jstor.org/stable/40264362.

Chapelle, Carol, and Shannon Sauro, eds. *The Handbook of Technology and Second Language Teaching and Learning*. Hoboken, New Jersey: John Wiley & Sons, Inc., 2017.

Chang, Shanton, and Catherine Gomes. "Why the Digitalization of International Education Matters." *Journal of Studies in International Education* 26, no. 2 (2022): 119–27. https://doi.org/10.1177/10283153221095163

Chen, Judy, F., Clyde A. Warden, David Wen-Shung Tai, Farn-Shing Chen, and Chich-Yang Chao. "Level of abstraction and feelings of presence in virtual space: Business English negotiation in Open Wonderland." *Computers & Education* 57, no. 3 (2011): 2126–34. https://doi.org/10.1016/j.compedu.2011.05.017

Chen, Yu-Li. "The Effects of Virtual Reality Learning Environment on Student Cognitive and Linguistic Development." *The Asia-Pacific Education Researcher* 25 (2016): 637–46. https://doi.org/10.1007/s40299-016-0293-2

Chien, Shu-Yun, Gwo-Jen Hwang, and Morris Siu-Yung Jong. "Effects of Peer Assessment within the Context of Spherical Video-Based Virtual Reality on EFL students' English-Speaking Performance and Learning Perceptions." *Computers & Education*, 146, (2020): 103751. https://doi.org/10.1016/j.compedu.2019.103751

Chun, Dorothy M. "Current and Future Directions in TELL." *Educational Technology & Society* 22, no. 2 (2019): 14–25. https://www.jstor.org/stable/26819614.

Chun, Dorothy, Richard Kern, and Bryan Smith. "Technology in Language Use, Language Teaching, and Language Learning." *The Modern Language Journal* 100, supplement (2016): 64–80. https://www.jstor.org/stable/44134996

Eutsler, Lauren and Christopher S. Long. "Preservice Teachers' Acceptance of Virtual Reality to Plan Science Instruction." *Educational Technology & Society* 24, no. 2 (2021): 28–43.

Farr, Fiona, and Liam Murray, eds. *The Routledge Handbook of Language Learning and Technology*. New York: Routledge, 2016.

Fisser, Petra and Michael Phillips, eds. *EDUsummIT 2019. Learners and Learning Contexts: New Alignments for the Digital Age.* EDUsummIT 2019 eBook, 2020. https://edusummit2019.fse.ulaval.ca/files/edusummit2019_ebook.pdf

Godwin-Jones, Robert. "Evolving technologies for language learning." *Language Learning & Technology* 25, no. 3 (2021): 6–26. http://hdl.handle.net/10125/73443

Handley, Zöe. "Replication Research in Computer-Assisted Language Learning: Replication of Neri et al. (2008) and Satar & Özdener (2008)." *Language Teaching* 51, no. 3 (2018): 417–29. https://doi.org/10.1017/S0261444817000040

Hanson-Smith, Elizabeth. "Teacher education and technology." In *The Routledge Handbook of Language Learning and Technology,* edited by Fiona Farr and Liam Murray, 210–22. New York: Routledge, 2016.

Hillman, Cornell. *UX for XR: User Experience Design and Strategies for Immersive Technologies*. New York: Apress, 2021. https://doi.org/10.1007/978-1-4842-7020-2

Ho, Caroline M.L., Mark Evan Nelson, and Wolfgang Müeller-Wittig. "Design and Implementation of a Student-Generated Virtual Museum in a Language Curriculum to Enhance Collaborative Multimodal Meaning-Making." *Computers & Education* 57, no. 1 (2011): 1083–97. https://doi.org/10.1016/j.compedu.2010.12.003

Hokanson, Brad and Amie Norden. "Second Thoughts: Understanding the Impact and Appropriate Use and Non-Use of Technologies." In *Educational Media and Technology Yearbook, vol. 42*, edited by Robert Maribe Branch, Hyewon Lee, and Sheng Shiang Tseng, special section on VR and AR edited by V.J. McClendon and David R. Squires, 13–18. Cham: Springer Nature Switzerland AG, 2019. https://doi.org/10.1007/978-3-030-27986-8

Kalyaniwala, Carmenne and Maud Ciekanski. "Autonomy CALLing: A Systematic Review of 22 years of Publications in Learner Autonomy and CALL." *Language Learning & Technology* 25, no. 3 (2021): 106–31. http://hdl.handle.net/10125/73452

Kaplan-Rakowski, Regina and Kay Meseberg. "Immersive Media and Their Future." In *Educational Media and Technology Yearbook, vol. 42*, edited by Robert Maribe Branch, Hyewon Lee, and Sheng Shiang Tseng, special section on VR and AR edited by V.J. McClendon and David R. Squires, 143–53.

Cham: Springer Nature Switzerland AG, 2019. https://doi.org/10.1007/978-3-030-27986-8

Kern, Richard. "Twenty-Five Years of Digital Literacies in CALL." *Language Learning & Technology* 25, no. 3 (2021): 132–50. http://hdl.handle.net/10125/73453

Kern, Richard and Dave Malinkowski. "Limitations and boundaries in language learning and technology." In *The Routledge Handbook of Language Learning and Technology*, edited by Fiona Farr and Liam Murray, 197–209. New York: Routledge, 2016.

Kessler, Gregg. "Technology Standards for Language Teacher Preparation." In *The Routledge Handbook of Language Learning and Technology,* edited by Fiona Farr and Liam Murray, 57–70. New York: Routledge, 2016.

Lan, Yu-Ju. "Guest Editorial: Language Learning in the Modern Digital Era." *Educational Technology & Society* 22, no. 2 (2019): 1–3.

Lan, Yu-Ju. "Immersion, Interaction, and Experience-Oriented Learning: Bringing Virtual Reality into FL Learning." *Language Learning & Technology* 24, no. 1 (2020): 1–15. http://hdl.handle.net/10125/44704

Lan, Yu-Ju, Shin-Yi Fang, Jennifer Legault, and Ping Li. "Second Language Acquisition of Mandarin Chinese Vocabulary: Context of Learning Effects." *Education Technology Research and Development* 63 (2015): 671–90. https://doi.org/10.1007/s11423-015-9380-y

Lan, Yu-Ju, Indy Y.T., Hsiao, and Mei-Feng Shih. "Effective Learning Design of Game-Based 3D Virtual Language Learning Environments for Special Education Students." *Educational Technology & Society* 21, no. 3 (2018): 213–27. http://www.jstor.org/stable/26458519

Lee, Hyun Gyung, and Joy Egbert. "Language Learning and Technology in Varied Technology Contexts." In *The Routledge Handbook of Language Learning and Technology*, edited by Fiona Farr and Liam Murray, 185–196. New York: Routledge, 2016.

Lee, Lina. "Autonomous Learning through Task-Based Instruction in Fully Online Language Courses." *Language Learning & Technology* 20, no. 2 (2016): 81–97. http://dx.doi.org/10125/44462

McClendon, V.J. and James Riggall. "VR as Library Technology: Early Faculty and Student Feedback on Educational Use of Immersive Technology." In *Educational Media and Technology Yearbook, vol. 42*, edited by Robert Maribe Branch, Hyewon Lee, and Sheng Shiang Tseng, special section on VR and AR edited by V.J. McClendon and David R. Squires, 129–42. Cham, Gewerbestrasse: Springer Nature Switzerland AG, 2019. https://doi.org/10.1007/978-3-030-27986-8

McClendon, V.J., and David R. Squires. "Introduction." In *Educational Media and Technology Yearbook, vol. 42*, edited by Robert Maribe Branch, Hyewon Lee, and Sheng Shiang Tseng, special section on VR and AR edited by V.J. McClendon and David R. Squires, 45–55. Cham: Springer Nature Switzerland AG, 2019. https://doi.org/10.1007/978-3-030-27986-8

Murray, Liam, Marta Giralt, and Silvia Benini. "Extending digital literacies: Proposing an agentive literacy to tackle the problems of distractive technologies in language learning." *ReCALL* 32, no. 3 (2020): 250–71. https://doi.org/10.1017/S0958344020000130

Ndubuisi, Anuli, Elham Marzi, Debbie Mohammed, Oluwatobi Edun, Philip Asare, and James Slotta. "Developing Global Competence in Global Virtual Team Projects: A Qualitative Exploration of Engineering Students' Experiences." *Journal of Studies in International Education* 26, no. 2 (2022): 259–78. https://doi.org/10.1177/10283153221091623

Ou Yang, Fang-Chuan, Fang-Ying Riva Lo, Jun Chen Hsieh, and Wen-Chi Vivian Wu. "Facilitating Communicative Ability of EFL Learners via High-Immersion Virtual Reality." *Educational Technology & Society* 23, no. 1 (2020): 30–49. https://www.jstor.org/stable/26915405

Parmaxi, Antigoni. "Virtual Reality in Language Learning: A Systematic Review and Implications for Research and Practice." *Interactive Learning Environments* 31, no. 1 (2023): 172–84. https://doi.org/10.1080/10494820.2020.1765392

Pegrum, Mark. "Augmented Reality Learning: Education in Real-World Contexts." In *Innovative Language Pedagogy Report*, edited by Tita Beaven and Fernando Rosell-Aguilar, 115–20. Research-publishing.net, 2021. https://doi.org/10.14705/rpnet.2021.50.1245

Peterson, Mark. "Virtual Worlds and Language Learning: An Analysis of Research." In *The Routledge Handbook of Language Learning and Technology*, edited by Fiona Farr and Liam Murray, 308–19. New York: Routledge, 2016.

Pomerantz, Jeffrey. "XR for Teaching and Learning: Year 2 of the EDUCAUSE/HP Campus of the Future Project." ECAR research report. Louisville, CO: EDUCAUSE, 2019. https://library.educause.edu/-/media/files/library/2019/10/2019hpxr.pdf

Sadler, Randall W. "The Continuing Evolution of Virtual Worlds for Language Learning." In *The Handbook of Technology and Second Language Teaching and Learning*, edited by Carol Chapelle and Shannon Sauro, 184–201. New Jersey: John Wiley & Sons, Inc., 2017. https://doi.org/10.1002/9781118914069.ch13

Sánchez Bolado, Javier. "A Pedagogical Model of Application of Augmented Reality in the Teaching of Spanish as a Foreign Language." *Proc. Jornadas sobre Tendencias en Innovación Educativa y su Implantación en UPM, 6ª Jornada: Realidad Aumentada y 3D*, Madrid, November 20, 2017.

Shadiev, Rustam, Xueying Wang, and Yueh Min Huang. "Promoting Intercultural Competence in a Learning Supported by Virtual Reality Technology." *International Review of Research in Open and Distributed Learning* 21, no. 3 (2020): 157–74. https://doi.org/10.19173/irrodl.v21i3.4752

Turner Lee, Nicol. "Can We Better Define What We Mean by Closing the Digital Divide?" Brookings: Techtank blog, January 11, 2022. https://www.brookings.edu/blog/techtank/2022/01/11/can-we-better-define-what-we-mean-by-closing-the-digital-divide/

Voogt, Joke, and Gerald Knezek. "About EDUsummIT." In *EDUsummIT 2019. Learners and Learning Contexts: New Alignments for the Digital Age*, edited by Petra Fisser and Michael Phillips, 1–3. https://edusummit2019.fse.ulaval.ca/files/edusummit2019_ebook.pdf

Voogt, Joke, and Gerald Knezek. "Guest Editorial: Technology Enhanced Quality Education for All—Outcomes from EDUSummit 2015." *Educational Technology & Society* 19, no. 3 (2016): 1–4. https://www.jstor.org/stable/jeductechsoci.19.3.1

Wang, Zhen. "On Computer Assisted Language Learning (CALL) and Change of Teachers' Role." *IOP Conference Series: Earth and Environmental Science* 632 (2021): 052049. 2020 Asia Conference on Geological Research and Environmental Technology. https://doi.org/10.1088/1755-1315/632/5/052049

Ziegler, Nicole, Detmar Meurers, Patrick Rebuschat, Simón Ruiz, José L. Moreno-Vega, Maria Chinkina, Wenjing Li, and Sarah Grey. "Interdisciplinary Research at the Intersection of CALL, NLP, and SLA: Methodological Implications from an Input Enhancement Project." *Language Learning* 67, no. S1 (2017): 209–31. https://doi.org/10.1111/lang.12227

CONCLUSION

PREPARING FOR THE FUTURE OF XR

Brian Beams and Lissa Crofton-Sleigh

The chapters in this volume are just a few examples of XR projects being implemented in the humanities, with many more being developed by scholars all over the world. The technology behind the XR paradigm is moving so quickly that it has become difficult to keep up with recent developments and innovations, making it challenging when trying to predict the future of XR in the classroom. When we think about arts and humanities, we can look historically at concepts or objects, like cave paintings in the Upper Paleolithic period, which were allowed to evolve over thousands of years. But a century ago, personal computers did not exist, much less virtual and augmented reality headsets. We do not know exactly what the future of this technology will look like, not in ten years and certainly not in a thousand years. But as experts in the humanities have observed, understanding the past can enable a more informed view of the present, and perhaps even the future. So the question is, how will the humanities adapt to this new technology? And how will these two disciplines play off of each other?

There are many cautionary tales about the risks of XR,[1] from a lack of access and accessibility, to fears of social and emotional manipulation due to XR's immersive potency,[2] and of course concerns about ceding control of the classroom to the large tech companies that control most of the XR market. Beyond the challenges mentioned in this volume, there are further challenges to consider when working with XR technology and education, or arts and humanities education more specifically. Tech is being concentrated largely into profit for corporations. More importantly for our considerations, companies do not necessarily have the humanities or arts in mind when they are developing this technology, and show little regard to maintaining a status quo upon which educators and researchers can develop projects that expect any sort of longevity. Scholars should also be wary of boom and bust cycles and not fall prey to them by getting on the bandwagon too early or missing out on that same bandwagon completely. This concern leads us to an even greater challenge, which is how to allow education to evolve without falling into the same traps as the tech industry. How quickly should educators, researchers, and scholars adopt VR and AR technology? Should the technology be integrated into the classroom as soon as possible, or should we wait until the technology is more mature? How do we develop content for these new platforms? These are questions that are not easily answered, and it often seems like technology is moving faster than anyone can adapt and effectively answer them. In this final chapter we hope to reflect on current trends in technology and how educators in the arts and humanities can prepare themselves for a potential future where XR technology can be seen as a helpful tool inside the classroom.

THE FUTURE OF HARDWARE

VR has come a long way since 1968 in Ivan Sutherland's lab. Computers in that time would take up entire rooms, and virtual reality headsets were so heavy that they needed to be bolted to the ceiling. When technology like this was used for academic purposes, whole labs were dedicated to the computer hardware, software was almost exclusively bespoke, and development/use was largely limited to large research universities. Since the beginning of the 21st century, however, there has been an increase in access to technology, with powerful computers and specialized human–computer interfaces within reach for almost anyone with the modest financial means to do so. At the time of writing, a person can visit their favorite electronics retailer and purchase a virtual reality headset of considerable quality and specifications for USD 400.

Augmented reality will likely follow this same trend. Commercial AR headsets are still quite expensive, but with similar investment in AR wearable technology they are likely to become more affordable in the near future. Some large companies have been planning to make AR headsets that are even more affordable and more technologically powerful than the existing ones in the near future. However, many technical hurdles must be overcome, and no amount of financial investment will bypass the need to let the technology mature organically. The needs of people must be met with solutions that make sense, and technologists who are developing the technology should avoid applying a one-size-fits-all approach to these new media. Not every problem can be solved with XR, but when a particular need can be met with a suitable XR solution, it has been proven to net powerful results for educators and students alike.

While overall accessibility has increased dramatically in a short time, it is harder to predict exactly how these technologies will fit (or continue to fit) into higher education or humanities education in general. Even though it is not an "early adopter," education tends to follow suit when technology is proven to be effective and economical. K-12 and postsecondary education began adopting iPads after Apple initiated the smart tablet market, making personal computing more accessible and giving students access to a wide array of tools and technology that could help them learn. Online teaching resources have also changed how students learn. Textbooks are often delivered digitally, if they are used at all. Study groups happen online, over video calls provided by Zoom, Microsoft, or Google, or in chat rooms hosted by Slack or Discord. With XR technology becoming more prevalent and accessible, could the classroom of tomorrow be hosted in a virtual headset?

Michael Abrash, chief scientist at Meta's Reality Labs, has theorized that VR will replace personal computers, and AR will replace smartphones.[3] This is a bold statement that should be met with an amount of skepticism, but it can potentially help us to understand the fundamental differences between VR and AR, and offers some clues as to how the technology could evolve. Based on our own experience working with this technology over the past ten years, it is clear that VR will continue to be an accessory to PCs, allowing users to quickly create and interact with digital worlds while switching quickly and seamlessly between computer screens and headset displays. Companies like Immersed are already looking into ways VR can improve productivity and blend between existing paradigms in computing.[4] One can easily imagine a reality where a person could extend their computer interface into a powerful immersive desktop, wander through detailed architectural spaces, or work from an office in an artificial virtual version of their favorite vacation destination. A mouse pointer could be easily paired with more organic forms of control based on speech recognition and hand gestures, and 3D objects could be sculpted naturalistically without the need for thousands of tiny mouse clicks. In a future where people are already working both in and out of virtual spaces, it would be a small step to ask a student to witness the

Roman Forum first-hand via a virtual reconstruction before writing a paper about the Arch of Septimius Severus.

While there are many challenges in the realm of AR wearables, massive adoption of AR within the smartphone ecosystem has already occurred.[5] Pokémon Go, a bona fide phenomenon, brought the idea of AR to the masses, and continues to be built around smartphone and internet-of-things (IoT) technologies.[6] Social media applications have built-in facial recognition and incorporate a wide range of different "filters," which can augment or alter the way a person looks, blurring the lines between a person's real face and their online persona. As smartphones advance and become even more integrated into our everyday lives, they will organically augment our perception of reality to a greater degree than seen before. AR will likely continue to revolve around smartphone technology, with internet connectivity and communications technology at its core.

THE METAVERSE

The term "Metaverse," as originally coined in the 1992 cyberpunk novel *Snow Crash* by Neal Stephenson, described an online VR world that people would log into for work, play, and everything in between. When tech companies discuss their own "metaverse" they are referring to an interconnected online presence, usually interfaced through some form of interactive immersive technology, where users can "interact with 3D assets and have hands-on experience."[7] While prognostication is precarious, what seems certain is that XR technology will become more internet-connected in the future as companies spend more time, effort, and money to get more people onto their platforms. Communication, exchanges of ideas, and even the classrooms themselves might be expected to migrate more into the virtual space. In the summer of 2021, Stanford University piloted the first class to be taught in virtual reality, appropriately titled "Virtual People."[8] This class was designed to teach students *about* VR, so the subject matter was a natural and even somewhat obvious topic to be taught *in* VR. However, it is not unreasonable to think that other subjects might also benefit from this format. The COVID-19 pandemic showed us that, while not always ideal, it is *possible* to teach—and teach well—online.

CREATING XR EXPERIENCES THAT WORK

Arts and humanities educators and researchers of the future will need to be content creators and curators as well as experts in their chosen field. They will be asked to come up with innovative ideas and collaborate with engineers, computer programmers, and designers to create compelling new ways to educate and ignite interest in the humanities. The greatest hurdle to content creation is the technical knowledge needed to build these experiences. Educators in the humanities and arts are subject matter experts in their chosen fields: disciplines such as philosophy, art history, or English literature require a significant amount of dedicated study to reach a level of understanding needed to teach students. Many of these experts, like those who contributed to this volume, have become multidisciplinary pioneers in both XR and the arts or humanities, developing the computer programming skills or learning the terminology enough to be able work alongside those who have experience in XR development. However, wider adoption in the classroom will necessitate changes in how content is developed.

In the future it is conceivable that tools built around generative AI (GAI) will allow educators to fill an empty 3D scene with a detailed model of the Roman Forum, built from a database of existing research based on ancient texts and extant structures, and filled with avatars whose actions are determined by parameters set by a knowledgeable Latin or ancient Roman expert. Code could be generated based on high level instructions ("Make this avatar walk to the Temple of Saturn," for instance) instead of esoteric programming languages. The technical minutiae of simple actions could take seconds instead of hours to create, moving the task of generating ideas and experiential design into the forefront. Applications such as ChatGPT have proven that this is theoretically possible,[9] and could help scholars in the humanities and arts create more elaborate and realistic virtual worlds without the need for large teams of engineers, digital artists, and programmers. Ethical considerations notwithstanding, it is possible that more content could be delivered to students at a fraction of the cost.[10]

CONCLUSION

These chapters present a bright future for the humanities and arts, one full of collaboration, innovation, and preservation of cultural ideas that without scholarly intervention could be lost to time. Consider, for instance, the cave paintings of the Upper Paleolithic mentioned earlier. We know now that human observation of these paintings has contributed to their ongoing deterioration.[11] Using XR technology, we can replicate them and allow students to explore these important human artifacts through noninvasive archaeology (similar to the methods mentioned in the first and second chapters of this book) and ensure preservation of the physical paintings. There are other threats to human culture in the last few thousand years that could be lost to time if we do not work on conservation; technology could help to bridge that gap, preserving these items and their physical forms while still allowing others to see them in their full splendor. But in order for these technological interventions to be successful, we have to view them as a conduit for cultural exchange, and not just conceive of them in terms of a showpiece for what the technology can do, which will require researchers to think seriously about the capabilities of the technology. Scholars who are familiar with the subjects that we are trying to preserve and who can inform us on how to accurately represent them in virtual spaces will be the key to creating new content and contexts for how we interface with XR technology.

NOTES

1. Heller and Castaño, "Artificial Intelligence, Virtual Courts."
2. Huang and Bailenson, "Close Relationships and Virtual Reality."
3. UploadVR, "Meta's top researcher."
4. https://immersed.com/
5. Niknejad et al., "Overview of smart wearables."
6. Wingfield and Isaac, "Pokémon go."
7. Siyaev and Jo, "Towards aircraft maintenance metaverse."
8. Bailenson et al., "Virtual People."
9. Kashefi and Mukerji, "ChatGPT for Programming."
10. Mhlanga, "Open AI in Education."
11. Geneste and Mauriac, "Conservation of Lascaux cave."

WORKS CITED

Bailenson, Jeremy N., Brian Beams, Cyan Deveaux, Daniel Akselrad, Eugy Han, Hanseul Jun, Mark Roman Miller, Mark York, and Tobin Asher. "Virtual People." Stanford University virtual reality class, 2021. https://stanfordvr.com/comm166/

Geneste, Jean-Michel, and Muriel Mauriac. "The conservation of Lascaux Cave, France." In *The Conservation of Subterranean Cultural Heritage*, edited by C. Saiz Jimenez, 165–72. London: CRC Press, 2014.

Heller, Brittan, and Daniel Castaño. "Artificial Intelligence, Virtual Courts, and Real Harms." Lawfare, March 14, 2023. https://www.lawfaremedia.org/article/artificial-intelligence-virtual-courts-and-real-harms

Huang, Sabrina A. and Jeremy N. Bailenson. "Close Relationships and Virtual Reality." In *Mind, Brain and Technology: Learning in the Age of Emerging Technologies*, edited by Thomas Parsons, Lin Lin, and Deborah Cockerham, 49–65. Educational Communications and Technology: Issues and Innovations. Cham: Springer, 2019. https://doi.org/10.1007/978-3-030-02631-8_4

Kashefi, Ali and Tapan Mukerji. "ChatGPT for Programming Numerical Methods." 2023. arXiv:2303.12093 [cs.LG]. https://arxiv.org/pdf/2303.12093

Mhlanga, David. "Open AI in Education, the Responsible and Ethical Use of ChatGPT Towards Lifelong Learning." February 11, 2023. Available at SSRN: https://ssrn.com/abstract=4354422 or http://dx.doi.org/10.2139/ssrn.4354422

Niknejad, Naghmeh, Waidah Ismail, Abbas Mardani, Huchang Liao, and Imran Ghani. "A comprehensive overview of smart wearables: The state of the art literature, recent advances, and future challenges." *Engineering Applications of Artificial Intelligence* 90 (2020): 103529. https://doi.org/10.1016/j.engappai.2020.103529

Siyaev, Aziz and Geun-Sik Jo. "Towards Aircraft Maintenance Metaverse Using Speech Interactions with Virtual Objects in Mixed Reality." Sensors 21, no. 6 (2021): 2066. https://doi.org/10.3390/s21062066

UploadVR. "Meta's Top Researcher: Why We'll Have Both AR & VR Glasses." YouTube, October 11, 2022. Video, 1 min. 40 sec. https://youtu.be/eBkOOzbtmlo

Wingfield, Nick, and Mike Isaac. "Pokémon Go Brings Augmented Reality to a Mass Audience." New York Times, July 11, 2016. Accessed April 3, 2023. https://www.nytimes.com/2016/07/12/technology/pokemon-go-brings-augmented-reality-to-a-mass-audience.html

Contributors

Brian Beams is currently the manager of the Virtual Human Interaction Lab (VHIL) at Stanford University. Prior to this he managed interdisciplinary projects for the Soft Interaction Lab at Texas A&M University, and later was virtual reality (VR) lab director and lecturer at Santa Clara University. Brian assisted in the development of creative anatomy virtual reality applications, interactive performance art, and research in the application of new technologies for art and education.

Matthew Brennan is a PhD candidate (ABD) in informatics at Indiana University. His research focuses on the application of technologies (particularly immersive technologies, like virtual reality) to fields traditionally within the "humanities," such as art history, archaeology, and architectural history. His background is in architectural design and architectural history, and he has taught undergraduate- and graduate-level courses at Indiana University. In 2019–2020, Matthew received a one-year Rome Prize in historic preservation and conservation at the American Academy in Rome, where he pursued research on his dissertation topic: the South Theater of Hadrian's Villa.

Lissa Crofton-Sleigh is Lecturer in Classics at Santa Clara University, where she also serves on the advisory council of the Digital Humanities Initiative. She earned a BA in Greek and Latin, with a minor in Music History, from UCLA, and her MA and PhD in classics from the University of Washington, Seattle. Her research spans Latin literature and ancient Roman culture, in particular the connections between poetry and built environments (which helped to spark her interest in the uses of extended reality (XR) in the humanities), to classical reception in music, especially opera and heavy metal.

Fabiola P. Ehlers-Zavala is professor at Colorado State University (CSU). She earned a BA in English from the Pontificia Universidad Católica de Valparaíso, Chile; and both an MA in English and a PhD in English studies from Illinois State University. She served as executive director (2014–2021) of INTO CSU (CSU's former English language center). She teaches in the MA in English program, preparing teachers of English as a foreign and second language. Her expertise includes language teacher preparation, internationalization for diversity, equity and inclusion, and leadership in higher education. She is Past President of the American Association for Applied Linguistics (AAAL).

Tim Gruenewald researches and teaches cultural and visual studies with a focus on popular culture, including virtual reality, film, television, graphic narrative, and museum exhibitions. He is the author of *Curating America's Painful Past: Museums, Memory, and the National Imagination*, which examines how memory of collective violence and the US national imagination intersect in historical museums of the National Mall. His documentary feature *Sacred Ground* explores the dynamics of remembering and forgetting traumatic national histories at the Mount Rushmore National Memorial and the Wounded Knee Massacre Monument. He is currently working on a new research project on narratives in virtual reality.

Elham Hajesmaeili is an artist-researcher and art educator who holds an MFA in painting and drawing from Penn State University. Her art focuses on identity issues for women post-migration. Elham received her Ph.D. in Art Education and Women's Gender, and Sexuality Studies (WGSS) from Penn State University in 2023. Her research links art education and social justice, focusing on Iranian women who migrated to the U.S. She employs AR technology and portrait painting as a research methodology to create interactive experiences for viewers to engage with marginalized communities. As an artist-researcher, Elham aims to raise awareness and promote empathy for diverse identities through her art and research.

Ryan Knapp started his career in IT at Indiana University where he worked for 21 years. In 2016 he applied for and received a federal grant to setup a 3D/VR service in the undergraduate campus library. In 2019 he began working with faculty to explore how the technology might be applied to facilitate their curriculum, and from 2019–2022 worked closely on developing custom VR builds with Dr. Elizabeth Thill for art history courses. Ryan is passionate about ancient art, archaeology, 3D technologies and, more recently, sound-money theory. He enjoys researching the latest technologies and understanding their implications on society.

Molly Kuchler (Pidgeon) received her bachelor's from Rutgers University and her master's from Bryn Mawr College in Greek, Latin, and classical studies. Her master's thesis, titled "Monumentality and Extra-Reality in Pindar," explores how the Greek lyric poet Pindar used scale and proportion to draw out the sublimity of extremes in order to better praise the victors of athletic games for whom he wrote. Her interests extend beyond Pindar to Greek architecture, religion, and digital humanities, which she explored as a Digital Scholarship Graduate Fellow at Bryn Mawr. She currently works for a company specializing in interactive and AR engagements.

David Chapman Lindsay is an arts administrator and artist, working in print, video, and animation. He has served as the graduate coordinator for the Master of Fine Arts program and the associate director for Texas Tech University, School of Art. He has also served as a member of the Student and Emerging Professionals Committee for the College Art Association. Currently, David is the director of Sites Set for Knowledge, a nonprofit arts organization which administers the Popwalk exhibition platform of site-specific art video. Popwalk has grown to exhibit in many locations across the United States.

Jay Schnoor is the CEO and co-founder of VEDX Solutions Inc. He has dedicated his life to international education and providing greater access to learning globally. He earned his master's degree from the University of Oregon in the field of international development, did research on community education in Cairo up to the revolution in 2012, and then worked for universities in the UK and US recruiting students to their programs. After being inspired to bring that same education to the students in their home country, he was inspired to build VEDX—adding virtual reality to educational curriculum.

Laura Surtees is a research and instruction librarian with a PhD in classical and Near Eastern archaeology from Bryn Mawr College. Trained as a field archaeologist, Laura taught at several Philadelphia-area colleges before transitioning to the field of librarianship where she manages the archaeology, classics, art history, and urbanism library. As a librarian, Laura focuses on developing students' information literacy while promoting engagement with the library, its collections, and spaces through active and passive programming, like Coloring the Past, to create a welcoming learning environment for all members of the community.

Dr. Elizabeth Wolfram Thill is a Roman archaeologist specializing in monumental sculpture and architecture, with a focus on the 2nd century AD city of Rome. She has worked extensively on the Columns of Trajan and Marcus Aurelius, as well as the Great Marble Map of Rome (*Forma Urbis Romae*). Her focus on such monuments, with their tension between awe-inspiring size and meticulous detail, first led her to virtual reality as a pedagogical and research tool. She currently serves as program director and associate professor of classical studies at Indiana University-Indianapolis.

Ian R. Weaver is an assistant professor of English in the professional writing program at the University of North Carolina Wilmington. He coordinates the post-baccalaureate certificate in science and medical writing, and he teaches undergraduate and graduate courses in technical and professional writing, grant writing, science writing, research methods, environmental writing, and technologies. His research investigates science communication, rhetorics of risk, and the use of participatory methods in developing technologies for community building.